Human Dimension of Total Quality Management

NAYANTARA PADHI
SASMITA PALO

ATLANTIC
PUBLISHERS & DISTRIBUTORS

Published by
ATLANTIC
PUBLISHERS & DISTRIBUTORS
B-2, Vishal Enclave, Opp. Rajouri Garden,
New Delhi-110027
Phones : 25413460, 25429987, 25466842

Sales Office
7/22, Ansari Road, Darya Ganj,
New Delhi–110002
Phones : 23273880, 23275880, 23280451
Fax : 91-11-23285873
web : www.atlanticbooks.com
e-mail : info@atlanticbooks.com

ISBN 81-269-0428-3

Printed in India
at Nice Printing Press, Delhi

The Book is dedicated to
Late Pratap Chandra Mishra
who was always a source of our
inspiration

Preface

In this epoch of ours, competition is rife and the prospects of sustainability augurs all in omen on part of the business houses. One does not need to go rather far than Tom Peters' book, *In Search of Excellence,* to find out how 'badly bruised' most of the companies are. In order to parry with the customers' pinch, distributors intimidation, and crashing margins, excellence in business is perhaps the only solution. Quality as a rule irrefutably is the surest way to achieve excellence.

With the passage of time, the quality fraternity has changed in its own paradigm. It is no longer in conformity to requirements. We are getting better and better in every way and yet lag behind. Decimation of global companies, which were scintillating like stars in the corporate firmament in yester years, is indicative of the fact that whatever has made you successful in the past will not be in the future. In nutshell, the meaning of quality has profoundly changed over the period. Today by quality, we mean creating products and services which are regarded as the best in the market and which delight the customers. Sustainable edge will come, in the words of Tom Peters, from "Our ability to provide awesome service of giving our customers an experience that enlivens their senses, instills their well-being, and fulfils even their unexpected wishes." The ultimate goal as a result is to satisfy the customers by achieving Total Quality in every activity, process, and product/service.

This has relevance specifically for the Indian steel industry, which constitutes one of the core sectors in the economic development of the country, but suffering from a declining fortune over the past few years because of severe pressure and challenges. Having taken the stock of the situation, prudence demands that the Indian steel companies must devise ways and means to overcome these global challenges and convert them into opportunities. One such opportunity is to produce quality goods, as even in the depressed market, a customer who has a wider choice of products/services would ultimately buy from a supplier who produces the best. Complementing this, the need of the hour is to concentrate on avoiding wastage in every area of operation and curtailing costs to the barest minimum possible. Perhaps, one of the best strategies to deal with this paradox is to adopt the novel management usage, **Total Quality Management** (TQM).

TQM now is regarded as the elixir of modern day business practices. Business corporations all over the world are adopting TQM mainly to meet the mass customization needs, e.g., capability to manufacture unique products with regard to customer needs without actually compromising on the cost, time or product standards and specifications. Implementation of TQM requires re-engineering of manufacturing processes and products (a part of BPR), adoption of Just-in-Time (JIT), production at zero-defect level, benchmarking with successful companies, and above all, bringing in a continuous improvement in the activities and processes through team spirit. As Mr. Alan Bradley, Secretary General, ISO in his recent visit to India on 20th April 2004 has pointed out, quality does not mean product quality, it refers to quality in the management systems as well.

The human component is always at the vanguard of TQM implementation. The ultimate strategy of TQM is not only to empower people, but also to turn every worker into a businessperson, where everybody thinks and acts to achieve total quality, everybody delights the customers, and everybody manages the bottom-line. This, in the words of Chris Turner of Xerox Business Services, TQM is the 'ultimate accountability strategy'. Thus, the hub of TQM strategy is people, i.e. 'Achieving Total Quality through People's Contentment'. This is possible only when all people in an organisation work in tandem, align their goals to the organisational goals, communicate and collaborate with each other, and strives to excel in their area of operations. In other words, total quality is achievable only when organisational goal becomes personal goal, organisation's mission becomes personal mission, and everyone's effort translates the corporate mission into reality. The crucial point therefore is that every member of an organisation, especially from the lower and middle levels, has to be committed to the total quality goal. Realising the relevance of people in achieving total quality, now CII has been directing its efforts towards harnessing and leveraging the power of people through its National HRD Committee. The National HRD Committee is looking at three major initiatives this year, namely, **Leadership Development, HR Competency Model, and People Capability Maturity Model** which are planned to be adapted and deployed widely in the manufacturing sector in India.

TQM as a management strategy and a corporate ploy seem fabulous, but more in theory. To put into practice, conversely, many well-run companies have one set of reservation or other about the efficacy and implementation of TQM programme in their organisations. Many companies have been brought to their knees by failed TQM programmes. Most TQM implementation disasters happened partly because the concept was thrust upon the companies as a big sellout and partly because companies brought into the concept without clearly understanding the basic issues relating to the complexities of its implementation, benefits and limitations, and the management processes they needed to have in place to get the maximum out of the programme. It is hard enough to launch a programme and run it successfully across the company. It is also a monumental task to achieve Total Quality in every activity and process across the organisation. If for example, the managers begin to make decisions basing on the wrong footing due to poorly managed TQM implementations, the company would be soon landing in big trouble. Adopting the programme is one thing and getting thousands of employees to massively change working styles they have followed for years is quite another. To sum up, the benefits of TQM are quite impressive, but at the same time, there is a need for extreme caution while implementing the programme. Once it is implemented vigilantly, indubitably it would be credited with bravura benefits to both the organisation as well its people in both tangible and intangible terms.

We would welcome constrictive comments, suggestions and feedback on the book, and new information or data on any further work in this area.

NAYANTARA PADHI
SASMITA PALO

ACKNOWLEDGMENTS

The book is not an outcome of our solo effort; it is a fruit of many people's labour, support and supervision. In writing this book we have been fortunate to have had help and inspiration from a lot of people. Sincere appreciation goes to the sample Respondents and Officials of RINL/VSP who had been very enthusiastic and ingenuously cooperative during the period of survey. We would like to thank all the people who have directly or indirectly helped in this endeavour. Thanks are also due to all our colleagues and friends for their skilled help, valuable suggestions and comments.

Finally we express our sincere thanks and gratitude to our families for their encouragement and support throughout the project. Without their love and trust this book would not have seen the light of day. Last but not the least thanks are due to Dr. K.R. Gupta and his entire team of Atlantic Publishers and Distributors for bringing out this book.

NAYANTARA PADHI
SASMITA PALO

CONTENTS

1

Total Quality Management: The Conceptual Framework

The volatile international competition in the corporate sector has forced the business houses either to shape-up or to ship-out, the only promising resolution. Corporate leaders and analysts are in a look out for new stratagems to endure. They are experimenting with various strategies like Business Process Re-engineering (BPR), managing core competencies, Benchmarking practices, and Total Quality Management (TQM), with a sudden sense of urgency.

In the contemporary period, a great deal has been written and said about TQM. That is why, TQM has been snubbed by some as just another fad, another catchphrase (Zemke, 1992). Yet, TQM programmes are very much alive and doing well in the workplace. *Training Magazine's* 1995 Survey of U.S. companies with 100 or more employees found that 58 per cent of them were pursuing TQM initiatives more than any other type of programme (Training, 1995). Therefore, dispense with the core principle of TQM because of apparent faddishness would be unwise as ignoring sound nutrition and guidelines because of endless discussion about dieting. TQM principles have profound practical implications for managing people today (Zemke, 1993).

TQM programmes have proven results in many organisations. But the bare fact about TQM is that it often receives the setback because of the barriers like impatience to achieve quick results, inexperience with implementing TQM, lack of commitment, and also the vicious protest by employees. In many instances such barriers force the management to shirk the programme as a 'failure'. Failure in conjunction with TQM is often defined as the 'inability to meet the high expectations'. Many TQM efforts have generated results, but not in the magnitude initially hoped by the organisations. A Survey of approximately 100 British firms found that only 20 per cent of them have achieved 'tangible results' (*The Economist*, 1992). It is therefore imperative to overcome such barriers to make TQM a real source of competitive advantage. A slight change in the perspective and interplay in the roles of the business personnel can orchestrate its growth leading to phenomenal success.

THE QUALITY SCENARIO IN THE INDIAN MANUFACTURING SECTOR

In India, the manufacturing sector has a meager share of 16% of the GDP of the country as compared to South-East Asia and Chinese economies that are having 25 to 35% share in their GDPs. This indicates that Indian manufacturing sector is at the rear, and one of its major downside is the poor quality management. The quality management contour of the Indian manufacturing sector is presented below based on the research findings of a handful researchers (Sinha & Willbourne, 1985; Sharma, 1997; Choudhary & Dhargawe, 2000).

(i) The top management of many Indian companies both in the public and private sector, which are earning huge profits, still have a conventional mindset "as long as we earn profit, why should we be perturbed for other matters"?

(ii) There are a few misconceptions about quality, one of which is "Better Quality Costs More". New insights into the mechanisms of quality building and manufacturing processes have shown that higher quality does not always cost more. Quality is first defined on paper which is translated into actual product on the basis of market needs. Investment in research and development (R & D) results in a marked improvement in product quality. Simultaneously, fine living and refining the manufacturing processes can lead to a substantial reduction in costs. This has been amply demonstrated in Japan and the West (GOI, *The Bureau of Information*).

(iii) Another allegory prevailing among production managers is that "Quality leads to reduced productivity". This has been handed down from the times when quality control consisted largely of physical inspection of the end product (GOI, *The Bureau of Information*).

(iv) The manufacturing strategy of most Indian companies is still not addressing certain fundamental problems of global competitiveness like quality improvement process to reduce the cost of operations and thereby the price of the product.

(v) Most Indian companies are unacquainted with the managerial approaches required company wide for quality assurance, development, assessment and improvement through TQM, which would also aid certification in the form of ISO-9000 Standards.

(vi) Poor work culture in Indian labour is often given by manufacturers as a reason for low quality of products.

(vii) Another wrong notion, which is widely held, is that organised quality improvement programme needs heavy investment in plant and machinery. Equipment are only a component of the total quality system. A number of companies in India have plants and machinery, similar to those used in the West although the quality of Indian products leaves much to be desired. There are also companies utilising indigenous equipment and manufacturing products acceptable in Europe and Japan.

(viii) Quality is generally regarded as a socially desirable objective but its contribution to profitability is considered marginal. In several units over 90 per cent of quality control manpower is deployed in *post-facto* checking activities. Hardly any people are deployed on preventive measures such as looking for potential causes of product defects or out of control processes so that these can be removed or rectified before defective material is actually produced (GOI, *The Bureau of Information*).

(ix) Indian managers have got some delusion about developing TQM system and practices, and thus adaptation of ISO-9000 standards.

(x) Most Indian companies have not assessed their capability to quip themselves with TQM tools and their adequacy in use. There is presently no status report on quality management in Indian companies industry-wise.

(xi) Most Indian Quality Assurance/Production Managers have not comprehended exactly the implication of TQM on functions like design engineering, purchasing management, maintenance management, materials planning and control, process engineering, post-production functions, customer servicing and developing human resources etc.

(xii) In most of the Indian companies, quality is not seen as a strategy to attain competitiveness. It is merely considered as a manufacturing sub-function with little focus on planning and improvement aspects of it. Most Indian managers find it difficult to formulate different elements of a corporate quality management strategy.

(xiii) It is now well-known that the majority of the defects are management controlled and therefore managers have wider role, responsibility and authority to execute the functions of quality assurance and improvement through mobilisation of human resources. Most of these managers do not communicate candidly with departments like marketing, finance and personnel with regard to quality as a core function.

(xiv) There has been a lack of workers commitment and assistance to the maintenance of quality systems, more so when there is no reward system. Even top management is not always committed in providing leadership and support to quality improvement efforts. Therefore what is needed is to create awareness among employees about meeting customer requirements, standardising processes, training operatives and enforcing technical discipline. All these do not require heavy financial investment. What is needed is a deep commitment to quality and intolerance of deviation.

(xv) Increased consumer rights and protection movements in the country have given greater importance to the concept of 'product liability', which is again an outcome of the total quality.

(xvi) Indian companies need to develop management strategies to tackle customer satisfaction and product liability issues. This becomes more relevant from the point of view of services packaged with product.

(xvii) India's competitive priority as on date lies in quality and structural change, which is directed towards manufacturing processes, but emphasis on R&D has gone down since 1997, which is definitely not a good sign in the global competitive scenario.

Nonetheless, progressively enterprises are discovering that quality management is the most effective enterprise strategy to realize the organisational goals of excellence and profitability and for winning and retaining customer confidence. Managers are concomitantly learning how to enhance quality and accurately measure the performance of the company in terms of quality, cost, flexibility, service and speed. Recently, a number of organisations from manufacturing and service sectors have demonstrated that espousal of TQM strategies guarantee attainment of the above cited goals. For instance, Sundaram Clayton Limited, the proud claimant of the 1998 Deming Award, Brakes India Limited, the Farm Equipment Sector, Mahindra & Mahindra Limited, Birla Cellulosic Limited which is a Unit of Grasim Industries Limited, the prestigious Deming Application Prize Winners for 2003, are the companies which have achieved distinctive performance improvement through the application of TQM technology.

So as to encourage Indian manufacturing and service organisations to endeavour for excellence, the Bureau of Indian Standards instituted the Rajiv Gandhi National Quality Award in 1991. The Award is designed in line with respected awards such as the Malcolm Baldrige National Quality Award in USA, the Deming Prize in Japan, and the European Quality Award. It is intended to generate interest and involvement of Indian industry in quality programmes, drive products and services to higher levels of quality and equip the Indian industry to encounter the challenges of domestic and International markets. The winners have included companies like BHEL, SAIL, L&T, Tata International, and Tata Bearings. Alongside, the demand on ISO to develop standards that are acceptable internationally, is amplifying by the Indian entrepreneurs. Some basic underlying factors for this state of affair are *globalisation of trade, de-localisation of procurement, security* and the *new emerging technologies*. Today, 6% of world's certificates for ISO-9000 are in India (*Quality News*, March-June 2004).

The Confederation of Indian Industry (CII) has now put high precedence on its renewed commitment to make the corporate sector, distinctively the SME sector that comprises a major segment of Indian industry, more competitive. With all these pooled uphill struggle of the Government, CII, and the companies, let's envision the Indian corporate sector as the future business leader *in terms of quality, productivity, and competitiveness.*

THE QUALITY SCENARIO IN OTHER SECTORS IN INDIA

Besides the manufacturing operations, emphasis is now placed on quality in Government and Government Departments. Phillip B. Crosby, the illustrious Quality Guru, in his last visit to India recommended an agenda for the country to have quality leadership in Government. Leading industrialist Mr. Rahul Bajaj has also advocated for a change in the management thought of the Government, and bureaucracy to meet quality revolution. A short time ago i.e., on March 2004, DGFT has obtained the ISO-9001:2000 Certificate. It is the first Government Department in India outside Ministry of Defence to obtain the ISO-9001:2000 Certificate. Over and above, progressively emphasis is placed upon achieving total quality in food industry, education sector, environment, tourism sector and even in the call centres. Accordingly, quality spreads out steadily to each and every realm of the societal network.

TQM IN RETROSPECT

Quality as a concept has been with us for millennia, but only recently, it has surfaced as a formal management function. In its original form, quality was reactive and inspection oriented, conversely in recent times, quality-related activities have been widened and are seen as *sine qua non* for premeditated success. In the past, quality was the one and only dominion of manufacturing and operational departments, but now, it incorporates functions as extensive as purchasing, engineering and marketing research.

The genesis of TQM can be structured into seven distinct phases[1]: Artisan, Mass Production, Inspection, Quality Control, Statistical Quality Control, Statistical Process Control, and Total Quality Management.

Stage I: Artisans

During the initial period quality control, as we understand it today, did not exist. Most manufacturing work was performed by artisans and skilled craftsmen or by journeymen and apprentices who were supervised by masters at the trade (Chandler, 1977). They used to produce goods and inspect the quality of their goods as well as that of their apprentices for supplying them to the customer. The artisan directly dealt the customer's complaint/dissatisfaction with the product. A well-performing product was viewed as the natural outgrowth of reliance or skilled tradesman for all aspects of design, manufacturing and service (Juran, 1976).

Stage II: Mass Production System

The upsurging of mass production amplified the need for the use of interchangeable parts. In 1798, Eli Whitney started designing and manufacturing muskets with interchangeable parts.[2] Earlier to that, firearms were created individually. If

1. A number of authors have divided the history of the quality movement in distinct periods, although they have frequently used only two categories, quality control and quality assurance. For details see, Abbot & Leaman, 1982; Adam, 1984, ASQC, 1986; Dorsky, 1984; Owens, Undated; and Reddy, 1980.
2. While the initial breakthroughs involving interchangeable parts have often been associated with Eli Whitney, recent research suggests that his role has been overrated. For details see, Woodbury (1960).

part of the musket broke, a new product was scrupulously put in order for that particular firearm or else that piece was discarded. Nevertheless, with the manufacturing of interchangeable parts by Whitney, firing mechanisms, barrels, or other parts could be used on any musket of the same design. Thus, by making parts interchangeable, Whitney created the need for **Quality Control** (Summers, 1997).

In a mass production setting, tasks essential to create a finished product were divided among many individuals and each individual was performing a specific task. Proper assembling of parts required two important conditions: First, with the purpose of being interchangeable, the parts must be identical. And the second, production is to be made 'with minimal variation and within specifications'. These conditions trounced the idea of interchangeable parts and so as to meet those two prerequisites, **Quality Principles** were evolved.

Stage III: Inspection

Inspection refers to those activities designed to uncover or find non-conformances existing in already completed products/services (Summers, 1997). The need for formal inspection arose only with the rise of mass production and the need for interchangeable parts. As volumes increased, parts could no longer be fitted to one another by hand. The process required a large pool of skilled labour and was both costly and time-consuming. This pressure gave rise to what has been called the American system of manufacturing, which means "the use of special-purpose machinery to produce interchangeable parts by following a pre-established sequence of operations" (Abernathy & Corcoram, 1983; Hounshell, 1984a; and Smith, 1977).

Most initial efforts were connected with the military demand for armaments. However, the major breakthrough was made with the development of rational jig, fixture, and gauging system in the early 1800s (Hounshell, 1984b). Inspection acquired a new respectability when activities that were previously conducted by eye were replaced by a more objective and verifiable process (Hounshell, 1984c).

Inspection became even more important in course of time. In the early 1900s, F.W. Taylor, Father of 'scientific management' invigorate it. In 1922, it was linked more formally to quality control, with the publication of G.S. Radford's (1922) *The Control of Quality Manufacturing*. For the first time quality was viewed as a distinct management responsibility and as an independent function. For several years, quality control was restricted to inspection and to such narrow activities as counting, grading, and repair etc. were considered outside the reach of available inspection department (Bicking, 1958).

Stage IV: Quality Control

Quality Control (QC) refers to the use of specifications and inspection of completed parts, subassemblies, and products to design, produce, review, sustain, and improve the quality of a product or service. QC goes beyond inspection by:

(i) establishing standards for the product or service, based on the customer needs, requirements and expectations;

(ii) ensuring conformance to these standards, poor quality is evaluated to determine the reasons why the parts or services provided are incorrect;

(iii) taking action in case there is a lack of conformance to the standards. These actions may include sorting the product to find the defectives. In service industries, action may involve contacting the customer and correcting the situation; and

(iv) implementing plans to prevent future non-conformance. These plans may include design or manufacturing changes and in a service industry, they may include procedural changes.

These four activities work together to improve the production of a product/service. QC efforts can be enhanced by the use of statistics.

Stage V: Statistical Quality Control

Edifying on these four tenets of QC, statistics were added to map the results of inspection of parts. In the 1920s, statistical charts to check and control product variables were developed by Walter A. Shewhart of Bell Telephone Laboratories. At the same time, Harold Dodge and Harry G. Romig of Bell Telephone Laboratories developed the area of sampling as a substitute for 100 per cent inspection. The use of statistical methods of production monitoring and parts inspection was known as **Statistical Quality Control (SQC)**, wherein statistical data are collected, analysed, and interpreted to solve quality problems.

Stage VI: Statistical Process Control

With the development of quality area, the need to become more proactive while dealing with quality problems was seriously felt. Thus, the emphasis was shifted from utilising SQC methods for the inspection or detection of poor quality to their use in the prevention of poor quality. Prevention of defects by applying statistical methods to control the process is known as **Statistical Process Control (SPC)**. Here prevention refers to those activities designed to prevent defects, defectives and non-conformance in products/services. Four separate elements were involved in defect prevention: quantifying the costs of quality, total quality control, reliability engineering and zero defects.

Stage VII: Total Quality Management

As the use of SPC got intensified in the 1980s, industry saw the need to monitor and improve the entire system of providing a quality product or service. Sensing that meeting customer needs, requirements, and expectations involved more than providing a product or service, industry began to integrate quality into all areas of operations from the receptionist to the sales and billing departments and to the manufacturing to shipping and even to the service departments.

Accordingly methods of quality management were developed and utilised to encourage the design, production, marketing, sales and service of quality products/services. This integrated approach involves all departments in a company in providing a quality product/service became known as **Total Quality Management (TQM)**. Thus TQM is a management approach that places emphasis on system improvement as a means of achieving customer satisfaction to ensure long-term success of a company (Summers, 1997).

However, Garvin (1988) organised the quality movement into four distinct 'Quality Eras': Inspection, Statistical Quality Control (SQC), Quality Assurance (QA) and Strategic Quality Management. According to him, the evolution pattern was strategic in nature with continuous improvement as the driving force in quality planning and employee involvement as the key objectives. The evolutionary pattern is tabulated in Table 1.1.

TABLE 1.1: Evolution Pattern of Quality Management

Phases of Quality Movement/ Identifying characteristics	Inspection	SQC	QA	Strategic Quality Management
Primary concern	Detection	Control	Coordination	Strategic view
Emphasis	Product uniformity	Product uniformity with reduced inspection	Entire production chain	Market and consumer needs
Methods	Gauging and measurement	Statistical tools and techniques	Programmes and systems	Strategic planning and setting
Role of Quality Professionals	Inspection, Acceptance, Sampling	Trouble shooting and the application of statistical methods	Quality measurement, planning, programme design	Goal setting, Education, Training and consultation
Who has responsibility for Quality	Inspection Department	Manufacturing, Engineering Departments	All Departments	Everyone in the organisation
Orientation and approach	Inspects in Quality	Controls in Quality	Builds in Quality	Manages in Quality

Source: Garvin, D.A. (1988). *Managing Quality*, The Free Press, Macmillan Inc., New York, p. 19.

Total Quality Management: The Theoretical Construct

Total Quality Management—the acronym represents three facets of an organisation—wide quality management, i.e., Total, Quality, and Management. The theoretical perspective of each facet is discussed below.

The 'Total' Perspective: The term 'Total' in TQM implies totality in three senses:

(i) every process (rather than mere manufacturing or production) such as, design, construction, R & D, accounting, marketing, repair, and every other function must also be involved in quality improvement;

(ii) every job, not merely those involved in making the project; and

(iii) each person is responsible for the quality of his or her work, and for the work of the group and the entire organisation.

Total involvement is recognition of the fact that every activity contributes or detracts from quality and productivity, and the people involved in those activities/processes are in best position to know what really needs to be improved (Cartin, 2000a).

The 'Quality' Perspective: 'Quality' means different things to different people. There is no exact definition, which can be used as a yardstick to measure quality. The established quality gurus offer a range of alternatives, such as:

- "Degree of uniformity and dependability at a low cost with quality suited to the market" ... (Deming, 1986).
- "Conformance to requirements" ... (Crosby, 1979).
- "Quality is a customer determination which is based on the customer's actual experience with the product or service, measured against his or her requirements—stated or unstated, conscious or merely sensed, technically operational or entirely subjective and always representing a moving target in a competitive market" ... (Feigenbaum, 1961).
- "Fitness for use" ... (Juran, 1988).
- "Quality is about constant improvement in all areas of operations" ... (Conway, quoted from Bank, John, 1988).
- "Quality is the totality of characteristics of an entity that bear on its ability to satisfy stated and implied needs." ... (ANSI/ISO/ASQL, A8402-1994).

Garvin (1984) has examined various quality definitions, and classified them into five principal categories:

- Transcendental: achieving excellence and the highest standard.
- Product-based: dependent on the attributes.
- User-based: satisfying the want of a customer.

- Manufacturing-based: conformance to requirements.
- Value-based: value for money.

Details of these five categories are given in Appendix 1.1. Of these five, the value-based view is becoming more popular day by day. While, ingredients and materials are the key quality indicators in such categories as food, clothing, personal care, and beauty products, reflecting a product-based approach to quality however, quality is increasingly apt to be discussed and perceived in relation to price.[3]

Garvin (1987) has also listed eight important quality dimensions which influence customers in determining quality levels: performance, features, reliability, conformance, durability, serviceability, aesthetics, and perceived quality.

Kelda (1996a) conducted an informal in-house survey on how the managers of different departments in various companies define quality. The following summarises the findings of the survey:

- For the marketing managers, the quality of the product is what makes it sell well.
- For the finance department, a quality product is one that is profitable for the company.
- For the production personnel, quality means conformance to specifications, standards, drawings, blueprints or other technical documents.
- For the workers advocate the quality gets defined when their line supervisors do not complain about their work/product.
- For the purchasing personnel, quality is perceived as a lower limit.
- For the research and development personnel, quality is defined as the state of art which is instrumental to develop the best possible products.
- For the representatives of certain government

---

3. This conclusion was drawn from a survey of consumer's perception of quality conducted in 28 product categories. For details see, *The Consumer Network Inc., Brand Quality Perceptions, Consumer Network,* Philadelphia, August, 1983.

organisations, a quality product is one that presents no threat to public safety and security.

- For the top managers, a quality product is one that enables them to satisfy the needs of the stockholders and the owners of the company.
- For the customers of the product quality represents the product's ability to satisfy their specific needs.

The examination of the above definitions and survey findings on quality reveal that, a quality product/service is one, which has fewer variations, lowers cost, more satisfied customers, and which enjoys more competitive advantage in the market.

From 'Quality' to 'Total Quality'

Until 1970, quality was mostly referred to product quality as defined by the customer and the customer alone. In the 1970s, Western companies started placing more emphasis on quality to keep hold of their market position or bring back lost shares in these markets. Nonetheless, the concept of total quality appeared in the 1980s only. This new hot topic has been variously defined over the years, thus engendering a great deal of bewilderment. Some articulate that '*total quality is a business strategy*'. Others contemplate it to be a '*new management philosophy*'. Yet others say, "*It's more than a program, it's a state of mind*", *or "It's not a program, it's a process*" (Kelda, 1996b). Even if these definitions are correct, the concept of total quality must be defined in a more concrete and measurable terms.

Total Quality (TQ) is a people focused management system that aims at continual increase in customer satisfaction. It is a total system approach (not a separate area or programme), and an integral part of high-level strategy which works horizontally across functions and departments by involving all employees from top to bottom and extending backward and forward to include the supply chain and the customer chain (Rampey & Roberts, 1992). The foundation of TQ is philosophical: the scientific method of TQ includes systems, methods and tools. TQ is anchored in values that stress the dignity of the individual and the power of community action" (Procter & Gamble, 1992).

Wakhlu (1994) has defined the term 'total quality' taking into consideration not only product quality, but also encompassing all facets of the organisation. He has defined total quality as, "*performance superiority in delighting customers. The means used are people, who are committed to employ organisational resources to provide value to customers by doing the right things right the first time, and every time.*"

This definition contains some important phraseology, which is discussed below:

Phrase # 1: Performance superiority: An organisation that is on the path of total quality has to strive towards being the 'best in the entire industry'. This is possible by constantly providing value to customers, which is possible only when the organisation is responsive to changes in customer requirements, technology and any other environmental factors that have a bearing on its ability to provide its customers the desired value.

Phrase # 2: Delighting customers: Today only those organisations excel who can anticipate their customers' requirements and strive to exceed them. This not only delights customers, but also provides firms with advantages that take time for the others to emulate, since they have a head start in figuring out what their customers seek.

Phrase # 3: Provide value: If a customer perceives that the product or service that he buys provides him value, then it can be assumed that quality of the goods relative to the cost incurred by the customer must be higher than that of competitors. The cost incurred by a customer could be the price or even the lifecycle cost, depending on the product. Thus, value may be defined as the ratio between quality and cost. Thus, $= \frac{\text{Quality}}{\text{Cost}}$

Phrase # 4: Doing the right things: It emphasizes the importance of ensuring that only those things be done in the organisation that add value to the final output. All else is wasted effort.

Phrase # 5: Right the first time: This suggests that organisations have to define their processes in such a way that the output is provided to the customer is exactly as planned, without errors of any kind.

Achieving Total Quality (TQ)

In order to achieve TQ, quality has to be 'built-into' and not 'inspected into' the product right from the quality at source to quality in manufacturing process to quality in customer's hands. In TQ, quality flows through different stages of the 'quality loop' as shown in Figure 1.1. This loop conceptualises that 'total quality' is an outcome of flow of quality through different activities namely, marketing, designing, engineering, purchasing, manufacturing, supervision and shop operation, inspection and testing, packing, distribution, installation and servicing to customer.

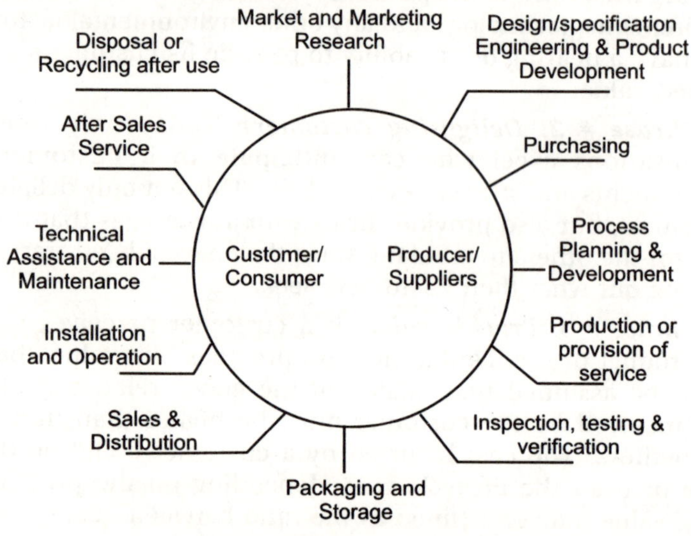

Figure 1.1. The Total Quality Loop

Source: Bureau of Indian Standards (1991). *Quality Management and Quality System Elements—Guidelines*, New Delhi.

The leading quality expert, Feigenbaum (1988) of General Systems Company Inc., USA has described seven characteristics of managing TQ. These characteristics are:

(i) TQ is not a technical function or department, but a systematic process that extends throughout the company.

(ii) TQ must be organised to recognise that while it is everybody's job in the company, it will become nobody's job unless quality process in the company is correctly structured to support both the quality of work of individuals and quality teamwork among departments.

(iii) TQ improvement must take place in marketing, development and engineering, in manufacturing and particularly in service department not merely in the production department.

(iv) TQ must be perceived to be what the buyer wants and needs to satisfy his requirements—not what the company needs to satisfy its requirements for marketing and production efficiency.

(v) TQ improvement requires applications of need technology ranging from quality design techniques to computer-aided quality management measures and control.

(vi) TQ improvement is achieved only through the help and participation from all the men and women in the workforce—not from just a few specialists.

(vii) For TQ attainment, the company has to establish a clear, and customer-oriented quality management system throughout the organisation which people can understand, believe in and want to be part of.

The House of Total Quality

The House of Total Quality presents an overview of the total quality philosophy and provides a comprehensive frame of reference, integrating key aspects of organisation design and operations. It consists of six components as depicted in Figure 1.2. These are,

(i) The roof or superstructure consists of four organisational systems within which the actual work of any organisation takes place: the management, social, technical and educational subsystems.

(ii) The four pillars of quality: customer satisfaction, continuous improvement, speaking with facts, and respect for people.

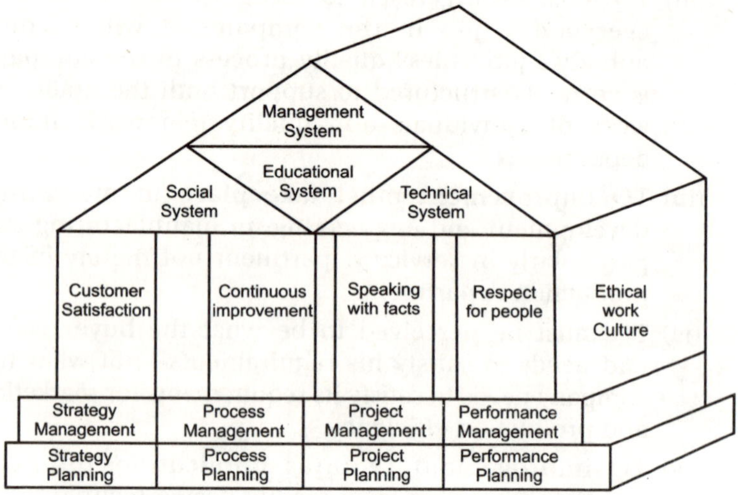

Figure 1.2. The House of Total Quality

(iii) The four foundations: strategy management, process management, project management, and individual task management.

(iv) The four cornerstones: strategic planning, process planning, project planning and task planning.

(v) The mortar of deployment between the joint of the roof, the pillars, the foundations and the customers.

(vi) The ethical work culture.

While the House of Total Quality provides the height and breadth of TQ, the organisational ethical work culture provides its depth and determines what it "feels like" to internal and external stakeholders who dwell there (Petrick & Furr, 1995). The ethical work culture of an organisation determines, whether the house becomes a home—a place where respect, cooperation, trust, caring, justice and high performance standards prevail on. Organisations with highly developed ethical work cultures demonstrate organisational integrity, which can be defined as "the collective alignment of moral awareness, judgment, intention and conduct around principled standards" (Petrick & Quinn, 1996, and Paine, 1996).

Classification of Organisations (in terms of quality concept): Big 'Q' and Small 'q' Organisations

(a) *Small 'q' – The Symbol for product focus in quality*

A lowercase 'q', usually known as 'Small q' is a symbol for a firms approach to quality. A 'small q' organisation emphasizes only on its products.

(b) *Big 'Q' – The Symbol for product, process and customer focus*

An uppercase 'Q' is the symbol used to denote a focus that goes beyond the product and encompasses the customers, the processes and the product.

Thus, while small 'q' firms have only the manufacturing orientation, big 'Q' firms have a holistic orientation, which includes all organisational activities, processes, products and services. Small 'q' denotes Quality Control (QC) and Big 'Q' denotes Company-Wide Quality Control (CWQC). A comparison between Big 'Q' and Small 'q' organisation is given in Table 1.2, and which is also represented in Figure 1.3.

TABLE 1.2: Comparison between Small 'q' and Big 'Q' Organisations

Sl. No.	Quality Element	Small 'q' Organisation	Big 'Q' Organisation
1.	The definition of quality is:	Product oriented	Customer oriented
2.	Emphasis is on:	Detecting errors	Preventing errors
3.	Costs are:	Raised when quality is emphasised	Lowered when quality is emphasised
4.	Cycle time is:	Lengthened to ensure quality work	Reduced dramatically through process improvements
5.	Responsibility of quality belongs to:	Quality Control/ Quality Assurance/ Inspectors or specialists	All employees
6.	The organisational culture tends towards:	Pointing fingers, finding blame and punishing risk takers	Continuous improvement, innovation and permission to fail
7.	Problem solving is by:	Those in authority, top of pyramid	Teams, all employee levels.

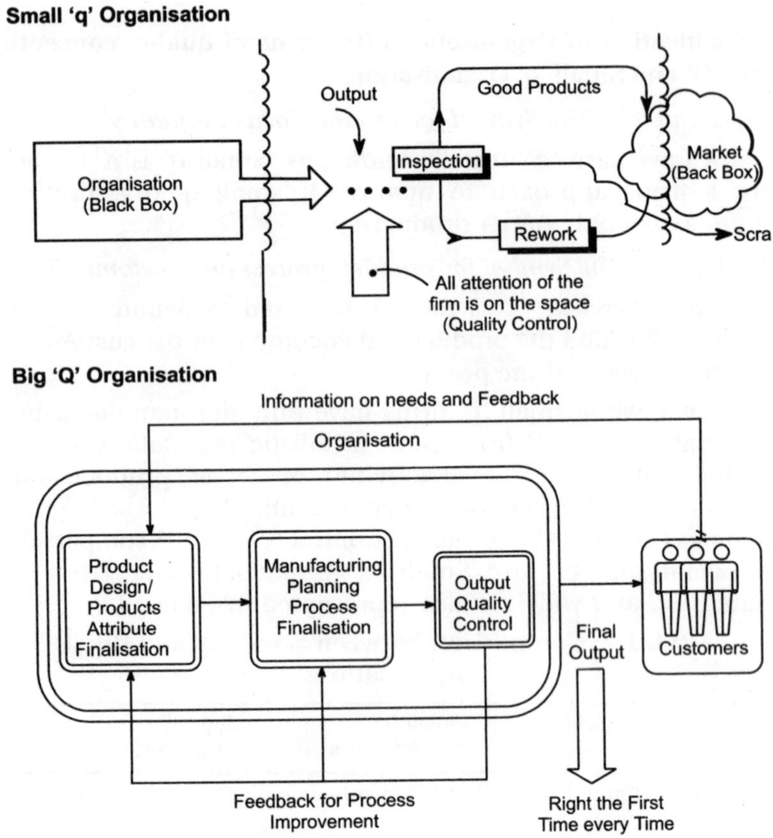

Figure 1.3. Small 'q' and Big 'Q' Organisations

The 'Management' Perspective

The 'M' in TQM implies that it is a management approach, not just a narrow quality control or quality assurance function. Someone from the quality control function may head-up and coordinate the TQM efforts, but to get away from this more traditional, and limited perspective, it would be more appropriate for someone from another department, someone who is respected and is a good communicator and "doer", to be the TQM project manager. The manager ideally should not only thoroughly understand and be able to train others in TQM, but also be a strong advocate and report directly to the General Manager/CEO (Luthans, 1995).

TOTAL QUALITY MANAGEMENT (TQM)

A descriptive analysis of these facets of TQM provides a crystal clear meaning to the term. Despite that, the concept lacks any universal definition. Practically every management author, consultant or practitioner has a different meaning for TQM (Luthans, 1993). Table 1.3 lists out some of the important definitions of TQM propounded by famous Quality Gurus and management experts.

These definitions capture in a few words what the objectives of a modern organisation should be. Meticulous examination of all these definitions divulges that:

> TQM is an holistic organisational approach to beget continuous improvement in products, services, and processes in conjunction with proper tools, technology and training to perpetually meet customers' expectations through total employees' involvement.

MODELS OF TQM

I. Integrated Model

Sohal, Tay and Wirth (1989) have discussed quality in terms of Total Quality Control rather than TQM, but refer control to the management of quality at various stages of the process. There are five elements in this model (Figure 1.4), which are essential to manage TQ.

- Customer (internal and external) focus;
- Management commitment;
- Total participation: Total Employment Involvement (TEI);
- Statistical Quality Control; and
- Systematic Problem-Solving Process; Plan-Do-Check-Act (PDCA) cycle.

II. Oakland's Model

The Oakland's (1989) model describes TQM as a pyramid representing five distinct components (Figure 1.5).

- Management commitment;
- Customer-supplier chains;

TABLE 1.3: Some Important Definitions of TQM

Definitions	Source
"A dynamic process involving all levels in an organisation to promote never ending improvement in the effectiveness and efficiency of all elements of business."	1
"The system of activities directed to achieving delighted customers, empowered employees, higher revenues, and lower costs."	2
"Continuous, customer-centred, employee-driven improvement."	3
"TQM means that the organisation's culture is defined by and supports the constant attainment of customer satisfaction through an integrated system of tools, techniques, and training. This involves the continuous improvement of organisational processes, resulting in high quality products and services."	4
"The TQM concept refers to company-wide quality assurance from suppliers to customers (external and internal) using systems approach of documented sets of procedures and control of process variability in a team spirit with top-management commitment."	5
"TQM refers to continuous profitability improvement."	6
"TQM is an integrated organisational approach for delighting the customers (both internal and external) by meeting their expectations on a continuous basis through everyone involved with organisation working on a continuous improvement in all products, services along with proper problem-solving methodology."	7
"TQM is an organisational strategy with accompanying techniques that deliver quality products and/or services to customers."	8
"Continuous improvement in quality through men and every other operational aspect of the organisation with customer at the centre of its activities."	9

Sources: 1. Deming, W. Edwards (1986). *Out of the Crisis*, Cambridge University Press, Cambridge.

2. Juran, J.M. and Gryana, F.M. (1995). *Quality Planning and Analysis*, 3rd edition, Tata McGraw Hill, p. 13.

3. Schonberger, R.J. (1992). "Total Quality Management Cuts a Broad Swath Through Manufacturing and Beyond",

- Systems approach of documented sets of procedures and standards;
- Statistical Process Control (S.P.C) tools; and
- Teamwork and continuous improvement.

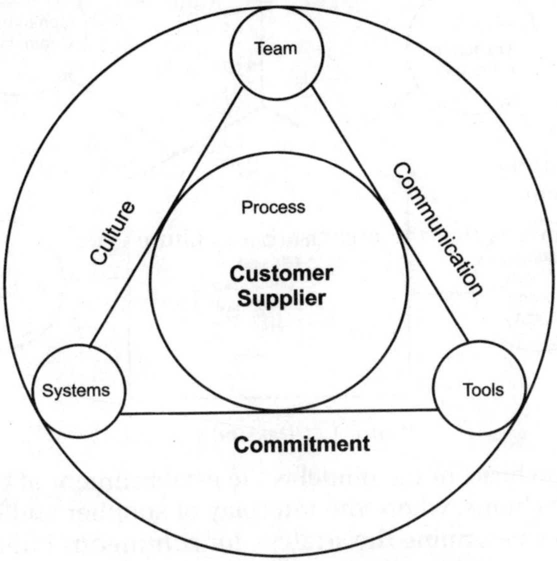

Figure 1.4. The Integrated Model of TQM

Organisational Dynamics, Spring, p. 18. Also see, Denton, D.K. (1995). "Creating a System for Continuous Improvement", *Business Horizon*, January-February, pp. 565-84.

4. Sashkin, M. and Kiser, K.J. (1993). *Putting Total Quality Management to Work*, San Francisco, Berrett-Koehler, p. 39.
5. Oakland, J.S. (1989). *Total Quality Management*, Heinemann Publishing Co., Oxford.
6. Stein, Robert E. (1994). *The Next Phase of TQM*, Marul Dekkel Inc., p. 4.
7. Anandaram, K.S. (2001). "Total Quality Management: A Goal for Organisations", *Indian Journal of Training and Development*, Vol. XXXI, No. 2, April-June, pp. 44-53.
8. Luthans, Fred (1995). *Organisational Behaviour*, McGraw Hill International Editions, Seventh Edition, Singapore, p. 30.
9. Khan, Praveen (2001). "Training Employees for Total Quality", *Indian Journal of Training and Development*, Vol. XXXI, No. 2, April-June, pp. 55-62.

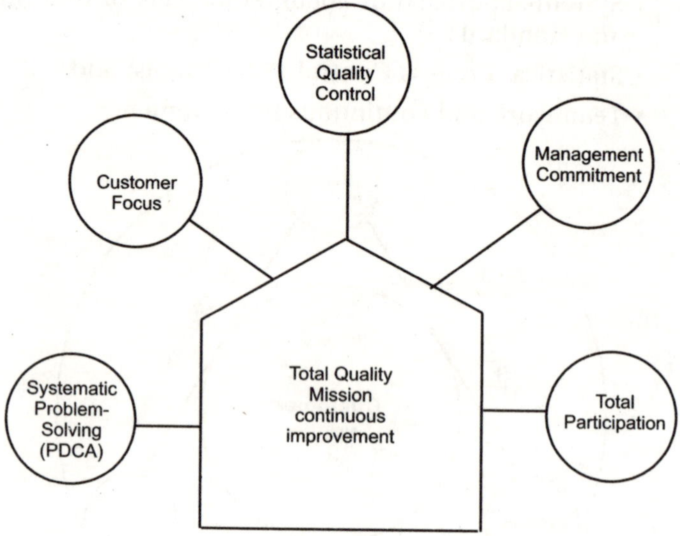

Figure 1.5. Oakland's Model

At the heart of the model is the establishment of customer-supplier chains, where the interplay of supplier and customer processes determine the strategy for continuous improvement through process feedback and customer feedback.

Oakland has enumerated the following thirteen strategies to represent a gradual progression towards implementing a TQM based culture. These are:

- Understanding quality
- Commitment to quality
- Policy on quality
- Organisation for quality
- Measurement costs of quality
- Planning for quality
- Design for quality
- System for quality
- Capability for quality
- Control for quality
- Teamwork for quality

- Training for quality
- Implementation of TQM

III. Quality-Sweating Theory

Kano (1989) has propounded the "Quality Sweating Theory" (Figure 1.6), which states that TQM is an effective tool for improving quality, but its success depends on making many

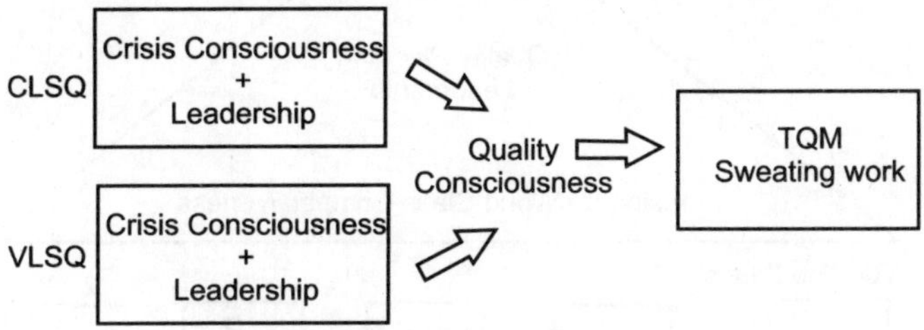

Figure 1.6. Quality Sweating Theory of TQM

employees sweat. This theory encompasses two alternative approaches: CLSQ (Crisis Consciousness and Leadership make people sweat for Quality) and VLSQ (Vision and Leadership encourage people to sweat for Quality).

IV. Building Blocks Model

Zairi (1991) at the Management Centre for Bradford University has developed the 'Building Blocks Model of TQM' (Figure 1.7).

This model proposes three kinds of building blocks to discuss total quality i.e., the foundation, pillars and the roof of TQ.

The Foundation of TQ: The three elements that constitute the foundation of TQM are:

- Continuous improvement;
- Value addition at each stage of every operation; and
- Employee involvement.

The Pillars of TQ: Pillars are the means by which the human creativity inputs can be converted into outputs for the benefit of the end customers. These are represented by various quality systems such as, procedures, documentation, use of Statistical Process Control (SPC), management control system, process flexibility provided by the use of computers, workplace design, ergonomics, and customer (both internal and external) supplier chain.

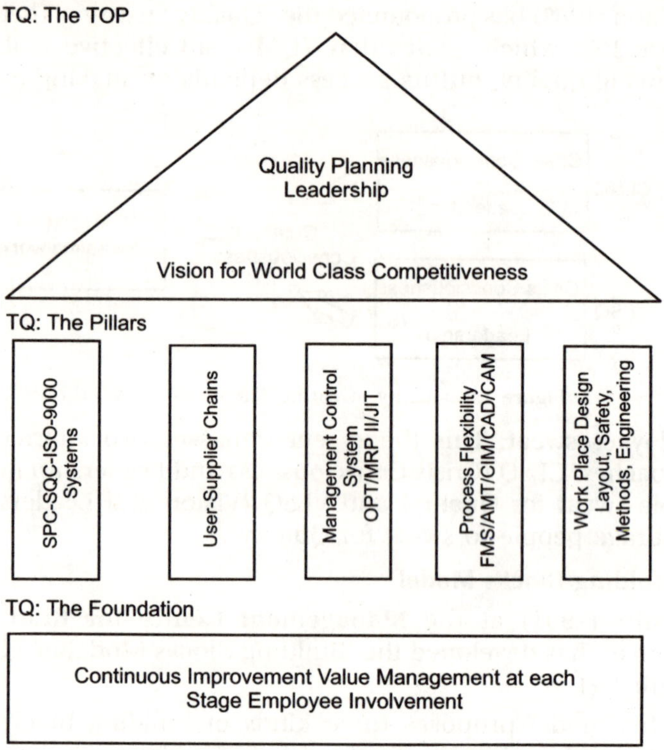

Figure 1.7. The Building Blocks Model of TQM

The Top of TQ: The topmost building block should shield the organisation from adverse external factors and protect it all the time. It should be weather proof (not affected by adverse changes in market place) and tangible (organisations are dynamic in nature and have to adapt to new market patterns). In this context, the senior managers must assume the responsibilities for:

- Quality planning;
- Leadership; and
- Vision for world-class competitiveness.

V. Theoretical Model

Anderson *et al.* (1994) have developed the 'Theoretical Model of Total Quality Management' on the basis of 'Deming's Management Method'. The theoretical essence of the Deming Management method uncovers the creation of an organisational system that fosters cooperation and learning to facilitate the implementation of process management practices. This in turn leads to continuous improvement of processes, products, and services and to employee fulfilment, both of which are critical to customer satisfaction and ultimately, to the survival of the organisation. The relational diagram of the theory of Total Quality Management underlying the Deming Management Method is illustrated in Figure 1.8.

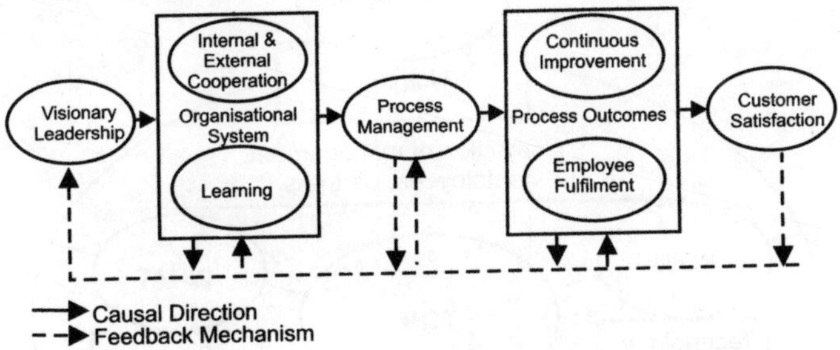

Figure 1.8. The Theoretical Model

The key concepts underlying the Deming Management Method are as follows:

- Visionary leadership;
- Internal and external cooperation;
- Learning;
- Process management;
- Continuous improvement;
- Employee fulfilment; and
- Customer satisfaction.

VI. Three-Dimensional Model

This model was developed by Joseph N. Kelda (1996) which emphasises upon the following three dimensions of TQM (Figure 1.9):

(i) The Human Dimension: psychological and political.

(ii) The Logical Dimension: rational and systematic.

(iii) The Technological Dimension: mechanical and systematic.

In his opinion, the human dimension is the most important one, yet is the least visible aspect of TQM.

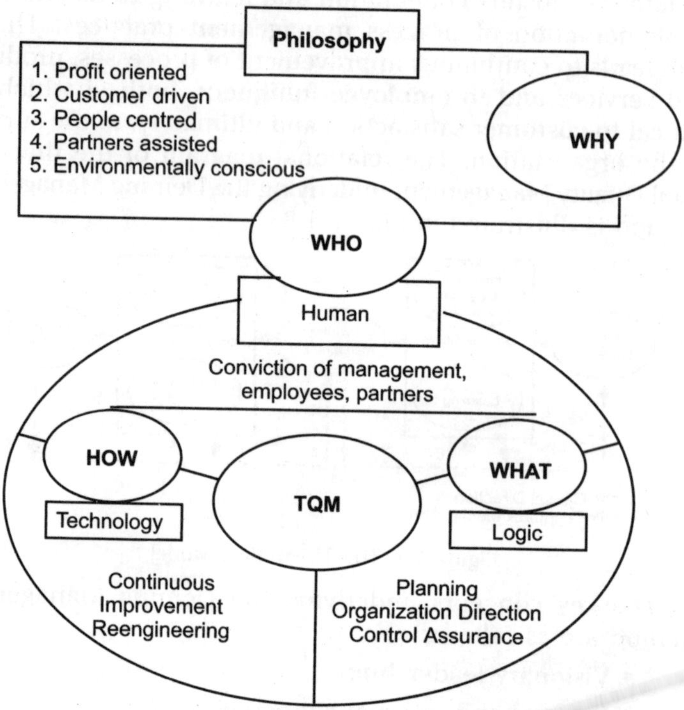

Figure 1.9. The Three Dimensional Model of TQM

VII. Pyramid Model

This model is developed by Kanji and Asher (1996a), who have defined TQM as, "a continuous process of improvement for individuals, groups of people, and the whole organisation". The model (Figure 1.10) illustrates TQM as a pyramid, the base of which is occupied by the four principles and two core concepts correspond to each side of the pyramid.

The model also indicates that organisation has to be guided through the TQM principles and core concepts of top management leadership.

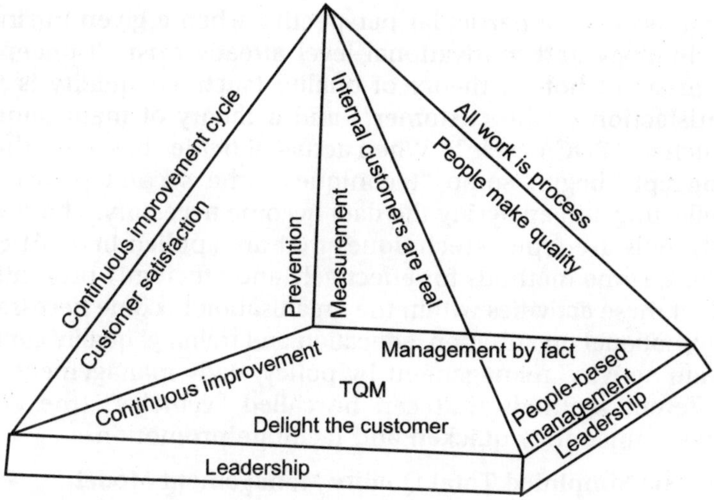

Figure 1.10. The Pyramid Model of TQM

VIII. The House of TQM

This model is developed by Kano (1997), which mostly deals with the structure of TQM (Figure 1.11).

From the figure, it is evident that the floor of TQM House symbolises "motivational approach" and the roof shows "customer satisfaction/quality assurance"—which is the ultimate purpose of TQM. The base is the "intrinsic technology", which refers to the driving technology specific to an industry. "Concepts" are of the pillars of the house which show how to

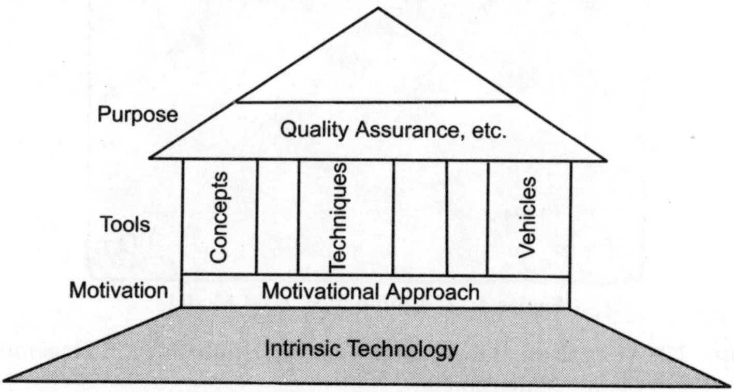

Figure 1.11. The House of TQM

proceed from a particular perspective when a given intrinsic technology and motivational level already exist. "Concepts" consists of both a theory of quality (such as "quality is the satisfaction of the customer") and a theory of management (such as "PDCA cycle"). When actual activities based on these concepts begin, some "techniques" (the second pillar) for collecting and analysing the data become necessary. The seven QC tools are typical techniques that are applied here. At this point, some methods for effectively and efficiently promoting all of these activities within the organisation become necessary. Promotional organisation, education and training, quality circles, team activity, management by policy, daily management are different methods that can be called "vehicles" (the third pillar) since they quicken and facilitate promotion.

IX. The Simplified Total Quality Management Model

Larry Green has developed this TQM model (Figure 1.12) on the basis of his experience over 15 years with TQM implementation in companies like GM, Crown International, Adams & Westlake, and many others. The Model is based upon the following assumptions, and supports the general

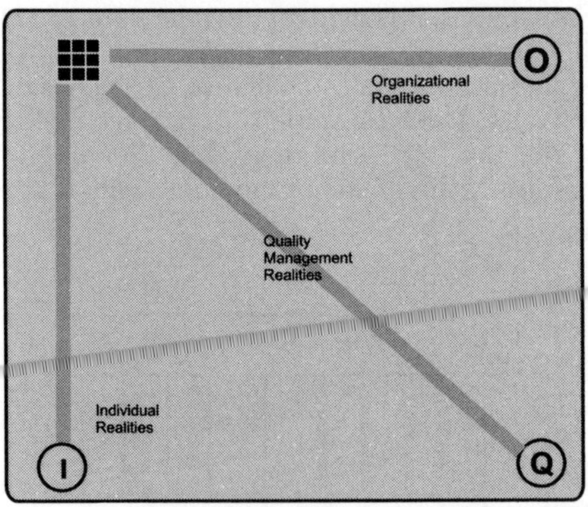

Figure 1.12. A Simplified TQM Model

Note: (O) Organisational Management; (I) Individual Management; (Q) Quality Management

Source: www. skyenet.net/~leg/tqm.htm - 8k

statements of Peter Senge's book (*The Fifth Discipline*) that leaders and managers must be generalists, understanding the systems they operate within.

Assumptions

- Simple Models are very powerful, easier to use, extremely effective, and needed by managers.
- Most companies already have over 75% of the elements needed for successful TQM in place.
- Implementing a successful TQM demands both immediate (profits) and strategic (cultural) planning.
- All three elements of Organisation, Individual and Quality Management must be in balance.
- Technology, Training and Teams are key, but teams, for teams sake, will fail every time.

The Model suggests that successful Total Quality Management requires both behavioural and cultural change. These three management systems must be aligned in a successful TQM initiative:

- OM (Organisational Management System),
- HRM (Human Resource Management Systems) and
- TQM (Total Quality Management).

A review of all these models reveal that they share eight common features (Nilakant & Ram Narayan, 1998). These are:

(i) Customer focus;
(ii) Strategic leadership;
(iii) Processes and systems;
(iv) Continuous improvement;
(v) Teamwork;
(vi) Empowerment;
(vii) Learning and experimentation; and
(viii) Complexity.[4]

---

4. In TQM jargon, complexity refers to unnecessary work or activities that do not increase quality. These could be extra process steps that are required to deal with external or internal errors. Reduction of these errors will eliminate unnecessary process steps leading to higher productivity. For details see, Fuller (1985).

PRINCIPLES AND CORE CONCEPTS OF TQM

There are variations in the language and scope of TQM programme. Different quality experts highlight upon different TQM principles. For instance, some have identified four common TQM principles:

(i) Do it right the first time to eliminate costly rework;

(ii) Listen to and learn from customers and employees;

(iii) Make continuous improvement on everyday matter; and

(iv) Build teamwork, trust and mutual respect (Bowen & Lawler III, 1992).

Some others have identified six common TQM principles (McShane, Steven & Glinow, 2001). Discussed below are these six principles that capture common themes in the field.

Customer Focus (CF)

Quality is always defined in terms of customers. A customer is anyone outside or inside the organisation to whom the employee supplies products, services or information (Goetsch & Davis, 1997; Milakovich, 1995; and Flood, 1993). The goal of satisfying customers is fundamental to TQM and is expressed by the organisation's endeavour to register decision and deliver products and services that fulfil customer needs. By being in close proximity to internal and external customers, employees feel a stronger sense of responsibility to ensure that the product/service is defect-free. Moreover, employees who receive high-quality services from others within the organisation tend to provide better service to external customers (Hallowell, Schelsinger & Zornitsky, 1996).

Employee Involvement (EI)

EI is an integral part of Quality Management because quality is the responsibility of all employees in everything they do. It is a practice within an organisation, whereby employees regularly participate in decision-making on how their work areas operate, including making suggestions for improvement, planning, goal setting, and monitoring performance. EI comes in different forms, but the trend is distinctly moving toward self-directed work-teams (Banker *et al.*, 1996).

Continuous Improvement (CI)

TQM is an unremitting system of improving work processes. CI is often called 'Kaizen', a Japanese word that literally means "good change" (Burlage, 1997). Originally a Buddhist term, Kaizen comes from the words, "Renew the heart and make it good." Therefore, adaptation of the Kaizen concept also requires changes in "the heart of the business", corporate culture and structure, since Kaizen enables companies to translate the corporate vision in every aspect of a company's operational practice. According to Imai (1986), an important advocate of Kaizen and who in fact coined the term, "Kaizen means improvement. Moreover it means continuing improvement in personal life, home life, social life, and working life. When applied to the workplace Kaizen means continuing improvement involving everyone—managers and workers alike." Believers of this theory maintain that managers of production operations cannot standstill; continuous development and improvement is critical to long term success. The 1995 Malcolm Baldrige National Quality Award criteria booklet states that, the term 'continuous improvement' refers to both incremental and 'breakthrough improvement'.

In practice, Kaizen can be implemented in corporations by improving every aspect of a business process in a step-by-step approach, while gradually developing employee skills through training education and increased involvement. Principles in Kaizen implementation are:

1. human resources are the most important company asset,
2. processes must evolve by gradual improvement rather than radical changes,
3. improvement must be based on statistical/quantitative evaluation of process performance.

Defect Prevention (DP)

TQM is built on the adage that 'a stitch in time saves nine'. A defect or error should be prevented at its origin, as the cost of repair increases exponentially as the defect moves further along the process. Thus, a central dogma of TQM is 'do it right the first time'. This quality philosophy also drives towards zero defects for the reason that even the smallest defect made may have extensive consequences.

Performance Measurement (PM)

Performance measurement is the core steerer for CI and defect prevention. By measuring the efficiency of work process and organisational outcomes, quality problems become noticeable and employees can see how their efforts are reducing these problems (Milakovich, 1995). This is in harmony with the trend towards fact-based management i.e., using objective rather than subjective information to assess quality and make corporate decisions.

Continuous Learning (CL)

'Learning' refers to acquiring knowledge, leading to new goals or approaches, and adaptation to change. TQM requires knowledgeable employees who have the ability to work in teams and adapt themselves to the dynamic work environment. In other words, TQM requires a heavy investment in employees' training and education. It envisages that learning should be a regular part of employees' daily work so that they can seek to eliminate problems at their source and be driven by opportunities to do better as well as by problems that need to be corrected.

TQM METHODS

TQM encompasses the above basic principles which can be put into practice by using suitable TQM methods. However, adopting the right kind of method is one of the most important jobs of the senior management and the degree of its success largely depends upon their knowledge and understanding of these TQM methods. All these methods can be classified into four Major categories:

- Management methods;
- Analytical methods;
- Idea generation; and
- Data collection, analysis and display (Kanji & Asher, 1996b).

A descriptive analysis of some of the important TQM methods is given below:

Design of Experiments (DOE)

DOE was first developed by Ronald Fisher in England in the 1920s to evaluate agricultural experiments in the natural conditions and was further developed by Taguchi in 1950s.

Purpose: DOE is a branch of applied statistics dealing with planning, conducting, analysing and interpreting controlled tests to evaluate the factors that control the value of a parameter or group of parameters. It is often used in conjunction with Quality Function Deployment.

Process: The following steps are important in using DOE.

- Obtain management support for the implementation of an experiment and approval for the required resources.
- Select a simple product and process to practice teamwork, methodology and interpretation of results.
- Organise the experiment team with people possessing both technical expertise and operating knowledge of the product and process to be studied.
- Establish team objectives, kinds of data and measurements required and method of operating.
- Perform the process analysis using appropriate QC tools to select the input factors for study.
- Formulate the experiment design and data sheets.
- Manipulate the process and run the experiment.
- Analyse the results and draw conclusions.
- Make an experimental confirmation run and identify requirements.

Benefits: DOE provides data that:

- Allow engineers to optimise the design characteristics so that performance variation can be minimised in the manufacturing and customer-use environments.
- Make products less sensitive to variations in their internal components.

- Identify best material, design or method that provides adequate performance.
- Provide the lowest cost design (avoid over-design).

Quality Function Deployment (QFD)

QFD was originated in 1972 at Mitsubishi's Kobe Shipyard site. Toyota began to develop the concept shortly thereafter and it has been used since 1977. Today, companies like GM, Ford, Xerox, and IBM are using QFD very successfully.

Purpose: QFD is used to translate customer requirements to engineering specifications. It is a link between customers–design engineers–competitors–manufacturing.

Process: QFD is a five-stage process that takes a design from customer requirements into a plan and schedule (Bossert, 1991; and Day, 1993):

1. Identifying customer needs or wants.
2. Translating requirements into technical specifications through the use of technical experts.
3. Turning the technical specifications into end-product specifications. These are called 'critical part characteristics'.
4. Designing the process to deliver the product or service.
5. Planning the activities necessary to produce the required output.

Figure 1.13 illustrates a typical QFD matrix, often called the 'House of Quality'. The left side of the matrix represents the first step, the top represents the second step, the right side shows the third step, the roof shows the fourth step and the central part represents the final step (Kanji & Asher, 1996c).

Benefits: QFD is very powerful as it incorporates the voice of the customer in the designs—hence it is likely that the final product will be better designed to satisfy the customer's needs:

- It provides an insight into the whole design and manufacturing operation (from concept to manufacture) and it can dramatically improve the efficiency as production problems are resolved early in the design phase.

- Improved communications and teamwork among all constituencies in the organisation.
- QFD helps to determine the causes of customer dissatisfaction.

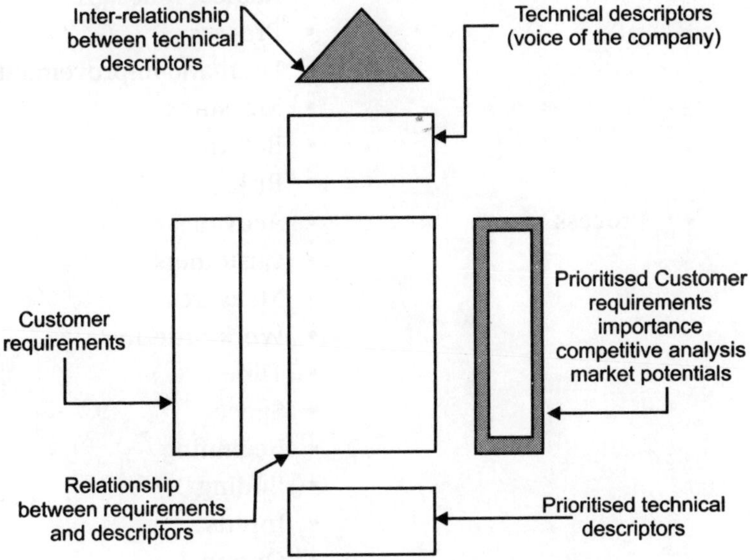

Figure 1.13. QFD Matrix

Re-engineering

Re-engineering has been a popular activity and another name for making major organisation-wide improvements. These are decisions by management based primarily on cost reduction.

***Purpose*:** Re-engineering is "the fundamental rethinking and radical redesign of business processes to achieve dramatic improvements in critical contemporary measures such as cost, quality, service and speed" (Hammer & Champy, 1992). Breakthrough redesign and process improvement, not structure reorganisation, are the common objectives of reengineering (Cartin, 2000b). Table 1.4 illustrates key reengineering concepts.

TABLE 1.4: Key Reengineering Concepts

Topic	Concept
• Reengineering	• Fundamental rethinking • Radical redesign • Process • Dramatic improvement • Measures • Return • Risk
• Process	• Activities • Customers • Measures • Work ordering • Time • Space • Beginning • Ending • Inputs • Outputs • Structure • Action • Baseline
• Redesign	• Process configuration • Design flows • Process transformation • Redesign alternatives

Source: Cartin, *op. cit.*, p. 102.

Process: There are usually two methodologies to reengineer business activities: (i) Critical Redesign Activities, and (ii) High-level Reengineering Activities. Both the methodologies are listed in Table 1.5 and Table 1.6.

TABLE 1.5: Critical Redesign Activities

Understanding and improving existing processes

1. Describe the current process flow
2. Measure the process in terms of the new process objectives.
3. Assess the process in terms of the new process attributes.
4. Identify problems with, or shortcoming of the process.
5. Identify short-term improvements in the process.
6. Assess current information technology and organisation.

Designing and prototyping a new process

1. Brainstorm design alternatives.
2. Assess feasibility, risk and benefit of design alternatives.
3. Select the preferred process design.
4. Prototype the new process design
5. Develop a migration strategy.
6. Implement a new organisational structures and systems.

Source: Davenport, T.H. (1993). *Process Innovation: Reengineering Work Through Information Technology*, Harvard Business School Press, Boston.

TABLE 1.6: High-level Reengineering Activities

1. Identifying process for innovation.
2. Identifying change levers (that is enabling or transformation technologies).
3. Developing process visions.
4. Understanding and improving existing processes.
5. Designing and prototyping the new process.

Source: Davenport, *op. cit.*

Benefits

- Reengineering helps in clarifying the responsibility between organisation functions about how work actually gets done, what processes are needed and how they should relate.
- It eliminates work not contributing to goals.

Just-in-Time (JIT)

JIT usage began in the USA in the late 1980s. The first success with JIT occurred in Japan i.e., in Toyota Company.

Purpose: JIT is an optimal material requirement planning system for a manufacturing process in which there is little or no manufacturing material inventory on hand at the manufacturing site and little or no incoming inspection.

Process: Figure 1.14 illustrates the themes and concepts of JIT and their interrelationships. All are treated as integral parts of JIT's application. The outer circle identifies the major elements and the inner circle notes the three areas of focus.

Figure 1.14. Elements of JIT and their Interrelationships

Source: Cartin, *op. cit.*, p. 128.

Benefits: JIT helps to eliminate stocks in order to prevent unproductive stock cost.

Zero Defects

Zero Defects is a performance standard developed by Philip B. Crosby (1984) to address a dual attitude in the workplace. People are willing to accept imperfection in some areas and at the same time they expect the number of defects to be zero. This dual attitude had developed because of the recognition of the fact that people are human beings and are prone to mistakes. However, the zero defects methodology states that, if people commit themselves to watching details and avoiding errors, they can move closer to the goal of zero.

Purpose: Zero Defects allows teams to experience the success involved in meeting over more demanding target without demotivating them by not achieving absolute success at once.

Processes: Zero Defects is a very simple concept described by Crosby (1984) using the team approach:

1. Identify and agree the current level of performance.
2. Agree a target and time-scale for the target to be met with milestones.
3. Monitor performance against the target and publish the results.
4. If the target is met on time, recognise the team's performance and step 2 is to be repeated.

Benefits: Zero Defects give a way of setting tougher targets and recognising the success of teams that meet them, so as to encourage future efforts.

Benchmarking

Xerox developed the concept of benchmarking in 1979 and subsequently it has been widely adopted by other companies. Benchmarking is an improvement process in which a company measures its performance against that of best-in-class companies. It determines how those companies achieved their performance levels and use the information to improve their own performance. The subjects that can be benchmarked include strategies, operations, processes and procedures.

Purpose: Benchmarking identifies and fills gaps in performance by putting in place best practice. Thus, it establishes superior performance.

Process: There are three distinct types of benchmarking which can be used by an organisation progressively to stimulate the improvement process. These are:

1. Internal benchmarking: It is the comparison between functions, departments or similar organisation as a means of improving performance.
2. Competitive benchmarking: It is a cross-comparison within one industry sector aimed at establishing best practice through the identification of gaps between own and competitor's performance.
3. Comparative benchmarking: It is the comparison across all business sectors aimed at establishing best practice in all areas of operation.

Figure 1.15 depicts an eleven-step process based on implementation of benchmarking as a sequence or a process.

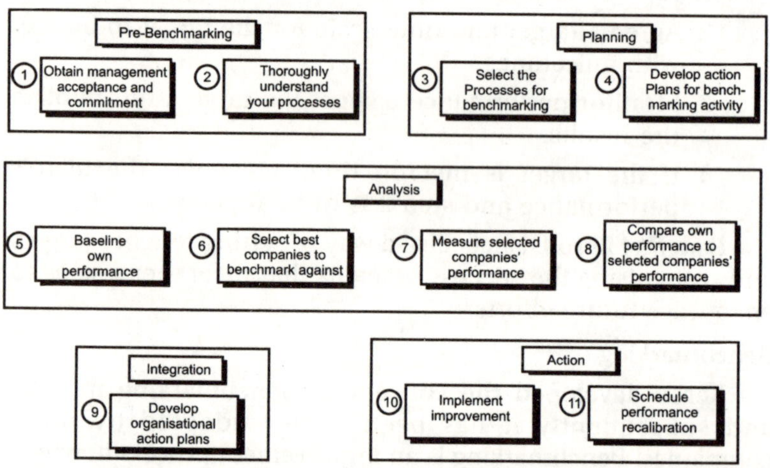

Figure 1.15. Eleven-Step Benchmarking Process

Source: Camp, R.C. (1989). *Benchmarking: The Search for Industry Best Practices that Lead to Superior Performance*, ASQC Quality Press, Milwaukee.

Benefits: Benchmarking accrues several valuable benefits such as:

- Highly motivating for an organisation to know that it is performing as well or better than the best.

- Provides an introduction to the idea of measurement.
- Helps organisations to move away from being introspective towards being externally focused and close to their markets.

Concurrent Engineering (CE)

CE refers to the cross-functional integration and concurrent development of a product or service and its associated processes (Swink, Scandvig & Mabert, 1996; Zangwill, 1993; and Owen, 1992).

Purpose: CE is a methodology for the design, development and manufacture of products that meet the market/customer demand for high quality, low cost and fast delivery.

Process: Generally, CE occurs by assigning product development to a cross-functional project team consisting of people from the key functional organisations like marketing, reengineering, manufacturing, quality engineering and suppliers. Figure 1.16 makes a comparison between how the product development process traditionally works and makes a comparison between how the product development process traditionally works and makes a comparison between how the product development process traditionally works and works under CE.

Benefits: The results as demonstrated by Japan and companies initiating CE in the West reveal that CE products are:

- More desired by the marketplace;
- More competitive;
- Involved with lower engineering and manufacturing costs; and
- Shorter design delivery cycle times (Cartin, 2000c).

Continuous Improvement (CI)

Purpose: CI includes the actions taken throughout an organisation to increase the effectiveness and efficiency of activities and processes in order to provide added benefits to the customer and organisation. It is considered as a subset of TQM and operates according to the premise that organisations can always make improvements.

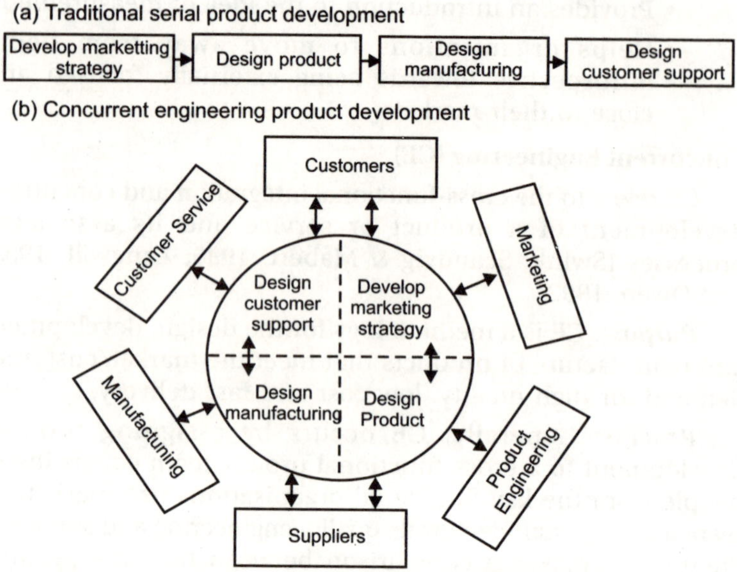

Figure 1.16. Traditional and Concurrent Product Development

Source: McShane *et al., op. cit.*, p. 325.

***Process*:** A number of tools have been developed over the years for achieving CI, beginning with the pioneering work of Shewhart at Bell Laboratories in the 1920s. Kaoru Ishikawa made the next major practical contribution to the QC tool kit in the 1960s by combining Shewhart's work with some of his own and describing seven Quality Control (QC) tools (Ishikawa, 1971). Also in the 1960s, the Union of Japanese Scientists and Engineers (JUSE) fostered the development of seven management tools for QC (Kamikubo, 1989). These are tools used to make qualitative analysis of problems of complex nature, which are not well defined. Both sets of tools are listed in Table 1.7 and the details about the tools are given in Appendix 1.2.

***Benefits*:** The seven management tools are linguistic and graphic for exploring problems, organising ideas, converting concepts into action plans, and designing criteria and so forth. The benefits that they accrue are as follows:

- They can be used in planning, R & D, designing and selling products.
- The seven QC tools are a graphic means for problem solving through group thinking and analysis of data.
- Use of all these tools facilitate orderly, organised and focused thinking from which we can distil information from a variety of sources.

TABLE 1.7: The Seven QC and Seven QC Management Tools

Seven QC Tools	Seven QC Management Tools
• Pareto diagram	• Affinity diagram (K-J)
• Cause-and-effect diagram	• Relationship diagram
• Flowchart	• Tree diagram
• Check sheet	• Matrix chart
• Histogram	• Matrix data analysis chart
• Scatter diagram	• Arrow diagram
• Graphs and Control charts	• Process decision

Quality Circle (QC)

The concept of QC was originated in Japan and was originally known as Quality Control Circle. QC is a small group of employees from the same work area performing similar work, who volunteer to meet regularly for one to one and half hour each week on company time.

Purpose: The purpose of QC is to identify the causes of work related problems, quality problems and to propose solutions to the management to take corrective actions. Improvement in the total performance leading to higher productivity and enrichment of the quality of work life are the ultimate goals of QCs.

Process: QC leaders and members should be trained in the techniques such as, brainstorming, tally charts, concentration diagrams, Pareto analysis, histograms, cause and effect analysis, and control charts to achieve the end.

Benefits: QC activities maybe helpful to the organisation in the following ways:

- Contribute to the improvement and development of the enterprise.
- Respect humanity and build a worthwhile-to-live-in, happy bright workshop.
- Exercise human capabilities fully and eventually draw out infinite possibilities (Udapa, 1986).

Suggestion Schemes

Purpose: To generate ideas for improvement.

Process: The following are guidelines for successful administration of suggestion schemes:

1. Set up a steering group to oversee the process.
2. Delegate as far down as practical the decision on whatever or not to implement the suggestion.
3. Give awards to supervisors and managers whose employees generate most ideas.
4. In the early stages go for quantity of ideas, rather than quality.
5. To generate ideas in manageable numbers try to set themes for ideas and change the themes regularly.
6. Ensure that all ideas are acknowledged quickly and that the person generating the idea is told whether it is to be implemented or not, what is the reason.
7. Look for reasons to say 'yes' rather than 'no'.
8. In the early stages be prepared for ideas to be about environmental aspects rather than operational ones.

Benefits: Suggestion schemes provide a way of moving to continuous improvement via small incremental changes.

ISO-9000 Series

The British Standard as BS 5750 originally created ISO-9000. The International Organisation for Standardization (ISO) now maintains the standard. ISO is a specialised international agency for standardization composed of the national standards of 91 countries in the year 1987. An overview of the ISO standards is shown in Appendix 1.3.

Purpose: ISO-9000 certification indicates that a company performs above a minimum level of quality and competence.

Process: The requirements for ISO-9000 Certification are depicted in Table 1.8.

TABLE 1.8: Requirements of ISO-9000

ISO-9001	ISO-9002	ISO-9003
1. Management responsibility	■	●
2. Quality system	■	●
3. Contract review	■	■
4. Design control	▲	▲
5. Document control	■	■
6. Purchasing	■	▲
7. Purchaser-supplied product	■	■
8. Product identification and traceability	■	●
9. Process control	■	▲
10. Inspection and testing	■	■
11. Inspection, measuring, and test equipment	■	■
12. Inspection and test status	■	●
13. Control of nonconforming product	■	●
14. Corrective action	■	●
15. Handling, storage, packaging and delivery	■	■
16. Quality records	■	●
17. Internal quality audits	■	●
18. Training	■	●
19. Servicing	■	▲
20. Statistical techniques	■	●

■ Full requirement ● Minimal ▲ Not required

Source: Cartin, *op. cit.*, p. 238.

Benefits: It ensures consistent quality for customers.

Six Sigma

Six Sigma is a quality manangement programme to achieve "six sigma" levels of quality. It was pioneered by Motorola in the mid-1980s and has spread to many other manufacturing companies. It continues to spread to service companies as well.

***Purpose*:** Six Sigma aims to have the total number of failures in quality, or customer satisfaction, occur beyond the sixth sigma of likelihood in a normal distribution of customers. Sigma stands for a step of one standard deviation; designing processes with tolerances of at least six standard deviations will, on reasonable assumptions, yield fewer than 3.4 defects in one million.

***Process*:** Basic methodology to improve the existing processes: **Define**: out of tolerance range. **Measure**: key internal processes critical to quality. **Analyze**: why defects occur. **Improve**: the process to stay within tolerance. **Control**: the process to stay within goals. And the basic methodology of introducing new processes. **Define**: the process and where it would fail to meet customer needs. **Measure**: and determine if process meets customer needs. **Analyze**: the options to meet customer needs. **Design**: in changes to the process to meet customers needs. **Verify**: the changes have met customer needs.

***Benefits*:** Achievement of six-sigma quality is defined by Motorola in terms of the number of Defects Per Million Opportunities (DPMO), that is, fewer than *four in one million customers* will have a legitimate issue with the company's products and service.

Internal Customer Satisfaction (ICS)

***Purpose*:** The purpose of ICS is to build positive relationship between customers and suppliers both inside and outside the organisation. In a quality organisation, employees must realise that providing outstanding service to the internal customers also enables the organisation to provide outstanding service to external customer.

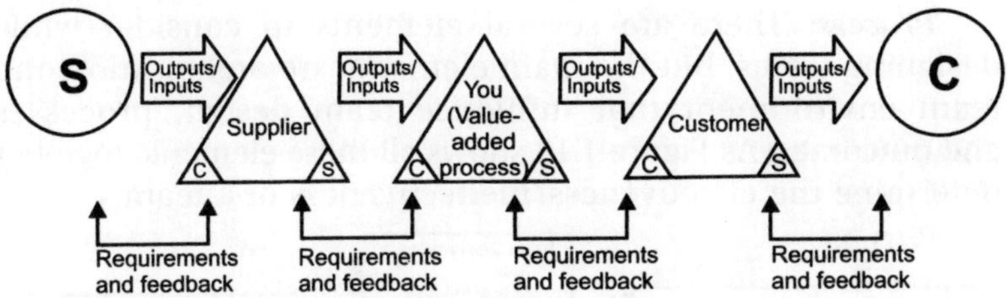

Figure 1.17. Customer-Supplier Chain

Process: The customer-supplier chain given in Figure 1.17 shows that any work can be seen as a customer-supplier chain in which customers receive inputs from their suppliers, value to those inputs and then pass those outputs on to their own customers. Therefore, everyone in an organisation must understand that,

- One becomes a customer when he gets materials, information or service from others inside the organisation or from outside.
- One becomes a supplier when he supplies materials, information or services to others inside the organisation or to external customers.
- As a customer, things received from others are inputs.
- As a supplier, things that are supplied are outputs.
- Customers and suppliers exchange information about their requirements and provide one another with feedback on how to meet those requirements.

Benefits

- Building positive relationship between customer and supplier which ultimately leads to doing right things right and is the key of adding value to the inputs.
- Workflow becomes smoother.

Team Work

Teams are groups of two or more people, who interact and influence each other, and are mutually accountable for achieving common objectives and perceive themselves as a social entity within an organisation (Cohen & Bailey, 1997).

Purpose: To provide expression to employee empowerment and involvement.

Process: There are several elements to consider while designing teams, but the main elements are organisation and team environment that influence team design, processes and outcomes. As Figure 1.18 shows all these elements together determine the effectiveness/ineffectiveness of a team.

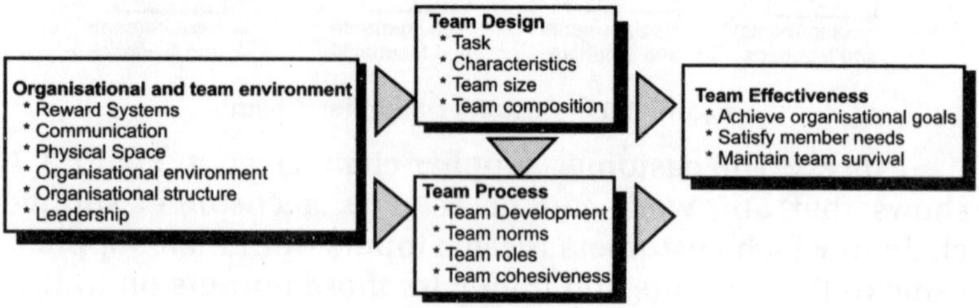

Figure 1.18. Team Effectiveness

Benefit: Teamwork helps to develop a quality strategy or to achieve solutions to a problem that is vital to the company.

THE HUMAN DIMENSION OF TQM

There is an important role for Human Resources (HR) in this sophisticated quality improvement process approach. The TQM initiatives are unlikely to come off without the support of people. TQM is in essence people-driven and profoundly reliant on the contribution that members make to the realization of organisational excellence. Without people being vigorously involved in the TQM process, no amount of 'jugglery' with any other factors that contribute to the attainments of quality objectives is likely to bring it any where near performance superiority.

What the Quality Gurus Speak

The Quality Gurus have made substantial contribution to the field of human dimension of TQM. Notable among them are: W. Edwards Deming, Joseph M. Juran, and Philip B. Crosby. Undoubtedly, the names of Ishikawa and Feigenbaum are also worth mentioning.

Deming's Legacy

TQM is resolutely established today, thanks in large part to the groundbreaking work of W. Edwards Deming.[5]

5. Deming's landmark work is Deming, W.E. (1986). *Out of the Crisis*, *op. cit.*

Paradoxically, the mathematician endorsed with Japan's post-World War II quality revolution rarely talked in terms of quality. He instead preferred to discuss "good management" during the hard-hitting seminars he delivered right up until his death at the age 93 in 1993 (Trumbull, 1993; and Hillkirk, 1993). Although Deming's passion was the statistical measurement and reduction of variations in industrial processes, he had much to say about how employees should be treated at workplaces.

One of Deming's most enduring lessons for managers is his 85-15 rule which states that very often, when things go wrong, there is roughly about 85% of the time (including management, machinery and rules) is at fault and only about 15% of the time individual employee is at fault. Unfortunately, as Deming observed, the typical manager spends most of his or her time wrongly blaming and punishing individuals for system failures. This management philosophy is captured in his famous 14 points (given in Table 1.9) and he has synthesised the underlying foundation behind the 14 points in what he called *"A system of profound knowledge"* (Deming, 1993). Thus he strongly argued that most errors and defects are the result of bad systems, not bad workers. His system eliminates adversarial relationships between departments and empowers workers. It promotes the anticipation and creation of customer needs well ahead of time.

Deming recommended the following measures pertaining to the human dimension of quality improvement:

- Formal training to employees in statistical process control techniques and teamwork.
- Helpful leadership, rather than order giving and punishment.
- Elimination of fear so that employees will be free to ask questions.
- Emphasis on continuous process improvements, rather than on numerical quotas.
- Teamwork.
- Elimination of barriers to good workmanship (Walton, 1990).

TABLE 1.9: Deming's 14 Points

1. Create and publish to all employees a statement of the aims and purposes of the company or other organisation. The management must demonstrate constantly their commitment to this statement.
2. Learn the new philosophy: top management and everybody.
3. Understand the purpose of inspection, for improvement of processes and reduction of cost.
4. End the practice of awarding business on the basis of price tag alone.
5. Improve constantly and forever the system of production and service.
6. Institute training.
7. Teach and institute leadership.
8. Drive out fear. Create trust. Create a climate for innovation.
9. Optimize toward the aims and purposes of the company the efforts of teams, groups, staff areas.
10. Eliminate exhortations for the workforce.
11. (a) Eliminate numerical quotes for production. Instead, learn and institute methods for improvement.
    (b) Eliminate M.B.O. instead, learn the capabilities of process, and how to improve them.
12. Remove barriers that rob people of pride of workmanship.
13. Encourage education and self-improvement for everyone.
14. Take action to accomplish the transformation.

Juran's Legacy

Dr. Joseph M. Juran, the son of an immigrant shoemaker from Romania, began his industrial career at Western Electronics' Hawthorne plant before World War-II and later he worked at Bell Laboratories in the area of quality assurance. Juran is the creator of many of the basic concepts of statistical quality control and authored a book titled *The Quality Control Handbook* (Juran & Gryna, 1988), which has become an international standard reference for the quality movement.

Juran believed that management and the system are responsible for quality improvement. He developed a perpetual spiral of progress or continuous striving towards quality. Juran's concept of quality included the managerial dimension for quality planning, quality control and quality improvement (known as Juran Trilogy) and focused on the responsibility of management to achieve quality. He called for the following regarding the human side of quality improvement:

- Create awareness of the need and opportunities to improve.
- Set goals for continuous improvement.
- Provide training to all.
- Give recognition.
- Communicate results.[6]

Juran suggested that by implementing his theories of quality improvement, not only the higher quality products are produced, but also the actual costs be lowered. His cost of quality principle is known as '*Gold in the Mine*'.

Ishikawa's Legacy

Prof. Kaoru Ishikawa (1915-89) is more popularly known as the 'Father of Quality Circles' for his role in launching Japan's quality movement in the 1960s. As the President of JUSE, he was instrumental in developing a unique Japanese strategy to total quality, i.e., the broad development of the entire organisation in its total sense—every worker, every process, and every job.

Ishikawa identified several critical human factors that are essential for the success of total quality control. These are:

- Participation by all members of the organisation in the company-wide quality control activities.
- Education and training in all aspects of total quality, which often accounts to 30 days per year per employee.

6. These five steps form part of "ten steps to quality" as suggested by Juran. The others are: organise to reach goals, carryout projects to solve problems, report progress, keep score, and maintain momentum. For details see, Juran and Gryna (1988). *Juran's Quality Control Handbook, op. cit.*

- Use of quality control circles to update standards and regulations, which are in constant need of improvement.
- Revolutionary mental attitude on part of both management and workers towards one another and toward the customer, including welcoming complaints, encouraging risk, and a wider span of control.[7]

Ishikawa believed that the management practices should be democratic. The top management must provide guidelines responsibility to guide people and implement the policies so that all uniformly follows them.

Feigenbaum's Legacy

A.V. Feigenbaum is best known for coining the term Total Quality Control and for his pioneering 850-page book on the subject (Feigenbaum, 1983). His teachings centre around the integration of people-machine-information structure in order to economically and effectively control quality and achieve full customer satisfaction. In his book, he uses the concept of the "9M's" to describe the factors that affect quality: (1) Markets, (2) Money, (3) Management, (4) Men, (5) Motivation, (6) Materials, (7) Machine and Mechanisation, (8) Modern information methods, and (9) Mounting product requirements. These methods led to increased quantification of total quality programme improvements during the 1970s and 1980s.

Crosby's Legacy

Unlike the other quality gurus, Philip Crosby, who hailed from the rank of an Inspector and ultimately became the Corporate Vice-President of a company, is known for his motivational talks and style of presentation. He first developed the concept of Zero Defects while working as a Quality Manager at Martin Marietta Corporation in Orland, Florida. Crosby does not believe that workers should take prime responsibility for poor quality. In the Crosby scheme of things, management

---

7. The other non-human critical factors Ishikawa identified for the achievement of quality are: quality audits, widespread use of statistical methods and a focus on problem prevention, and nation-wide quality control promotion activities. Kaoru, Ishikawa (1985). *What is Total Quality Control – The Japanese Way,* Prentice Hall, Englewood Cliffs, NJ.

sets the tone on quality and workers follow their example; whilst employees are involved in operational difficulties and draw them to management's attention, the initiative comes from the top.

He has developed fourteen steps for a quality improvement programme, which are set out in Table 1.10.

TABLE 1.10: Crosby's Fourteen Steps to Quality Improvement

Step–1	*To make clear management's commitment to quality.
Step–2	*To set up quality improvement teams with representatives from each department.
Step–3	To set in place quality measurement to provide a display of current and potential non-conformance problems.
Step–4	To determine the 'cost of quality' and explain how to use it as a management tool.
Step–5	*To raise the level of quality awareness and personal concern for the company's quality reputation for all employees.
Step–6	To take corrective action on the problems raised in the previous steps.
Step–7	To plan a zero defects programme.
Step–8	*To train the supervisors actively to carry out their part in the total quality improvement process.
Step–9	*To hold a zero defects day to create an event that will let all employees through a personal experience that there has been a change.
Step–10	*Goal setting and encouraging individuals and groups to set improvement goals.
Step–11	*To encourage employees to communicate to management the difficulties they have in achieving their improvement goals in the error-cause removal campaign.
Step–12	*To recognise and appreciate all those who participate in the programme.
Step–13	*To establish quality councils to communicate on a regular basis.
Step–14	To do it all over again to emphasise that quality programmes never end and that they are indeed a journey not a destination.

Note: *Implies emphasis given by Crosby on human aspects of quality improvement programme.

Source: Crosby, *op. cit.*

Crosby's goal is to give all staff the training and the tools of quality improvement, to apply the basis precept of Prevention Management in every area. This is aided by viewing all work as a process or series of actions conducted to produce a desired result. His basic elements of improvement include: determination, education and implementation. By determination, he meant that the top management must be serious about quality improvement. Everyone should understand the absolutes and this could be accomplished only through proper education and guidance. Finally, every member of the management team must understand the implementation process (Evans & Dean, Undated).

The above analysis indicates that all the quality gurus intrinsically highlight on the humanistic dimension of quality management and clamour for treating people fair and square at the workplace.

Position of Human Resources under Different Quality Awards

Today, nearly sixty quality awards exist internationally, many based on criteria of the Malcolm Baldrige National Quality Award. Moreover, forty-three states in the United States have now established quality awards (compared to only ten in 1991) (Smart, 2001). Therefore the discussion is made with reference to the Baldridge Award only.

The US Congress created the Malcolm Baldrige National Quality Award, named after the late Secretary of Commerce of the United States, in 1987. It is the highest level of national recognition for quality performance and practices that a US organisation can receive. The U.S. Commerce departments and National Institute of Standards and Technology (NIST) control the programme. The Baldrige criteria are built upon a set of core values and concepts that include visionary leadership, customer-driven excellence, valuing employees and partners, management by fact, and a focus on results and creating value. These core values are embodied in the seven Baldrige Categories and each award category is briefly explained, along with the role human resource (HR) professionals have in the quality improvement process.[8]

1. ***Leadership***: Examines how executives and management create and sustain visible quality values with goals and plans to integrate quality principles and with training and rewards for quality efforts. HR professionals must assure that the top

8. The discussion is based upon the writings of Kemelgor, Bruce and Mears, Peter, "HR's Role In The CQI Process", *Journal for Quality & Participation*, Oct/Nov 95, Vol. 18.

management is committed to improving quality. The emphasis needs to be on actions taken, not simply what management says they are doing. They have to organise workshops on changing the organisation's culture, training in coaching and counselling skills, and assistance in clearly communicating the organisation's goals and objectives.

2. *Strategic Planning*: Strategic Planning addresses strategic and action planning, deployment of plans and how accomplishments are measured and sustained. The Category stresses that customer-driven quality and operational performance are key strategic issues that need to be integral parts of the organisation's overall planning.

HR professionals should ensure that all employees participate in the planning process. One way of realizing this is to have departments conduct periodic meetings devoted to quality improvement. Focus the discussion on what can be done to improve customer satisfaction with your services during the coming year.

3. *Customer and Market Focus*: Assesses the company's knowledge of and responsiveness to customers, customer satisfaction, and customer and market requirements and expectations. The category stresses relationships as an important part of an overall listening, learning, and performance excellence strategy.

Here the role of HR Professionals is to make the employees to learn how to identify the customers needs, and to satisfy them. HR professionals have long recognized the importance of human relations skills in employees who come in direct contact with customers. Factors, such as rendering a service with a smile, thanking a customer, and being courteous are examples of such skills, which influence customer satisfaction. The HR department is in an excellent position to assist other departments in identifying key factors influencing customer satisfaction, so that specific training programmes focused on quality service can be developed.

4. *Measurement, Analysis and Knowledge Management*: This category is the main point as it examines all key information about effectively measuring and analyzing performance and managing organisational knowledge to drive improvement and organisational competitiveness. HR professionals need to become facilitators by bringing members of various departments together, and assisting them as a group in identifying the critical factors influencing their quality.

5. ***Human Resource Focus***: Human Resource Focus addresses key human resource practices—those directed toward creating and maintaining a high-performance workplace and toward developing employees to enable them and their organisation to adapt to change. The category covers human resource development and management requirements in an integrated way, i.e., aligned with the organisation's strategic objectives.

The Human Resource Professionals in this context must strive for building the employee support climate. They must assure that all employees are informed of quality goals, trained in the use of quality techniques, evaluated based on quality criteria, and that employees are recognized for quality accomplishments.

6. ***Process Management***: It is the focal point within the criteria for all key work processes built into the Category are the central requirements for efficient and effective process management: effective design; a prevention orientation; linkage to customers, suppliers and partners and a focus on value creation for all key stakeholders; operational performance; cycle time; and evaluation, continuous improvement, and organisational learning. Agility, cost reduction, and cycle time reduction are increasingly important in all aspects of process management and organisational design. In simplest terms, "agility" refers to ones ability to adapt quickly, flexibly, and effectively to changing requirements. Depending on the nature of the organisation's strategy and markets, agility might mean rapid changeover from one product to another, rapid response to changing demands, or the ability to produce a wide range of customized services. Flexibility demands special strategies, such as implementing modular designs, sharing components, sharing manufacturing lines, and providing specialized training. Cost and cycle time reduction often involve lean process management strategies. It is crucial to utilize key measures for tracking all aspects of the overall process management.

TQM system includes internal departments such as the HR department itself. HR management can be a role model in the quality improvement effort by developing their own systems to collect internal customer data that reflect key quality factors. Besides they have to act as change agents and help employees to adapt to the change process.

7. ***Business Results***: This category provides results focus that encompasses the customers' evaluation of the organisation's products and services, the overall financial and market performance, the governance structure and social responsibility and results of all key processes and process improvement activities. Through this focus, the criteria's purposes-superior value of offerings as viewed by the customers and the marketplace, superior organisational performance as reflected in the operational legal, ethical and financial indicators, and organisational and personal learning—are maintained.

Particular concerns are quality levels of empowered teams. HR professionals are in the best position to understand group processes, and can help develop these teams and measure their performance.

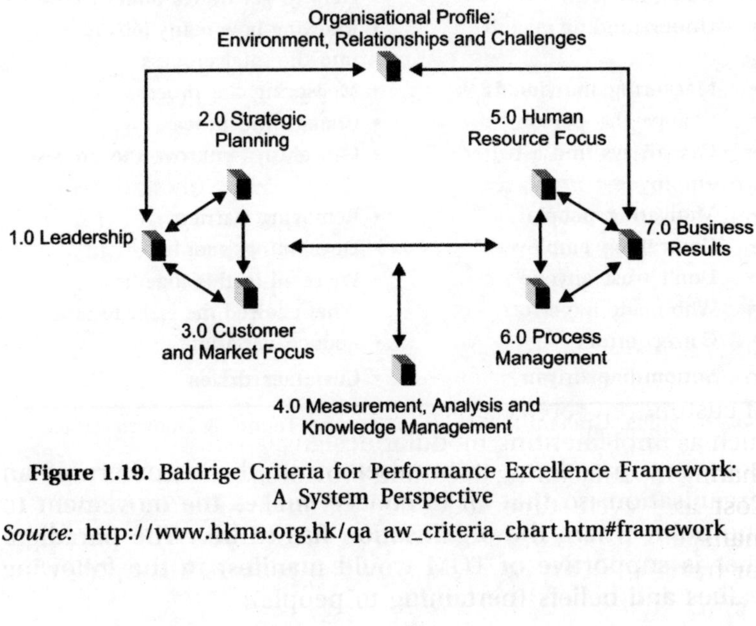

Figure 1.19. Baldrige Criteria for Performance Excellence Framework: A System Perspective

Source: http://www.hkma.org.hk/qa aw_criteria_chart.htm#framework

CHANGING HRM APPROACHES UNDER TQM

As discussed above, the role of Human Resource Professionals change drastically under TQM because of changing expectations of stakeholders specifically customers, employees, and management concerning HRM responsibilities. To begin with, they have to be yet more customers focused. Secondly, a tricky task is to be performed by them, i.e., to bring psychological transition in employees. Psychological transition refers to the mental condition that people go through when they come across a new situation. The psychological transitions that usually take place in the aftermath of TQM implementation are presented in Table 1.11. They have to create a new and collective mindset also. A number of experts, especially amongst Japanese, consider the pursuit of total quality to be a philosophy. TQM has to be creation of a new

TABLE 1.11: Psychological Transitions

Traditional Organisation Mindset	New Process Mindset
• Employees are the problem	• The process is the problem
• Doing my job	• Help to get things done
• Understanding my job	• Knowing how many jobs fit into the total process
• Measuring individuals	• Measuring the process
• Change the person	• Change the process
• Can always find a better employee	• Can always improve the process
• Motivating people	• Removing barriers
• Controlling employees	• Developing people
• Don't trust anyone	• We're all in this together
• Who made the error?	• What allowed the error to occur?
• Correct errors	• Reduce variation
• Bottom-line driven	• Customer driven

Source: Shiba, Graham & Walden, 1993; and Tenner & Detorro, (1993).

collective paradigm or mindset in all the members of an organisation, so that all in concert makes the movement to the point where the organisation has to be. The paradigm that is supportive of TQM would manifest in the following values and beliefs (pertaining to people):

Value 1 : People, working independently or in teams create excellence

Value 2 : Within the organisation people have to work across functional and hierarchical boundaries

Value 3 : Everyone has to participate in attaining total quality (Wakhlu, 1994).

Third, in regard to the management, total quality human resource strategic management has to be reciprocally interdependent with business strategic management (Schuler and Jackson). This is the most important contribution to the total quality orientation of human resource management. Total quality HR strategy managers must shape, introduce, maintain, and review the total quality initiatives in the organisation. Table 1.12 catalogues the activities to be performed by the HR managers in pursuit of successful TQM implementation.

To summarize, HR Professionals ought to:

- **Care:** customer satisfaction both external and internal.
- **Enable:** people to be customer-focused as the satisfied customer is the ultimate objective.
- **Create:** a TQM Culture to in which innovation, team working and total quality can flourish.
- **Draft:** a change management/communications plan that addresses the people side of the TQM.
- **Help:** people to be process-oriented i.e., how they do their work.
- **Convince:** people that they are the most valued resource.
- **Assist:** people to adapt quickly to change that occurs in the process of TQM implementation.
- **Motivate:** people through proper rewards and recognition for good results.
- **Consult:** around structure, strategy, process and people issues for achieving quality.
- **Counsel:** managers on how their behaviour can help or hinder TQM's acceptance throughout the organisation.
- **Coach:** people around personnel issues.

TABLE 1.12: The Total Quality HRM Strategies

Role of HR professionals	Changing HRM strategies
Shaping TQM	• Preparing and synthesizing reports from other organisations that have experience in TQM in conjunction with the management team. • Assisting with choices about which TQM approach to adopt. • Identifying any internal sources of expertise. • Utilizing the expertise of practitioners from other organisations. • Ensuring that an appropriate infrastructure is put into place and takes sufficient account of both customer feedback and HRM issues. • Reviewing current practices, behaviour and attitude in the organisation and assessing their degree of fitness with TQM. • Shaping the type of organisational structure, culture, and ethical climate appropriate for introducing and sustaining TQM. • Designing and delivering senior management development courses that set the proper tone for TQM. • Developing a TQM directory of internal resources and expertise.
Facilitating and adopting TQM	• Encouraging and facilitating a total quality partnership between company and union leadership.

TABLE 1.12 (*Contd.*)

Role of HR professionals	Changing HRM strategies
	• Training all formal leaders in the principles of TQM. • Identifying the conditions necessary for the successful use of quality management tools and techniques. • Training and coaching facilitators, mentors and team members in interpersonal skills and how to manage the improvement processes. • Designing communication events and vehicles to publicize the launch of TQM and early success. • Consulting with employees about the introduction and development of TQM. • Proactively contributing to vision and mission statements and preparing quality objectives for dissemination to staff, customers and suppliers.
Maintaining and reinforcing TQM	• Adopting selection processes that target and screen for conceptual, technical, ethical and social skills that support a TQM environment. • Introducing and upgrading the Total Quality Management component. • Ensuring training in relation to Total Quality Management. • Redesigning appraisal procedures so that they contain criteria relating to Total Quality Management.

TABLE 1.12 (*Contd.*)

Role of HR professionals	Changing HRM strategies
	• Assisting continuous improvement and project teams to work effectively and innovate.
Reviewing TQM	• Contributing to or leading the preparation of an annual TQM report.
	• Assessing the effectiveness of TQM infrastructure.
	• Preparing and administering employee attitude and ethical climate surveys and disseminating their results.
	• Coordinating customers' comments on the organisation's progress.
	• Benchmarking the effectiveness of the organisation's TQM with that of competitors and global best practices.
	• Identifying the barriers to continuous quality improvement.
	• Conducting HR, quality and ethical audits.

Source: Dale and Cooper, 1992; and Wilkinson, Marchington and Dale, 1993.

- **Train:** people in regard to quality matters.
- **Improve:** individual competence, core processes and internal systems (to be able to "do more with less resources"); and
- **Involve:** people through delegation of authority and decision-making to lowest possible levels.

Nonetheless being included in TQM merely because HR professionals can play a vital role in the success of TQM does not inevitably follow that they will be called for participation. HR can greatly increase its chances of being included in the total quality initiative only when they are regarded as a partner in all business initiatives, and the organisation is ensured that the HR professionals have the right skills and knowledge so as to make potential contribution to the TQM initiative. Accordingly to begin with they should endeavour to develop the right skill and knowledge and also be actively involved in the formulation of a coherent set of personnel and business policies which would jointly reinforce the organisation's strategies for achieving business needs and improving performance. This is the real challenge for the HR managers in a total quality organisation. In other words, the traditional approach to HRM as a stand-alone function with specialized standards should be replaced with a more generalist approach that will require the HR function to help create competitive advantages for organisations. This is indispensable as in a recent Harvard Business Review article, HR author Dave Ulrich affirmed "the activities of HR appear to be and often are disconnected from the real work of the organisation". He also said that "the new HR agenda is one in which every HR activity in some concrete way helps the company better serve its customers or otherwise increase shareholder value". As the search for QUALITY has become the single most important force leading to organisational success and growth, and this trend business environment reshape organisational life, HR professionals must respond with new strategies, practices and competencies.

SUMMARY

TQM is a holistic organisational approach to bring continuous improvements in organisational activities, processes and products to satisfy the customers. Quality experts have propounded different TQM models describing various components, core methods and principles of TQM. A review of all these models reveal that 'customer' is the heart of TQM and the interplay of customer and supplier determines an organisation's strategy for its continuous improvement.

TQM is a people-driven management approach. People play a pivotal role in successful TQM implementation. Therefore, all the quality gurus underline the humanistic aspects of TQM. They insist on the management to provide a fair treatment to people at work place. The HRM strategies have to be muddle through so as to abet the TQM implementation. TQM requires a new and collective mindset of people and it is the responsibility of HR professionals to bring a paradigm shift in their conventional mindset. Besides, they must shape, introduce, maintain, and periodically review the total quality initiatives introduced in the organisation.

APPENDIX 1.1: Approaches to Define Quality

Sl. No.	Approach	Major Focus	Definitions	Source
I.	Transcendent	'Quality is a simple, unanalysable property that can be recognised only through experience.'	• "Quality is neither mind nor matter, but a third entity independent of the two...even though quality cannot be defined, you know what it is."	1
			• "... a condition of excellence implying fine quality as distinct from poor quality.... Quality is achieving or reaching for the highest standard as against being satisfied with the sloping or froudent."	2
			• "Innate excellence."	3
II.	Product-based	'Quality as a precise and measurable variable.'	• "Difference in quality amount to differences in the quantity of some desired ingredient or attribute."	4
			• "Quality refers to the amounts of the unpriced attributes contained in each unit of the priced attribute."	5
III.	User-based	'Quality lies in the eyes of the beholder.'	• "Quality consists of the capacity to satisfy wants."	6
			• "...the quality of a product depends on how well it fits patterns of consumer preference."	7
			• "...the goods that best satisfy consumers' preferences are the ones having the highest quality."	8

APPENDIX 1.1 (Contd.)

Sl. No.	Approach	Major Focus	Definitions	Source
			• "Quality has led to the notion of ideal points: precise combinations of product attributes that provide the greatest satisfaction to a specified consumer."	9
			• "Quality differences are captured by shifts in a product's demand curve."	10
IV.	Manu-facturing-based	'Quality is concerned with engineering and manufacturing practices i.e., the supply side of the equation.'	• "Quality is the degree to which a specific product conforms to a design or specification."	11
			• "Quality improvements (which are equivalent to reductions in the number of deviations) laid to lower costs for preventing defects is viewed as less expensive than repairing or reworking them."	12
V.	Value-based	'Quality in terms of costs and prices.'	• "Quality is the degree of excellence of an acceptable price and the control of variability at an acceptable cost."	13
			• "Quality-product is one that provides performance on conformance at an acceptable price or cost."	14

Sources: 1. Prising, Robert M. (1974). *Zen and the Art of Motorcycle Maintenance*, Bentham Books, New York, pp. 185-213.

2. Tuchman, Barbara W. (1980). "The Decline of Quality", *New York Times Magazine,* November, Vol. 2, p. 38.

3. Prising, Robert M., *op. cit.,* pp. 183-228; and Tuchman, Barbara W., *op. cit.,* pp. 38-41.

4. Abott, Lawrence, *Quality and Competition,* Columbia University Press, New York, pp. 126-27.

5. Leffler, Keith B. (1982). "Ambiguous Changes in Product Quality", *American Economic Review,* December, p. 256.

6. Edwards, Carwin D. (1968). "The Meaning of Quality", *Quality Progress,* October, p. 37.

7. Kuchn, Alfred A. and Day, Ralph L. (1962). "Strategy of Product Quality", *Harvard Business Review,* Nov-Dec., p. 101.

8. Edwards, Corwin D., *op. cit.,* pp. 36-39; and Kuchn and Day, *op. cit.,* pp. 100-10.

9. Kuchn & Day, *op. cit.,* pp. 101-08; and Johnson, Richard M. (1971). "Market Segmentation: A Strategic Management Tool", *Journal of Marketing Research,* February, pp. 13-18.

10. Chamberlain, Edward H. (1953). "The Product as an Economic Variable", *Quarterly Journal of Economics,* February, pp. 1-29; Dorfman, Robert and Steiner, Peter O. (1954). "Optimal Advertising and Optimal Quality", *American Economic Review,* December, pp. 822-36; and White, Lawrence J. (1972). "Quality Variation When Prices Are Regulated", *Bell Journal of Economics and Management Science,* Autumn, pp. 425-36.

11. Glimore, Harold L. (1974). "Product Conformance Cost", *Quality Progress,* June, p. 16.

12. Campanella, Jack and Corcoran, Frank J. (1983). "Principles of Quality Costs", *Quality Progress,* April, p. 21.

13. Broh, Robert A. (1982). *Managing Quality for Higher Profits,* McGraw Hill, New York, pp. 3-4.

14. *Ibid.*

APPENDIX 1.2: The Seven QC and Seven QC Management Tools

Tool	Description
Pareto Diagram	Developed by Juran in 1950. It suggests that 80% scrap or rework quality costs come from 20% of the possible causes. It is a basic tool used to graphically rank causes from most significant to least significant. It utilises a vertical bar graph in which the bar height reflects the frequency or impact of causes.
Cause and Effect Diagram	Also refer to as Ishikawa Diagram, as it was developed by Kaoru Ishikawa, and the Fishbone diagram, as the complete diagram resembles to a fish skeleton. It is a tool for analysing process dispersion. The diagram illustrates the main causes and sub-causes leading to an effect (symptom).
Flowchart	It is a graphical representation of the steps in a process. Flowcharts can vary from the elementary, identifying just the order of key process activities, to the complex, including information feedback paths and activity performance measures such as cycle time.
Check Sheet	Check Sheets are designed and structured formats for recording process data in a manner that can readily interpret results.
Histogram	It is a graphical representation of summarising variation in a set of data. It is used when process variables are to be measured (Grams, Millimetres, Volts, Dollars).
Scatter Diagram	It is a graphical technique to analyse the relationship between two variables. Two sets of data are plotted on a graph, with the y-axis being used for the variable to

APPENDIX 1.2 (Contd.)

Tool	Description
	be predicted and the x-axis being used for the variable to make the prediction. The graph will show possible relationships (although two variables might appear to be related, they might not be: those who know most about the variables must take the evaluation).
Control Chart	It is a basic tool, which consists of a chart with upper and lower control limits on which values of some statistical measure for a series of samples or subgroups are plotted. It frequently shows a control line to help detect a trend of plotted values toward either control unit. It is used to monitor and analyse variation from a process to see whether the process is in statistical control.
Affinity Diagram	It is used to organise large amounts of data into natural groupings in a way that stimulates new, creative ideas.
Relationship Diagram	It illustrates the relationship between problems and ideas in complex situation. Also identifies meaningful categories from a mass of ideas when relationships are difficult to determine.
Tree Diagram	It identifies the tasks and methods needed to solve a problem and reach a goal. It systematically traces the means and clarifies the problem to be solved by exposing its complete structure. From this analysis, the problem-solving method can be identified.
Matrix Chart	This chart shows the relationships among various groups of data. It yields information about the relationships and the importance of task/method elements of the subjects.

APPENDIX 1.2 (Contd.)

Tool	Description
Matrix Data Analysis Chart	It provides a picture of numerical data from a matrix diagram in an effective way.
Arrow Diagram	It shows the time required to solve the problem and which items can be done in parallel. It is simplified critical path method of planning and scheduling designed to show the optimum schedule for fulfilling a plan and tracking its progress.
Process Decision Programme Chart	This is used for contingency planning. It focuses on possible sequences to help lead to a desirable result. It was developed to plan for the future while still in the development stage of problem solution planning.

APPENDIX 1.3: Overview of ISO-9000 Series

ISO-9000 is a series of three informational standards and supplementary guidelines in quality management and quality assurance, which were first published in 1987 and revised in 1994. The standards are not specific to any particular products and can be used by both manufacturing and service industries.

The ISO-9000 series has evolved over several revisions.

- The initial 1987 version, **ISO-9000:1987**, originally issued as BS 5750, focused on quality control retroactive checking and corrective actions. This version was strongly influenced by the existing US Department of Defence Military Standards ("MILSPECS") on manufacturing, and so was well-suited to the demands of a rigorous, stable, factory-floor manufacturing process.
- The 1994 version, **ISO-9000:1994**, emphasised quality assurance via preventive actions, and required evidence of compliance with documented procedures. Unfortunately, companies tended to implement its requirements by creating shelf-loads of procedure manuals, and becoming burdened with an ISO bureaucracy. Adapting and improving processes could be particularly difficult in this kind of environment.
- The 2000 version, **ISO-9000:2000**, introduced the concept of process effectiveness via process performance metrics, and so reduced the emphasis on having documented procedures if clear evidence could be presented to show that the process was working well. Expectations of continuous process improvement and tracking customer satisfaction were made explicit at this revision.

REFERENCES

- Abernathy, William J. and Corcoram, John E. (1983). "Relearning from the Old Masters: Lessons of the American System of Manufacturing", *Journal of Operations Management,* August, pp. 155-68.
- Abobott, R.A. and Leaman, D.C. (1982). "Quality Control and Quality Assurance", in Car, H. ed., *The Encyclopedia of Management,* Third edition, Van Nostrand Reinhold, New York, pp. 998-1009.

- Adam Jr., Ever, H. (1984). "Quality Assurance Broadens the Concept of Quality Control, *The Pulse Report,* American Productivity Center, January, p. 4.
- Anderson, John C., Rungtusaratham, Manus, and Schroeder, Roger G. (1994). "Theoretical Model of Total Quality Management", *Academy of Management Review,* Vol. 19, No. 3, July, pp. 472-509.
- ANSI/ISO/ASQL, A8402-1994, "Quality Management and Quality Assurance Vocabulary."
- ANSI/ISO/ASQL, A8402-1994, "Quality Management and Quality Assurance Vocabulary."
- Bank, J. (1998). *The Essence of Total Quality Management,* Prentice Hall of India Pvt. Ltd., New Delhi, p. 81.
- Bicking, Charles A. (1958). "The Technical Aspects of Quality Control", *Industrial Quality Control,* March, p. 7.
- Bossert, J.L. (1991). *Quality Function Deployment: A Practitioner's Approach,* ASQC Quality Press, and Milwaukee.
- Bowen, D.E. and Lawler III, E.E. (1992). "Total Quality Oriented Human Resource Management", *Organisational Dynamics,* Spring, pp. 29-41.
- Burlage, F. (1997). "Master the Art of Kaizen", *The European,* Vol. 20, February, p. 12.
- Cartin, Thomas J. (2000). *Principles and Practices of Organisational Performance Excellence,* Prentice Hall of India Pvt. Ltd., New Delhi.
- Chandler Jr., Alfred D. (1977). *The Visible Hand;* Harvard University Press, Cambridge, pp. 50-64.
- Choudhary, Abhaya & Dhargawe, Gautam (2000). "The Strategies for Indian Manufacturing Industry for the New Era of Globalization" retrieved from www.indiainfoline.com/ *bisc/stma.*
- CII (2004). *Quality News,* March-June, Vol. 15, No. 2.
- Cohen, S.G. and Bailey, D.E. (1997). "What Makes Teams Work: Group Effectiveness Research from the Shop Floor to the Executive Suite", *Journal of Management,* Vol. 23, May, pp. 239-90.
- Crosby, P.B. (1979). *Quality is Free,* McGraw-Hill, New York.
- Crosby, Philip B. (1984). *Quality Without Tears,* McGraw-Hill, New York.
- Day, R.G. (1993). *Quality Function Deployment: Linking a Company with its Customer,* ASQC Quality Press, and Milwaukee.
- Deming, W. Edwards (1986). *Out of the Crisis,* Cambridge University Press, Cambridge.
- Dorsky, L.R. (1984). "Management Commitment to Japanese Apple Pie", *Quality Progress,* February.

- Feigenbaum, A.V. (1961). *Total Quality Control: Engineering and Management*, McGraw-Hill, New York.
- Feigenbaum, A.V. (1983). *Total Quality Control*, 3rd Ed., McGraw-Hill, New York.
- Feigenbaum, A.V. (1988). "Total Quality Management into the 1990s—An International Perspective" in Chase, R.L. (ed.), *Total Quality Management*, Springer-Verlag, New York.
- Flood, R.L., *Beyond TQM*, John Wiley, UK.
- Fredendall, L.D. and Robbins, T.L. (1995)."Modelling the Role of Total Quality Management in the Customer Focused Organisations", *Journal of Management Issues*, Vol. 7, Winter, pp. 403-19.
- Fuller, T.F. (1985). "Eliminating Complexity from Work: Improving Productivity by Enhancing Quality", *National Productivity Review*, Autumn, pp. 327-44.
- Garvin, A.D. (1984). "What Does Product Quality Really Mean?" *Sloan Management Review*, Fall.
- Garvin, A.D. (1987)."Competing on the Eight Dimensions of Quality", *Harvard Business Review*.
- Garvin, D.A. (1988). *Managing Quality*, The Free Press, Macmillan Inc., New York.
- GOI, "QUALITY—MYTH & REALITY", by Menon, S.V., *Bureau of Information*, retrieved from http://pib.nic.in/feature/feyr98/fe1298/f0312982.html
- Hammer, M. and Champy, J. (1992). *Reengineering the Corporation: A Manifesto for Business Revaluation*, Harper Business, New York.
- Hillkirk, J. (1993). "World-Famous Quality Expert Died at 92", *USA Today*, December 21, pp. 13-23.
- Hounshell, David A. (1984). *From the American System to Mass Production*, 1800-1932, John Hopkins Press, Baltimore, pp. 15-17.
- Imai, M. (1986). *Kaizen: The Key to Japan's Competitive Success*, Random House and New York.
- Juran, J.M. (1976). "Consumerism and Product Quality", *Quality Progress*, July.
- Juran, J.M. (1988). *Juran on Planning for Quality*, Free Press, New York, pp. 5-7.
- Juran, J.M. and Gryna, Frank M. (1988). *Juran's Quality Control Handbook*, McGraw Hill, New York.
- Kamikubo, H. (1989). "New Way of Management Tools", *ASQC Annual Quality Congress Transactions*, Milwaukee.

- Kanji, Gopal K. and Asher, Mike (1996). *100 Methods for TQM*, Response Books, New Delhi.
- Kano, N. (1989). "Quality Sweating Theory: Crisis Consciousness, Vision and Leadership", *Quality (Journal of the Japanese Society for Quality Control*), Vol. 19, pp. 32-42.
- Kano, N. (1997). "A Perspective on Quality Activities in American Firms", in Michael L. Tushman and Philip Anderson (eds.), *Managing Strategic Innovation and Change (A Collection of Readings)*, Oxford University Press, pp. 402-16.
- Kelda, Joseph N. (1996). *Integrating Reengineering with Total Quality*, ASQC Press, USA, pp. 25-26.
- Kemelgor, Bruce and Mears, Peter (1995), "HR's Role In The CQI Process", *Journal for Quality & Participation*, Oct/Nov, Vol. 18, Issue 6, p. 66.
- Luthans, Fred (1993). "Meeting the New Paradigm Challenges Through Total Quality Management", *Management Quarterly*, Spring, pp. 2-13.
- Luthans, Fred (1995). *Organisational Behaviour*, McGraw Hill International Editions, Seventh Edition, Singapore, p. 30.
- McShane, Steven L. and Glinow, Mary Ann Von, *Organisational Behaviour*, Tata McGraw-Hill Publishing Co. Ltd., New Delhi.
- Milakovich, M.E. (1995). *Improving Service Quality*, St. Lucie Press, Delray Beach, FL.
- Niepce, W. and Molleman, E. (1998). "Work Design Issues in Lean Production from a Sociotechnical Systems Perspective: Neo-Taylorism or the Next Step in Sociotechnical Design?", *Human Relations*, Vol. 51, March, pp. 259-87.
- Nilakant, V. and Ram Narayan S. (1998). *Managing Organisational Change*, Response Books, pp. 132-34.
- Oakland, J.S. (1989). *Total Quality Management*, Heinemann Publishing Co., Oxford.
- Owen, J.V. (1992). "Concurrent Engineering", *Manufacturing Engineering*, Vol. 109, November, pp. 69-73.
- Owens, D.A. (Undated). "QA / QX and ASQC History", *Harvard Business Review*, March-April.
- Paine, Lynne S. (1996). "Managing for Organisational Integrity", *Harvard Business Review*, March-April, pp. 110-15.
- Petrick, Joseph A. and Quinn, John F. (1996). *Management Ethics and Organisation Integrity*, Sage Publications, Newbury Park, CA, pp. 56-60.
- Petrik, J.A. and Furr, D.S. (1995). *Total Quality in Managing Human Resources*, St. Lucie Press, Delrayeach, pp. 26-32.

- Procter & Gamble (1992). "Report to the Total Quality Leadership Steering Committee and Working Commits", Cincinnati, Ohio.
- Radford, G.S. (1922). *The Control of Quality in Manufacturing,* Ronal Press, New York.
- Rampey, J. and Roberts, H. (1992). "Perspectives in Total Quality", *Proceedings of Total Quality Forum IV,* Procter & Gamble, Cincinnati, Ohio, November.
- Reddy, J. (1980). "Incorporating Quality in Competitive Strategies", *Sloan Management Review,* Spring.
- Sharma, S. (1997). *TQM in Indian Engineering Industries,* Business Publications Inc., Mumbai, pp. 9-10.
- Shiba, Shoji, Graham, A. and Walden, D. (1993). *A New American TQM: Four Practical Revolutions in Management,* Productivity Press, Cambridge MA, pp. 107-88.
- Sinha, M.N. and Willbourne, W.W.O. (1985). *The Management of Quality Assurance,* John Willey and Sons, New York.
- Smart, Karl L. (2001), Column Editor, *Recognizing Quality Achievement,* September/October, p. 36.
- Smith, Merritt Roe (1977). *Harpers Ferry Armory and the New Technology,* Cornell University Press, New York, Chs. 3-5.
- Sohal, A.S., Tay, G.S. and Wirth, A. (1989). "Total Quality Control in an Asian Division of a Multinational Corporation", *International Journal of Quality and Reliability Management,* Vol. 6, No. 6, pp. 60-74.
- Summers, D.C.S. (1997). *Quality,* Prentice Hall, USA, pp. 7-13.
- Swink, M.L., Scandvig, J.C. and Mabert, V.A. (1996). "Customising Concurrent Engineering Processes: Five Case Studies", *Journal of Product Innovation Management,* Vol. 13, pp. 229-44.
- Tenner, Arthur R. and Detorro, Irving J. (1993). *Total Quality Management,* Addison-Wesley, Reading, MA, pp. 97-124.
- *The Economist,* 1992.
- *Training,* 1995.
- Trumbull, M. (1993). "What's Total Quality Management?" *The Christian Science Monitor,* May 3, p. 12.
- Udapa, S.R. (1986). *Quality Circles in India: Participation for Progress,* Tata McGraw-Hill, New Delhi, pp. 6-8.
- Wakhlu, Bhara (1994). *Total Quality-Excellence through Organisation-wide Transformation,* Wheeler Publishing, New Delhi, pp. 11-13.
- Walton M. (1990). Deming Management at Work, Putnam/Perigee, New York.

- Woodbury, R.S. (1960). "The Legend of Eli Whitney and Interchangeable Parts, *Technology and Culture,* Summer.
- Zairi, M. (1991). *Total Quality Management for Engineers,* Woodland Publishing Ltd., UK.
- Zangwill, W.I. (1993). *Lighting Strategies for Innovation: How the World's Best Firms Create New Products,* Lexington, New York.
- Zemke, R. (1992). "TQM: Fatally Flawed or Simply Unfocused?" , *Training,* October.
- Zemke, R. (1993). "A Buffers' Guide to TQM", *Training,* April.

2

LITERATURE REVIEW AND RESEARCH METHODOLOGY

The discussion in the previous chapter about the philosophy, methods and practices of TQM almost subscribe to the contention that in order to coalesce customer needs and leverage the existing systems and resources, TQM is of absolute importance. While it is greatly acknowledged that TQM is not easy to be implemented in Indian organisations, still attempts are being made in several organisations with the belief that it would help them in achieving the competitive advantage. Studies on the efficacy of the programme in Indian organisations and its interface with Key Human Factors show mixed results. This experience sounds an alarm of caution for not to jump into any foregone conclusion without an empirical verification. It is therefore essential to empirically study TQM and its interface with human resources to get a wholesome picture of their interrelationship. The present study is designed to serve the above purpose. The study on its face appears to be limited because it focuses its attention on the implementation of TQM in a single unit, namely **Rashtriya Ispat Nigam Limited (RINL)/Vishakhapatnam Steel Plant (VSP)**.

In the present chapter, discussions have been made in two separate sections. The first section analyses the findings of previous research studies conducted on various issues relating to TQM with a specific emphasis on its human dimension. The second section focuses upon the research design and methodology adopted for the study.

LITERATURE REVIEW

Plethoras of studies have been made both in India and outside covering different aspects of TQM. All these studies may be categorised into two major headings: (a) TQM *vis-à-vis* Organisational Performance; (b) Prerequisites and Barriers to successful TQM implementation.

TQM *vis-à-vis* Organisational Performance

Many researchers have tried to explore the relationship between TQM and functional and business unit performance. In recent literature, the majority of useful evidence is based on case studies (Kristensen, *et al.*, 1992; and Bossink *et al.*, 1992).

The study by Sink (1991) shows that the performance of an organisation system is composed of seven interrelated criteria: effectiveness, efficiency, total quality, productivity, quality of work life, innovation, and financial performance.

Little (1992) conducted a survey of 500 American manufacturing companies and found that only a third felt that their TQM programmes were having a 'significant impact' on organisational performance. Another survey of approximately 100 British firms found that only 20 per cent of the organisations achieved 'tangible results'. The major reasons for the failures are: impatience to achieve quick results; inexperience with implementing Total Quality Management; and losing sight of the ultimate customer.

Shea and Gobeli (1995) surveyed ten small organisations in Oregon, USA that had successfully implemented TQM and found that implementation of TQM has got a positive bearing on the organisations' success and growth.

Sinclair and Zairi (1996) highlight a case study, which examined the implementation of a total quality based performance measurement system. The review of the study reveals that there is a gap between information sought by people and what they tend to receive, and personal involvement is vital for effective performance measurement. The performance measurement criteria, which they mention are: quality, productivity, financial performance, customer satisfaction, employee factors, and environmental performance.

Madu *et al.* (1996) attempted an empirical study to test if there is any significant association between quality dimensions (such as, customer satisfaction, employee service quality) and organisational performance. They used middle managers' perceptions to make some inferences about the association between the variables that are compared and validate some of the claims made by quality experts and practitioners regarding the importance of TQM to organisational success.

Nilakant and Narayan (1998) have made a survey in Mahindra & Mahindra Ltd. and found that TQM programme had significantly improved the company's performance. By 1996, it had achieved a 75 per cent increase in sales per employee, doubled its productivity, reduced quality related complaints by 90 per cent, reduced lead time and increased inventory turnover. They have also made a survey in Larsen & Toubro Ltd. and found that TQM programme has a significant impact on the company's financial performance.

Singh *et al.* (2000) have conducted a sample survey of 50 different organisations with a view to gain a deep insight into application of TQM in Indian industries and also to assess whether the application of TQM increases the profitability and productivity of the organisations or not. The conclusion drawn was, proper and effective application of TQM could bring about miraculous changes in the performance of the organisational workforce, especially in context of Indian industries where the concept of TQM is at the growing stage.

Wali *et al.* (2000) from the literature review found that TQM helps in achieving the primary goal of enhancing productivity and reducing costs. However, on this account a system of performance measurement has to be developed commensurate with the objectives of TQM. They have identified various critical success factors for supporting performance metrics in a TQM environment.

Prerequisites and Barriers

Whether TQM in an organisation would work or not—largely depends upon certain individual and organisational factors. In order to identify these factors, many research studies have been conducted. The analysis of these research studies provides an understanding of prerequisites and barriers to successful TQM implementation. The findings of these studies can be grouped under the following headings:

Management Focused

Deming (1982) instituted a process approach to continual improvement based on statistical analysis of the firm's operations. He reiterated that all levels of management are to be involved in the quality programme. Managers are to improve supervision, train employees, retrain employees in new skills, and create an organisational structure that supports the quality programme.

Saraph *et al.* (1989) by using data collected from 162 General Managers and Quality Managers from 20 companies in the Minneapolis/St. Paul area have identified eight critical factors for quality management practice. These factors are: the role of management leadership and quality policy, role of quality department, training, product/service design, supplier quality management, process management, quality data and reporting, and employee relations.

Lorinc's (1990) study in Reimer Express, one of the Canada's largest trucking firms, found that for successful implementation of TQM, management must put emphasis on training, learning and consistency of purpose.

Schmidt and Finnegan (1992) following the management approaches of Baldrige Award recipients suggest that in order to make TQM successful, the leadership commitment and their plan for change are highly essential. They offer five key management strategies for making TQM successful: establishing supportive organisational structure, using the proper tools, making a long-term investment in training, creating a meaningful recognition and award system, and encouraging communication.

Gilbert (1992) presented three case studies in which TQM was implemented in response to major problems with production. In the first case, TQM failed due to poor management and lack of training. In second case, TQM met the same fate for similar reasons. And, in the third case, the time and management support the TQM programme received was enough to save the company that was experiencing problems just as severe as those in the first two cases.

Barclay's (1993) survey of some sample large service and manufacturing organisations indicates that most executives perceive quality as a very important strategic advantage, but they fail to communicate this well to employees. Majority of firms in the sample have company-wide quality definition, defective product definitions or quality characteristic measures. Top executives somewhat supported cross-functional teams, but most employees were not involved in such things. The author recommends that a common 'quality vocabulary' is a must for successful TQM implementation.

Lu and Sohal (1993) identified some common myths concerning TQM and its implementation in Australian organisations. They recommended that management must reorient its strategies for: identification of the strategic direction of the business (mission, vision and policies); determination of customer expectations, and measurement of perceptions (market research, surveys and focus groups); definition of strategy for implementation of the programme (time-frame, resources to provide leadership and training); formal structure to control, monitor and maintain improvement initiatives (steering committee, improvement teams); train the trainer on TQM concepts (participants to train own staff eventually); quality assurance system (ISO-9000); and use of external consultants.

Oakley and Doug (1994) report on a survey conducted by Cook Associates. The consulting firm interviewed 25 quality leaders from 20 Fortune 500 companies that have pursued TQM. The survey indicates that leaders who effectively apply TQM principles combine effective leadership characteristics with an "open" approach to learning. Effective leaders look for ways to help with problem solving and take personal responsibility for the implementation of TQM. Therefore, they recommend that managers of every organisation must establish support systems that make their core values visible, and teach people the skills that quality leaders seem to master intuitively.

Heller (1994) made a survey of Directors and Managers of large U.K. firms and found that 70 per cent of respondents were familiar with quality improvement concepts. The author concludes that managers may be doing well in improving products and are working on process, but are not paying similar attention to other 'pillars' of TQM (such as organisation, leadership and commitment). Perhaps this is because these pillars require changes in the behaviour of leaders and organisational objectives, which may be unwelcome on the part of managers.

Similar result was found in the study of Deevy (1995), which reveals that 75 per cent of TQM efforts failed because of the failure of the management to deliver on their promises.

Capon *et al.* (1996) carried out a study in one of the industries of U.K. by forming different teams and checked the effects of six monitors based on National Malcom Baldridge Award. This study provides the evidence that measuring and displaying results by management increase the chance of success of TQM programme.

Sharma's (1997) study on 66 Indian engineering organisations reveal that the committed leadership from the top and appropriate management strategies are the preconditions for TQM implementation.

Das (1998) conducted two case studies on the TQM culture scenario in India. From his study he identified few barriers to TQM implementation at macro and micro levels, such as, lack of support of top management and casual approach in filling up decision-makers' posts. He has concluded that in absence of the coordinated actions, it will only be a ritual for industrial organisations to transplant the imported concept of TQM from outside as a legacy of management decision.

The June 1998 issue of the *AS Magazine Quality Progress* carried an article describing the results of a survey to identify the main causes of failure of TQM implementation. In this survey, 65 per cent of the managers opined that the failure was due to the fact that meeting improvement objectives was not tied to management compensation. Managers, like anyone else, respond to the real reward payoffs.

People Focused

Majumdar *et al.* (1991) from their study in SAIL discovered two unique challenges associated with implementation of TQM in India. First, the possibility of downsizing which is particularly a sensitive social issue, since any employee who is terminated would lose his housing as well as wages. Second, illiteracy is another issue, since many of the workers do not speak, read or write Hindi and/or English.

Wolley and Kowalski (1992) surveyed a representative sample of Hewlett-Packard employees in U.K. and found that employees tend to get involved with the total quality because of their desire for improvement in their work areas, identification of specific problems and their solutions by using total quality techniques, and management instructions. The recommendations which they provide for quality training include: making training relevant to individual work situations; helping employees learn to choose appropriate total quality projects; and using training to communicate more information about the competitive environment within which the organisation exists.

Caudron (1992) points out that human resources system often get in the way of cultural change that is one of the goals of TQM. Organisation needs to align human resource systems with quality goals. To achieve this end, the author suggests different methods like: communicating about quality through the human resources department; communicating information about quality efforts work best when done in a small group setting it can be personalized; training offered should focus on building quality skills with equal attention paid to behavioural skills and quality tools need for change in performance-management systems; and recognition.

Caudron (1993b) also conducted a survey of human resource practices in companies that have won Baldrige Award. The result indicates that human resources must partner with other departments in the organisation to support TQM effectively. Options include, using human resource representatives as internal consultants to other departments, as members of cross-functional teams, or restructuring the whole department so that individual business units are billed directly for personal services they use.

Thompson's (1993) study in the chemical group of Monsanto found out that total quality process is guided by three basic principles: customer focus, continual improvement as goal, and involving employees in the process.

Hege-Kleiser (1993) described the Traveller's Check Group's (TCG) total quality approach, which is based on five quality ordinals: prevention-based work process and data systems; a commitment to training; empower employees to improve service; stop errors before they happen; and a commitment to customers' service. TCG emphasises upon training employees as customers, using employees input, measuring employees satisfaction, benchmarking, and incorporating better practices. TCG has been very innovative in implementing newer skills and programmes to help employees to balance work and family responsibilities.

Woods (1993) conducted his study in the Katherine Plant located in Chester, South Carolina. The plant has implemented TQM process since 1990. It has been quite successful in the plant due to training, team-oriented work environment, establishment of achievement teams to address special concerns, wide employee participation, effective two-way communication, and effective recognition and rewards system.

Artzt (1994) conducted a study in the Esso Research Centre, a part of the Exxon Corporation, the petrochemical giant located in South of Oxford (U.K.). The study reveals that the Centre has recognised the importance of the concepts of TQM and the use of quality assurance standards since the mid-1980s. It has developed a 'two dimensional model' which views the quality process as a mixture of 'hard' quality (business goals, driving process control, and improvement) and 'soft' quality (values driving people's behaviour and practices).

Hayes *et al.* (1994) administered a personality inventory measure to 136 factory workers to identify the personality characteristics of individuals, who were successful employees in the total quality-manufacturing environment. The results were quite surprising. It was found that more successful employees tended to be more reserved, prudent, conscientious and less interested in intellectual pursuits.

Schonberger (1994) from his study found that the conventional HRM practices conflict with TQM and should be changed. In terms of people and their roles, things that need to shift are: to make process improvement part of everyone's job (not just a management/specialist responsibility); for managers to evolve into facilitators; and use of multifunctional teams instead of single teams. In terms of Human Resource Department, the shift needed are: letting line people handle most personnel functions; shrink the number of job classifications; focus on training for everyone; and spend less time on employee relations and wage/classification issues.

Sharma's (1997) study found that most of the quality problems in an organisation arise due to attitude, resilience, mind-set and work culture of employees rather than knowledge and skills. Resistance to change was another inhibiting factor for effective TQM implementation. Therefore, he recommends for training in quality for all employees irrespective of hierarchical levels, training the trainers, extensive job enrichment programmes, appreciations of employees' work as the essential factors for successful TQM implementation.

Parth Sarathi (1997) conducted a study on the ramifications of TQM and the role that HRD department has to play when a company embarks upon TQM. He found that the TQM approach emphasises planned changes through human resources, hence the HRD professionals are the ideal resource persons to start with.

Kumar (1999) opines that the major quality imperative for any organisation is 'employership', which is all about building a workplace—where people develop a sense of commitment and more importantly sense of mattering.

According to Poonawalla (1999), the only route to achieve total quality in any organisation is through people and quality circle is a very dependable medium to do so.

Ojha (2000) conducted a study on implementation of TQM in two hospitals in Canada by administering a questionnaire to 574 respondents. He examined the role of vision, leadership, momentum of change, teamwork, allocation of resources, focus, and training on the effective implementation of TQM leading to desired medical and financial outcomes.

Wali *et al.* (2000) carried out a case study in one of the leading manufacturing organisations in India producing products used in agro-processing. They found that ability to meet customer needs, understanding of the organisational process, and ability to reduce waste have been considered as the most important factors in quality improvement journey.

Organisation Focused

Olian and Rynes (1991) looked at: supportive organisational process (like communicating a quality vision, setting quality goals, training, team building) that encourage people to adopt behaviour that support quality; the outcome measure (like quality assurance programmes, financial measures, and measures of employees' contribution) that track manufacturing and service processes; and provide information to be used in continuous improvement, and sources of both support (provided by top management) and opposition (by middle managers) to changes which lead to a total quality culture.

Becker *et al.* (1994) found that adoption of TQM leads to flatter organisations with larger spans of control in supervision, more cross-functional problem-solving teams, a decrease in number of employees with an increase in output (as measured by revenues), a shift in incentive system from emphasis on the individual to group reward, more frequent involvement in planning by lower-level employees, and more open communication.

TQM and Organisational Change

Dodson (1991) from his study found that the change in employees' attitude and overcoming resistance to TQM programme are very important in a successful TQM effort.

Heilpern and Nadler (1992) found that success in implementing TQM and receiving a return on investment depends upon understanding, positioning, and managing TQM as a large-scale organisational change. TQM does impact almost all of an organisation's components (work, people, structure, culture, values etc.). Organisations' need transition strategies in moving towards TQM and the responsibility is entrusted upon the senior management.

Green (1993) emphasises that any quality approach used by an organisation must be treated as an organisational change. He has listed 13 principles of organisational change in general and followed a list of 23 fundamental quality principles.

Sharma's (1997) empirical study reveals that all the companies in which TQM was implemented faced resistance. The main OD intervention strategies employed by 85 per cent of the companies counteracting resistance to change were bringing cultural transformation in the company with the help of external change agents followed by internal change agents/ facilitators and extensive training programme. The rest 15 per cent companies used T-Training and/or process consultation.

IDENTIFICATION OF KEY HUMAN FACTORS (KHFs) FOR SUCCESSFUL TQM IMPLEMENTATION

From the above review of literature, the researcher has identified a few KHFs which are critical to the success of TQM. These KHFs have been enlisted in Table 2.1. The literature review also suggests that up till now, there has been only a few systematic attempts to organise and synthesize the various KHFs identified by different researchers. Hence, the present research study has been undertaken with a view to find out a workable model that would depict the interrelationships among TQM, KHFs, and organisational performance.

TABLE 2.1: Key Human Factors (KHFs) for Successful TQM Implementation

• Quality awareness	• Recognition and Reward
• Vision	• Maturity and Breadth
• Leadership	• Attitude and Morale
• Creativity and Innovation	• Customer Satisfaction Sensitivity
• Ethics	• Team work
• Perception	• Training
• Communication	• Empowerment
• Mental Condition (stress and delight)	• Commitment and Involvement

THE PROPOSED TQM MODEL ADOPTED FOR THE STUDY

The study is based on the premise that the 'stimuli' provided by implementing TQM tools in an organisation would have a significant impact on its performance level. In other words, the organisational performance largely depends on the effectiveness of TQM tools implemented in the company. Thus, in the proposed model (given in Figure 2.1) for TQM implementation, TQM tools have been taken as 'independent variables' and organisational performance as the 'dependent variable'. The KHFs are taken as 'intervening variables' that would help to facilitate the implementation of TQM process in an organisation.

SCOPE AND OBJECTIVES OF THE STUDY

The scope of the present study is limited to RINL/VSP, Vishakhapatnam, which has been rated as the 68th largest steel producing company in the world.

Two types of objectives have been set up for the purpose of the present study:

A. Primary Objectives

(i) To study the practice of TQM principles, tools, and techniques.

(ii) To identify the key human factors relevant for the success of TQM.

(iii) To identify, conceptualise and analyse the interface between TQM and human factors.

(iv) To assess the need, capability, and potential of human factors to achieve competitiveness in the global market through TQM approach.

(v) To examine the strategic roles that the Human Resource Professionals can play for successful implementation of TQM in an organisation.

(vi) To find out various human resource challenges associated with TQM implementation.

(vii) To assess the opinion of employees regarding various dimensions of TQM.

B. Secondary Objectives

(i) To present a brief profile of the organisation.

(ii) To critically examine the present quality profile of the organisation.

(iii) To assess the process climate of the organisation.

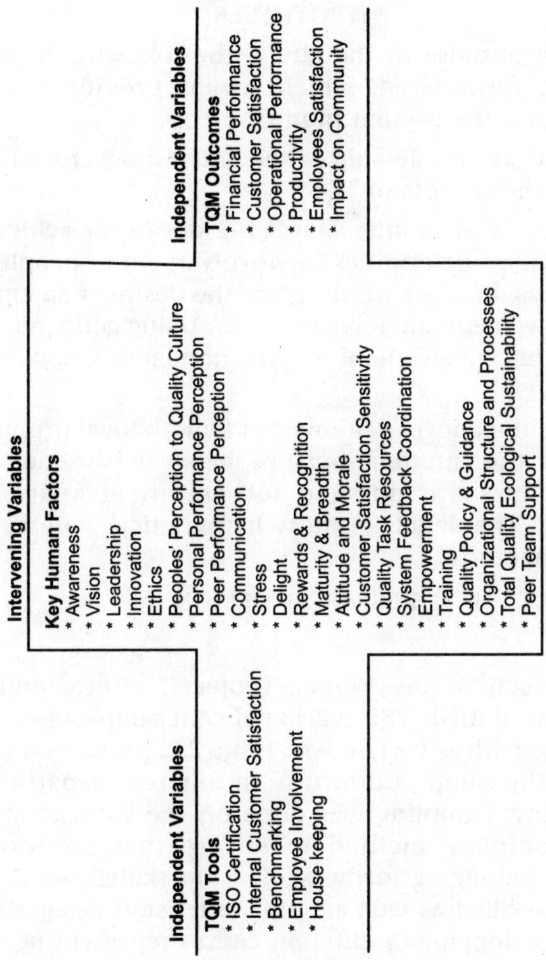

Figure 2.1. Proposed Model for TQM Implementation

(iv) To make a qualitative and quantitative analysis of the leadership style in the organisation.

(v) To diagnose the weak areas pertaining to TQM-HR interrelationship and suggest action plans for their remedy.

HYPOTHESES

For the purpose of the study, the following hypotheses have been formulated, which would provide the broad framework for the present inquiry:

Hypothesis[1]: Leadership is one of the most crucial human factors for the success of TQM.

Hypothesis[2]: The intensity of the desire for achievement and recognition determines the involvement of people in the TQM process. In other words, more the desire of an employee to get achievement and recognition for doing good job, greater would be his involvement in the implementation of TQM process.

Besides the above, a number of hypothetical propositions concerning the interrelationships between varieties of key human factors are pursued for empirical analysis and verification. The details of those hypothetical statements are given in Chapter 4.

RESEARCH DESIGN

Sampling

From each of the Works, Projects, Mines, and other departments of RINL/VSP, a 2.43 per cent sample of executives and non-executives was drawn. Table 2.2. provides a detailed picture of the samples drawn from different departments of the company. Sampling was done on the basis of stratified random sampling method to ensure that non-executive employees belonging to the skilled, un-skilled, semi-skilled, and highly-skilled as well as ministerial staff categories, and executives belonging to different cadres representing various functional areas were included in the sample almost proportionately. Thus, *in toto*, 372 sample respondents, that is 248 non-executives and 124 executives were selected and a specially-designed questionnaire was administered to them.

TABLE 2.2: Composition of the Sample

Name of the Unit	Category of Employees					
	Executives and Junior Officers			Non-Executives		
	TS	ST	% of Sample	TS	ST	% of Sample
Works	2,700	85	3.1	11,326	215	1.89
Projects	173	4	2.3	82	2	2.4
Mines	66	2	3.0	308	6	1.9
Others	1,258	33	2.6	1,093	25	2.28
Total	4,197	124	2.75	12,809	248	2.11

Note: 'TS' represents Total Strength
'ST' represents Sample Taken

Besides the above sample respondents, 45 executives from the HRD and Personnel Department, 6 executives from the TQM-ISO Cell, and 15 Union Representatives who were members of different Quality Circles and Quality Action Teams were contacted on a random basis for the purpose of seeking their opinions on various issues relating to TQM.

METHODOLOGY

I. Data Collection

The present research project is of a descriptive-cum-diagnostic type. The data collection methods have been planned in such a manner so that every bit of information pertaining to TQM-HR interface has been collected.

Tools for Data Collection

The following tools have been used in data collection for the present study:

Primary Data: Primary data have been retrieved from the sample respondents through:

(a) Plant Visits;

(b) Structured Questionnaire; and

(c) Individual Depth Interviews.

(a) *Plant Visits*

After a good preparation and planning in order to obtain meaningful and reliable data, the researcher made plant visits several times from January 2001 to May, 2002. At the preliminary stage, an elaborate schedule was prepared for collection of relevant information from the management of RINL/VSP. This schedule was designed covering such aspects as profile of the organisation, its human resource policy, manpower position, quality policy, structure and functions of HRD Department, Personnel Department, TQM-ISO Cell, TQM practices etc.[1] The HRD department of RINL/VSP was of great help during this stage. It provided the list of different categories of employees (both executives and non-executives) with whom preliminary discussions relating to implementation of TQM in the company were held. The TQM–ISO Cell provided the list of TQM executives with whom preliminary discussions were made. On the basis of this discussion, a tentative model questionnaire was designed for administration to the sample respondents.

(b) *Structured Questionnaire*

Pre-Testing of Questionnaire: To pretest the questionnaire, a tentative model of 90 questions were prepared and administered to 30 sample respondents selected on unstratified random basis. Thereafter, personnel interview was made with those sample respondents to assess their problems in understanding some questions. They were also given opportunity to suggest modifications. Two professional experts in the area were also requested to suggest changes in the questionnaire with regard to the type of questions and scales of measurement used therein. The questionnaire was accordingly revised on:

(i) Suggestions received from respondents in the pre-test administration;

(ii) Suggestions received from the professional experts in the area.

Contents of the Questionnaire: As a result of pre-testing and feedback from respondents, many questions were added,

1. For details of the Schedule, see Annexure-I.

redesigned, and simplified for the purpose of objective assessment of the responses and their easy administration. The final questionnaire was spread over 6 sections. The areas covered in the questionnaire encompassed virtually every aspect of TQM-KHFs interface.[2]

Measurement Scale: Different measurement scales have been used in different sections of the questionnaire depending on the kind of information required. For instance, for assessing employees' attitude and opinion towards the quality profile of the organisation, a 5-Point Rating Scale has been used with a maximum rating of 5 and minimum rating of 1 for each question with interval scale of 2.[3]

(c) *Individual Depth Interviews*

Individual depth interviews have been conducted with executives of TQM-ISO Cell, Union members, and HR professionals of the company. It was thought that individual in-depth interviews could provide more detail information and indicates personal preferences and idiosyncrasies, desirable subtleties, and nuances of difference that normally masked in group settings (Tull, 1976). In most of the cases, interviews lasted for 15 minutes to 1 hour. The interviews with TQM-ISO Cell Executives and Union members were unstructured and direct in nature in the sense that interview respondents had been first made aware of the underlined purpose of the survey and then interviewed in order to observe their attitudes, opinions and behaviours towards TQM in an exploratory manner. However, the interviews with HR professionals had been well structured and the interview guide was followed for the purpose.[4]

Secondary Data: The secondary data have been retrieved from the sources like the files, records, documents, Annual Reports of the Company, monthly House Magazine *(Ukkuvani)*, and occasional publications of RINL/VSP like *Prerana*. Other secondary sources were books, research journals, periodicals and unpublished research materials etc.

---

2. For details of the questionnaire see Annexure-II.
3. For details of the measurement scales used, see different parts of the questionnaire appended in Annexure-II.
4. For details of the Interview Guide see Annexure-III.

II. Data Analysis

The data collected have been analysed by using the following statistical exercises:

(i) *Calculation of sample means and standard deviations*

On the basis of the scores obtained on individual question in each section, calculation of sample means and standard deviations has been made in respect of each dimension of TQM.

(ii) *Item Analysis*

Item analysis is a methodology for assessing the accuracy of measurements that are obtained in social sciences, where precise measurements are often hard to secure. The accuracy of measurement are broken into two main categories: validity and reliability. The validity of an instrument refers to whether it accurately measures the attributes of interest. The reliability of an instrument concerns with the identical results in repeated applications. An instrument may be reliable, but not valid. However, it cannot be valid without being reliable.

In this study, Cronbach's Alpha (or Coefficient Alpha) method is used to determine the internal consistency among the collected data. Similarly, Kaiser-Moyer-Olkin (KMO) measure has been used to test sampling adequacy.

(iii) *Bivariate Correlations*

Pearson's Correlation Coefficient (PCC) with their significance levels have been used to measure how variables or rank orders are related to each other.

(iv) *Independent-Sample t-Test*

The Independent-Sample t-Test has been used to compare means of two groups i.e., executive and non-executive sample respondents. This test is done to find out the significance of the difference between two sample means regarding a particular TQM attribute.

For statistical computation, processing and analysis of surveyed and tabulated data, two computer software such as MS Excel and SPSS for Windows, Release: 10.0.5. (27 November, 1999) have been used.

LIMITATIONS OF THE STUDY

Though the researcher has not directly perceived any serious limitation *per se* of the study, the following points, however, deserve special attention and might have posed some limitations inadvertently:

(a) The study has been made mainly from the perspective of Human Resource Management. An in-depth study relating to the technical aspects of TQM such as implementation of various TQM tools, technical barriers to effective TQM implementation etc. could not be made.

(b) While measuring the performance of the company in the aftermath of TQM implementation, information relating to certain parameters such as, resource allocation to TQM-ISO Cell, TQM training, quality workshops could not be obtained because of the unwillingness of the management to part with the information.

(c) The sample respondents have been selected on stratified random basis. However, some samples were also selected on the basis of convenience. Thus, the sample may not be cent–per cent random and normal, but predominantly it is so.

THE ORGANISATION

The entire study is presented in six chapters.

As is evident, the first chapter has primarily dealt with the conceptual framework for Total Quality Management. Various models of Total Quality Management are presented and a theoretical discussion on the Human Dimension of Total Quality Management has also been made.

In the second chapter, discussion has been made in two separate sections. The first section reviews existing research work on Total Quality Management. Based on that, attributes or Key Human Factors (KHFs) that are crucial to introduction, development, and implementation of Total Quality Management have been identified. The second section deals with the scope and objectives of the study, research design, and limitations of the research done.

The third chapter presents a brief profile of **Rashtriya Ispat Nigam Limited (RINL)/Vishakhapatnam Steel Plant (VSP)** as a backdrop to this study. It also presents the implementation of TQM process in VSP. An attempt has also been made to measure the performance of the company in the aftermath of Total Quality Management by using different indicators and parameters.

The fourth chapter, titled as 'The Human Dimension of Total Quality Management' tries to bring an interface between Total Quality Management and human factors.

The fifth chapter compiles and makes statistical analysis of the collected data from the sample respondents with regard to different dimensions of Total Quality Management as well as Total Quality Management-Human Resource interface.

The sixth and last chapter deals with the summary of findings and their implications for practice.

The Annexes include the schedule, questionnaire, and interview guide used for the purpose of data collection.

APPENDIX 2.1: Summary of Literature on Total Quality Management *vis-à-vis* Organisational Performance and Pre-requisites and Barriers to Total Quality Management

Category	Author (Year)	Methodology	Findings
(1)	(2)	(3)	(4)
I. Organisational Performance	Sink (1991)	Discussion	Lists seven criteria measuring the performance of an organisation and way to implement quality management.
	Little (1992)	Survey	Provides three reasons for failure of Total Quality Management.
	Shea & Gobeli (1995)	Survey	Finds positive bearing of Total Quality Management on the organisation's success and growth.
	Sinclair & Zairi (1996)	Case Study	Shows how personal involvement in performance measurement is vital for effective performance measurement system.
	Madu *et al.* (1996)	Empirical Study	Finding on association between quality dimensions (CS, ES, ESQ) and organisational performance and proving these dimensions are valid and reliable.
	Nilakant & Narayan (1998)	Empirical Study	Find a positive correlation between Total Quality Management programme and company's performance.
	Singh *et al.* (2000)	Survey	Shows how proper application of Total Quality Management can bring miraculous changes in the performance of workforce.
	Wali *et al.* (2000)	Discussion	Lists various critical success factors for supporting performance matrix in a Total Quality Management environment.

(Contd.)

APPENDIX 2.1 (Contd.)

Category	Author (Year)	Methodology	Findings
(1)	(2)	(3)	(4)
II. Pre-requisites and Barriers			
A. Pre-requisites			
1. Manage-ment Focused	Saraph *et al.* (1989)	Empirical Study	Lists eight critical factors as the pre-requisites.
	Lorinc (1990)	Case Study	Emphasises upon training, learning and consistency of purpose.
	Schmidt & Finnegan (1992)	Discussion	Offers five-way management strategies for making TQM successful.
	Gilbert (1992)	Case Study	Finds an association between time, management support and successful TQM implementation.
	Barclay (1993)	Empirical Study	States that a common quality vocabulary is essential.
	Lu & Sohal (1993)	Empirical Study	Recommends re-orientation of management strategies towards 7 key areas.
	Oakley & Doug (1994)	Reporting on a Survey	Emphasise upon establishing support system by the TQM organisation to make their core values visible and teach people the necessary skills.
	Heller (1994)	Empirical Study	Recommends attention should be paid on leadership quality and commitment.
	Capon *et al.* (1996)	Empirical Study	Study the effects of six monitors of NMBA on teams. Find that measuring and displaying results by management increase the chance of TQM success.
	Sharma (1997)	Empirical Study	Identifies committed leader-ship from top and appropriate management strategies as the pre-conditions.

APPENDIX 2.1 (Contd.)

Category	Author (Year)	Methodology	Findings
(1)	(2)	(3)	(4)
2. People Focused	Walley and Kowalski (1992)	Empirical Study	Provides training of employees as a pre-condition.
	Caudron (1993a)	Discussion	Emphasises upon proper alignment between human resources system and quality goals.
	Caudron (1993b)	Survey	Recommends human resources must partner with other departments in the organisation to support TQM.
	Thompson (1993)	Empirical Study	Finds three basic principles that guide total quality process.
	Woods (1993)	Case Study	Emphasises upon role of training, teamwork, employees' participation, effective two-way communication, recognition, and reward system as pre-requisites.
	Hege-Kleiser (1993)	Discussion	Emphasises upon treatment of employees as customers, measuring employee satis-faction and encouraging employees to innovate as pre-conditions.
	Artzt (1994)	Empirical Study	Views quality process as mixture of "hard" quality (organisation related) and "soft" quality (people related).
	Hayes *et al.* (1994)	Empirical Study	Finds an association between personality characteristics and success implementation of TQM.
	Schon-berger (1994)	Discussion	Necessity for shifting the role of employees, managers and human resource department to make TQM successful.
	Parth Sarathi (1997)	Empirical Study	Emphasises upon the role of HRD professionals.

(Contd.)

APPENDIX 2.1 (Contd.)

Category	Author (Year)	Methodology	Findings
(1)	(2)	(3)	(4)
	Kumar (1999)	Discussion	Identifies "Employership" as a major quality imperative for any TQM organisation.
	Poonawalla (1999)	Discussion	Identifies quality circle as a dependable medium to achieve total quality.
	Ojha (2000)	Empirical Study	Emphasises upon the role of 7 key factors relating to people for effective TQM implementation.
	Wali *et al.* (2000)	Case Study	Emphasise upon more involvement of employees through small improvement teams and quality circles.
3. Organisation focused	Olian & Rynes (1991)	Discussion	Provides that supportive organisational process is necessary to encourage people to adopt behaviour that supports quality.
	Becker *et al.* (1994)	Empirical Study	Find TQM leads to flatter organisation, larger spans of control, more cross-functional problem solving teams and open communication.
4. TQM and Organisational change	Dodson (1991)	Empirical Study	Finds change in employees' attitude and overcoming resistance to TQM as the most important factors.
	Heilpern & Nadler (1992)	Discussion	Finds an association between TQM and organisational change.
	Green (1993)	Discussion	Finds an association between TQM and organisational change and has enlisted 13 principles of organisational change and 23 fundamental quality principles.
	Sharma (1997)	Empirical Study	Emphasises upon the role of external change agents followed internal change

APPENDIX 2.1 (Contd.)

Category	Author (Year)	Methodology	Findings
(1)	(2)	(3)	(4)
			agents/facilitators and extensive training programme for overcoming resistance to change.
B. Barriers	Majumdar *et al.* (1991)	Case Study	Find the possibility of downsizing and illiteracy of TQM as the key barriers.
	Gilbert (1992)	Case Study	Attributes failure of TQM to poor management and lack of training.
	Deevy (1995)	Empirical Study	Finds TQM efforts failed due to failure of the management to deliver on their promises.
	Sharma (1997)	Empirical Study	Identifies conventional mind-set, lack of positive attitude and resistance to change as the inhibiting factors.
	Das (1998)	Case Study	Identifies lack of management support and casual approach to fill-up decision-makers' posts as the barriers.

REFERENCES

- Artzt, Edwin L. (1994). "TQM in the Research and Development Environment: A Balanced Approach Between 'Hard' and 'Soft' Quality: Esso Research Centre", *Cases in Total Quality Management*, Butterworth-Heinemann, Oxford, UK, pp. 52-59.
- Barclay, Charles A. (1993). "Quality Strategy and TQM Policies: Empirical Evidence", *Management International Review*, Vol. 33, First Quarter, pp. 87-98.
- Becker, Selwyn, Golomski, Selwyn W. and Lorry, C. (1994). "TQM and Organisation of the Firm: Theoretical and Empirical Perspectives", *Quality Management Journal*, Vol. 1, No. 2, pp. 18-24.
- Bossink, B., Gieshes, J. and Pas, T., "Diagnosing TQM" Part I, *Total Quality Management*, Vol. 3.
- Capon, N., Kaye, M. and Wood, M. (1996). "Measuring the Success of a TQM Programme", *International Journal of Quality and Reliability Measurement*, Vol. 12, No. 8.

- Caudron, Shari (1993a). "How HR Drives TQM", *Personnel Journal*, Vol. 72, No. 8, August.
- Caudron, Shari (1993b). "Change Keeps TQM Programs Thriving", *Personnel Journal*, Vol. 72, pp. 104-09.
- Das, H. (1998). "Total Quality Management: A Management Legacy?" *Personnel Today*, January-March, pp. 21-28.
- Deevy, E. (1995). *Creating the Resilient Organisation: A Rapid Response Management Programme*, Prentice Hall, New Jersey.
- Deming, W. Edwards (1982). "Improvement of Quality and Productivity Through Action by Management", *Productivity Review*, pp.12-22.
- Deming, W. Edwards (1982). *Quality, Productivity and Competitive Position*, MIT Centre for Advanced Engineering, Cambridge MA.
- Dodson, Robert L. (1991). "Speeding the Way to Total Quality", *Training and Development*, Vol. 45, pp. 35-42.
- Gilbert, James D. (1992). "TQM Flops: A Chance to Learn from the Mistake of Others", *National Productivity Review*, Vol. II, No. 4, pp. 491-99.
- Green, Richard Tabor (1993)."Organisational Change Approaches for Implementing Quality", *Global Quality: A Synthesis of the World's Best Management Methods*, ASQC Quality Press, Milwaukee, pp. 608-21.
- Hardie, N. and Walsh, P. (1994). "Towards a Better Understanding of Quality", *International Journal of Quality and Reliability Management*, Vol. II, No. 4.
- Hayes, Theodore L., Roehm, Harper A., and Castellono, Joseph P. (1994). "Personality Correlates of Success in Total Quality Manufacturing", *Journal of Business Psychology*, Vol. 8, Summer, pp. 397-411.
- Hege-Kleiser, Carmen (1993). "American Express Travel Services: A Human Resources Approach to Managing Quality", in: *Managing Quality in America's Most Admired Companies*, Brett-Koehler Publishers, San Francisco, pp. 205-12.
- Heilpern, Jaffery and Nadler, David (1992). "Implementing Total Quality Management: A Process of Cultural Change", *Organisational Architecture: Design for Changing Organisations*, Jossey-Bass, San Francisco, pp. 137-54.
- Heller, Robert (1994). "Putting the Total into Total Quality", *Management Today*, August, pp. 56-60.
- Kristensen, K., Pahigard, J. and Kanji, G.K. (1992). "Quality and Economic Development Project", *Total Quality Management*, Vol. 3, No. 1, 1992.
- Kumar, Pradeep (1999)."Employership: The Quality Imperative for Employers", *Quality for Business Transformation, Challenges of Sustainable*

Excellence in the 21st Century, Institute of Directors, New Delhi, pp. 76-79.

- Little, Arthur D. (1992). "The Cracks in Quality", *The Economist,* 18 April, pp. 63-64.
- Lorinc, J. (1990). "Dr. Denming's Traveling Quality Slow", *Canadian Business,* Vol. 63, pp. 38-42.
- Lu, E. and Sohal, A. (1993). "Success Factors, Weaknesses and Myths Concerning TQM Implementation in Australia", *Total Quality Management,* Vol. 4, No. 3.
- Madu, C.N., Kue, C.H., and Jacob, R.A. (1996)."An Empirical Assessment of the Influence of Quality Dimensions on Organisational Performance", *International Journal of Production Research,* Vol. 34, No. 7.
- Majumdar, Amit, Smolenyak, Megan and Yencho, Naney (1991). "Planting the Seeds of TQM", *National Productivity Review,* Vol. 10, pp. 491-97.
- Nilakant, V. and Narayan, Ram (1998). *Managing Organisational Change,* Sage Publications, New Delhi.
- Oakley, Ed and Doug, Krug (1994). "Open Learners", *Training and Development,* Vol. 48, May, pp. 14-19.
- Ojha, Abhoy K. (2000). "Total Quality Management: How Can We Make the Implication Effective?", *Vikalpa,* Vol. 25, No. 2, April-June, pp. 19-29.
- Olian, Judy D. and Rynes, Sara L. (1991). "Making Total Quality Work: Aligning Organisational Processes, Performance Measures and Stakeholders", *Human Resource Management,* Vol. 30, pp. 303-33.
- Partha Sarathi (1997). "Enhancing Readiness for Total Quality Management: The Role of Human Resources Development", *Management & Labour Studies,* Vol. 22, No. 3, July, pp. 133-45.
- Poonawalla, Lila (1999). "Total Quality through People Participation", *Quality for Business Transformation, Challenges of Sustainable Excellence in the 21st Century,* Institute of Directors, New Delhi, pp. 85-90.
- Saraph, J.V., Beneson, P.G. and Schroeder, R.G. (1989). "An Instrument for Measuring the Critical Factors for TQM", *Decision Sciences,* Vol. 20.
- Schmidt, Warren H. and Finnegan, Jerome P. (1992). *The Race Without a Finish Line,* Jossey-Bass, San Francisco.
- Schonberger, Richard J. (1994). "Human Resources Management Lessons from a Decade of Total Quality Management and Reengineering", *California Management Review,* Vol. 36, Summer, pp. 109-23.
- Sharma, Sunil (1997). *TQM in Indian Engineering Industries,* Business Publications Inc., Mumbai.

- Shea, John and Gobeli, David (1995). "TQM: The Experiences of Ten Small Businesses", *Business Horizons*, January-February, Vol. 38, No. 1, pp. 71-77.
- Sinclair, D. and Zairi, M. (1996). "Assessing the Effectiveness of Performance Measurement Systems: A Case Study", *Total Quality Management*, Vol. 7, No. 4.
- Singh, Deepali, Suchi Priya, Pillai, Santosh, Sharma, Shweta and Mehta, Sandeep (2000)."TQM on Crossroads", *JIMS 8 M*, Vol. 5, No. 2, April-June.
- Sink, D.S. (1991). "The Role of Measurement in Achieving World Class Quality and Productivity Management", *Industrial Engineering*, June.
- Thompson, Fred L. (1993). "Monsanto: Employee Empowerment through Total Quality Management", in: *Managing Quality in America's Most Admired Companies*, Brett-Koehler Publishers, San Francisco, pp. 103-14.
- Wali, Ayoob Ahmed, Deshmukh, S.G. and Gupta, A.D. (2000). "Quality Initiatives in a Manufacturing Unit: A Case Study", *Productivity*, Vol. 41, No. 2, July-September, pp. 210-16.
- Wali, Ayub A., Deshmukh, S.G. and Gupta, A.D. (2000). "Framework for TQM Performance Measurement System", *Productivity*, Vol. 41, No. 1, April-June.
- Walley, Paul and Kowalski, Emil (1992). "The Role of Training in Total Quality Implementation", *Journal of European Industrial Training*, Vol. 16, No. 3, pp. 25-31.
- Woods, Robert (1993). "Springs Industries Inc., Quality Through Improved Use of Human Resources", *Managing Quality in America's Most Admired Companies*, Brett-Koehler Publishers, San Francisco, pp. 241-50.

3

TQM Practices in RINL/VSP

The present chapter presents a brief profile of the organisation i.e., RINL/VSP and analyses the TQM practices followed in the company. At the outset, an attempt has been made to trace the evolution of TQM in the company. Afterward, TQM practices in terms of implementation of various TQM tools such as, Quality Improvement Projects, Memorandum of Understanding, ISO Certification, Employee Involvement Schemes, Benchmarking, and Housekeeping etc. have been critically examined on the basis of the factual data collected from the company. At the closing stage, using certain parameters and performance indicators the efficacy of TQM implementation has been assessed.

RINL/VSP—A BRIEF PROFILE

RINL/VSP is one of the 'main steel' producers of India, located on the coast of Bay of Bengal in the State of Andhra Pradesh. It is a very dynamic and vibrant organisation, which is performing exceedingly well both in steel production as well as in sales. It produces different steel products such as angles, billets, beams and so on, their by-products such as granulated slag, lime fines and so on and markets them both inside and outside the country.

The company procures its raw materials such as, iron ore, limestone, dolomite, manganese ore, and coal from different parts of India as well as from abroad. Its technology with the modernized plans sustains production of high quality steels. RINL/VSP has the capacity to produce 3 MT liquid steel per annum. There are seven major production units, two non-production units and twenty-five supporting units in RINL/VSP.

The CMD heads the company and he is assisted in his task by an army of officers. Unlike other PSUs, managers at all levels upto the CMD are actively involved in the day-to-day operation of the company. Another major strength of the company lies in its approachable management philosophy.

The total manpower strength of the company is 17,006, out of which executives; junior officers and non-executives comprise 16.45%, 8.22%, and 75.33% of the total workforce respectively. Being the latest addition to the Indian public sector, the company enjoys the twin advantages of joining of the experienced personnel as well as young enthusiastic and educated workforce.

RINL/VSP has made remarkable strides in improving its techno-economic indices. As a result, its techno-economic indices are regarded as the best in the country and some of them are of international standards. To its credit, it has achieved a number of significant awards since its inception. Steel production of 5.0 MT with the existing manpower, labour productivity of 231 tonnes/man-year, and generating profit by the next year are some of the future concerns of the company.

EVOLUTION OF TQM IN RINL/VSP

In June 1993, Mr. J. Mehra, Director (Operations) took over the charge as CMD of RINL/VSP. "When I assumed office as CMD, there were three areas that needed most of top management's time and attention.... The need for changing the mindset of employees (which was rooted in the past), restructuring the company's finances (to offset the adverse impact of the heavy financial charges), and the need to achieve rated capacities quickly and reduce costs," said Mehra. Consequently, in order to make RINL/VSP viable, Mehra adopted the following consolidation strategies:

(i) Mindset-Change;

(ii) Cost Management; and

(iii) Financial Restructuring.

The inordinate delay in commissioning the project, the massive cost overrun, the Government's decision to withdraw the project, all taken together had lowered the morale of

RINL's 17,000-odd executives and workmen. An organisation survey was commissioned by RINL/VSP in 1993 to study the attitude of employees. The survey report revealed the common perception among the workforce were,

(a) RINL/VSP can never achieve its rated capacity.

(b) RINL/VSP has unusually low manpower.

(c) RINL/VSP can never make profits.

In order to remove these mental blocks, Mehra started sending teams of executives and workmen abroad to study technological process and work practices in world-class steel plants in Korea, Japan and USA to make them understand how world class production standards could be achieved. These teams then made presentations to their colleagues back home in groups, followed by question-answer sessions and intense discussions. It took RINL about a year to internalise these learning. The process of mindset change was reinforced by the adoption of TQM system that introduced several changes in the form of employee involvement, inviting suggestions from employees, an innovative incentive and reward package that was designed to boast productivity levels etc. This ultimately improved the morale of employees. Thus TQM tools were implemented in the company as a survival stratagem.

The journey of TQM in RINL/VSP took off on 15 September, 1995 with the establishment of the TQM Cell. At the foundation stage, TQM Cell was under the control of Works Department, which comprised only three executives—one Deputy Chief Manager and two Deputy Managers. "The TQM movement in the Works Division has been given a major thrust with the formation of full time TQM Cell. The rationale of this Cell was to propagate Total Quality Movement in Works Division, so that the quality of work process and whatever we do, continuously improves," said R.C. Jha, the erstwhile Director (Operations).

To provide further impulsion to the programme, the CMD together with the other top managers took on a policy decision to institute a full-fledged TQM department in the company. As a result, the TQM-ISO Cell was born on January 1997. In order to provide a more methodical approach to TQM activities, it was decided to implement the programme in a phased manner. Details of these phases are illustrated below.

Phase-I: Creating Quality Awareness among Executives

At the beginning phase, awareness among executives was created about the necessity of introducing TQM in the organisation and how well it has to be implemented. This was done to ensure that all executives in the organisation think and talk alike, when they refer to total quality. To meet the objective, the management hired the services of the Singapore-based Organisation Development Inc. (ODI) as the Consultant. The ODI conducted a 5 days workshop on 'Total Quality Advantage', which was attended by the CMD, all Directors, General Managers, and all Senior Executives. The training programme was then cascaded downwards up to Junior Officers level, thereby creating quality awareness among all executives.

Accordingly, training in TQM was provided to employees in two phases. The first phase was commenced on 17th March, 1997. During this phase, 6 days training was provided to 44 executives from different departments, who were groomed as facilitators. Afterwards, these facilitators taught the quality mantras they have learnt to other executives in a phased manner. *In toto,* 2900 executives were trained in the first phase, which was continued upto June 1997. During the second phase, a 7-days training programme was organised to provide training to 75 executives from different departments on 'Total Quality Advantage'. During the Phase, a common language of 'Quality' was created across the company.

Phase-II: Formation of Cross-Functional Quality Action Teams (QATs)

A number of QATs were formed to solve specific problems and help employees to observe practical demonstration of substantial benefits that will flow from adopting TQM practices and problem-solving methodology.

Phase-III: Creating a Voice of Employee Index

A survey was conducted in the organisation through administering a specially designed questionnaire to collect data relating to the level of motivation, job satisfaction, commitment and morale of employees. The collected data was analyzed to render meaningful inferences about employees' attitude towards this novel practice.

Phase-IV: Exposing Workmen

During this phase, the executives who had already been trained in TQM were assigned the responsibility to educate and train employees at the grass-root level to make them understand the meaning of quality as well as establish in them a willing commitment to work in the lines of quality.

At the beginning phase, Mr. J. Mehra, the then CMD, took keen interest to spread the TQM movement in the company with an aim that it will help to maintain high product standard. The HRD department was actively involved in conducting the awareness as well as training programmes for TQM. The Director (Operations) was closely monitoring its progress. Besides one Core Group, Quality Council, and Steering Committee were constituted to synchronize the overall TQM efforts within the organisation and review its progress. The constitution and functions of these teams are described below.

(a) *Steering Committee*

The Steering Committee (SC) was constituted on 24 August, 1995 in the Works Division with a view to improve the quality of work through total employee involvement. The SC constituted 10 members—that included, General Manager (Works) as the Chairman of the Committee, General Manager (Management Services), Additional General Manager (Steel), (Iron), (Mills), Deputy General Manager (Maintenance), (Quality Assurance & TD), (CO & CC)), (SP & RMTTP), and Additional Chief Manager (HR).

(b) *Core Group*

The Core Group was set up on 28 January, 1997 with a view to coordinate the overall TQM efforts and support the Quality Council and the Steering Committee in their functioning. The Chief (Technical and R&D) and the Assistant General Manager (HRD) were the members of the group.

(c) *Quality Council*

To ensure that the implementation process is carried out on schedule and in an effective manner, one Quality Council

(QC) was set up on 28 January, 1997. It consisted of the following members: CMD as the Chairman of the Council, Director (Operations) & (Finance and Control), Executive Director (Vigilance) & (Works), Chief (PECs), General Manager (Management Services), (Personnel), (Services), (Operations), (Mills), CMO, Chief (T & R&D), Corporate Planning, Additional General Manager (Industrial Relations), (RM & Mines), (Maintenance), Joint General Manager (Finance), (Marketing), (Materials Management), (Training), and Assistant General Manager (HRD) as the member conveners. The first meeting of QC was held on 8 February, 1997 and normally it met once in a month.

The details of the roles and responsibilities of these Councils and Committees are given in Table 3.1.

At present, these three committees are no more in existence. Their role and responsibilities have been shifted to the TQM-ISO Cell.

QUALITY MANAGEMENT SYSTEM

Successful TQM implementation has enabled RINL/VSP to obtain ISO-9001:2000 certification from 4 January, 2001 onwards. In accordance with the provision of ISO-9001:2000, the company has established, documented, implemented and maintained a Quality Management System.

To meet the quality planning requirements of the organisation and also to facilitate continuous improvement, the Quality Management System (QMS) has been established, documented, implemented and maintained in RINL/VSP in accordance with the requirements of the international standards. Figure 3.1 depicts the process involved in the implementation, organisation and review of QMS.

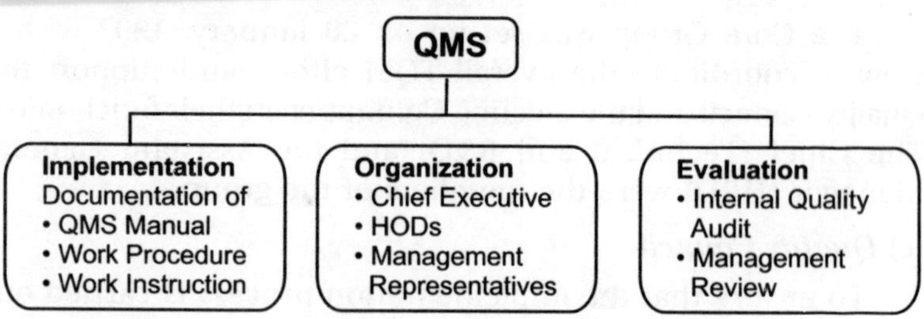

Figure 3.1. QMC Process

TABLE 3.1: Roles and Responsibilities of Steering Committee Core Group and Quality Council

Steering Committee	Core Group	Quality Councils
Constitution		
The steering committee consists of 6-7 senior managers/HODs at each division. The committee meets once a month to review the progress in their division.	It is a two-manager team.	This is the executive management team, usually consisting of 8-12 members representing all functions of the organisation.
Responsibility		
(a) Generate a list of improvement projects for review.	(a) Coordinating the overall TQM efforts in the organisation.	(a) Establish organisational and project goals.
(b) Select team leaders and members.	(b) Supporting the Quality Council and Steering Committees.	(b) Identify priority processes to improve.
(c) Establish a system for measuring and monitoring.	(c) Becoming the key change agents of the company.	(c) Approve budget and other resources.
(d) Handle implementation problems.	(d) Serve as facilitators for both Total Quality Advantage (TQA) and the Quality Action Teams (QATs).	(d) Review status of teams on a regular basis.
(e) Determine the team's reporting requirements.	(e) Provide regular update and reports to the senior management.	(e) Provide recognition.
(f) Provide publicity, recognition other support.		

Source: Compiled from the data collected from TQM-ISO Cell, RINL/VSP.

Implementation

The QMS operates through manual, work procedures and work instructions affecting the product, process and quality system. The 'Quality Management System Manual' is an apex-manual documented for having the overall control on the QMS. It refers to the system procedure and outlines the structure of the documentation used in the QMS. The second level documents contain various work procedures in conformity with QMS manual. These work procedures are prepared, controlled and issued by the Management Services department. They contain work procedures relating to the continual improvement in product, process and quality system, procedures relating to the internal communication between various levels and processes of the QMS as well as communication with the customers and suppliers etc. And, the third level documents are work instructions for different jobs and are the detailed documents being followed to meet requirements of the work procedures. Thus, all the aspects relating to product including its inspection, process, and quality systems are covered in the work procedures and work instructions. The documented work procedures and work instructions define how the quality requirements of the organisation are met.[1]

Organisation

The Chief Executive, Management Representatives, and Heads of various departments are entrusted with the responsibility to implement QMS. The details of the inter-relationship of the personnel involved in its implementation are given in Figure 3.2.

Chief Executive (CE)

The Executive Director (Works) has been appointed as the Chief Executive of the QMS of the Works Division. He exercises full control on all activities for ensuring quality in

---

1. Applicable documents of external origin and documents of permanent nature which undergo revisions rarely such as equipment's operation and maintenance manuals, equipment drawings, repair cycles and other documents of similar nature are referred in the respective work procedures and the work instructions as 'document'.

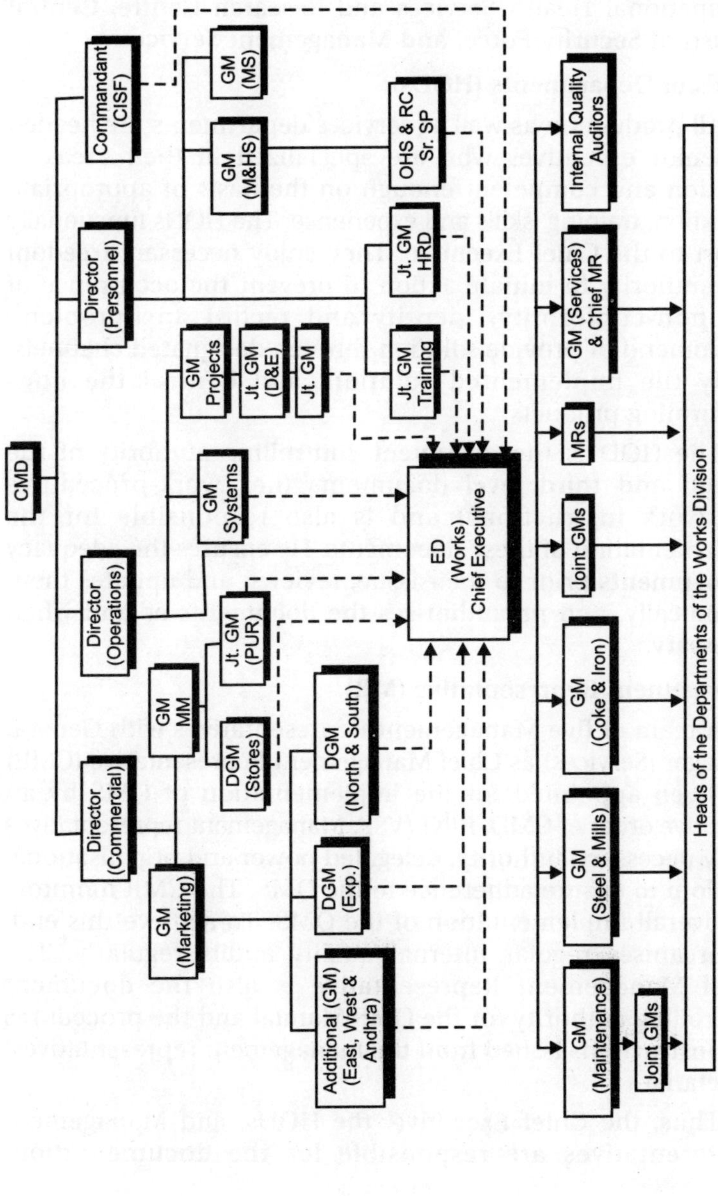

Figure 3.2. Organisational Chart of QMS

Note: Dotted lines show functional reporting relationship.

product, process, and quality system in the Works Division and other related departments such as, Marketing, Materials Management, Systems, Training, HRD, Receipt, Inspection, Occupational Health Services and Research Centre, Central Industrial Security Force, and Management Services.

Heads of Departments (HODs)

All production as well as services departments are headed by senior executives who are specialized in their areas of function and competent enough on the basis of appropriate education, training, skills and experience. The HODs functionally report to the Chief Executive. They enjoy necessary freedom and authority to initiate action to prevent the occurrence of any non-conformity, identify and record any problem, recommend or provide solution through designated channels, verify the implemented solution, and control the non-conforming products.

The HOD is the document controlling authority of the second and third level documents (i.e., work-procedures and work instructions) and is also responsible for the implementation of these documents. He ensures the adequacy of documents prior to their issue, reviews, and updates them periodically, and preauthorises the documents as and when necessary.

Management Representative (MR)

A team of five Management Representatives with General Manager (Services) as Chief Management Representative (CMR) has been appointed for the implementation of QMS by an executive order of CMD, RINL/VSP. Management representatives enjoy necessary authority, delegated power and organisational freedom to ensure adherence to the QMS. The CMR monitors the overall implementation of the QMS. To achieve this end, he organises regular internal quality audits regularly. The Chief Management Representative is also the document controlling authority for the QMS Manual and the procedures and instructions issued from the management representatives' secretariat.

Thus, the Chief Executive, the HODs, and Management Representatives are responsible for the documentation, implementation, and monitoring of the QMS. The detailed responsibility matrix of different executives involved in the QMS is presented in Appendix 3.1.

Evaluation

Review of QMS is done through regular internal quality audits and management reviews.

Internal Quality Audit

In order to verify and determine the effective implementation and maintenance of the QMS, quality audits are carried out at regular intervals by the Internal Quality Auditors. For this purpose, 50 qualified executives from different departments have been identified and trained in three batches by the Bureau Veritus Quality International (BVQI), U.K. The BVQI organised a five days training programme inside the organisation. Only those executives, who do not have direct responsibility for any of the activity being audited, are eligible for appointment as Internal Quality Auditors.

Management Review

The management review of the QMS is done once in every two months to ensure its continuing suitability, adequacy and effectiveness. The Chief Executive, the COMMERCE, and HODs are responsible to conduct the management review. QMS review includes, assessing opportunities for improvement including the quality policy, and quality objectives. Inputs to QMS review include information on:

(i) Results of audits;
(ii) Customer feedback;
(iii) Process performance and product conformance analysis;
(iv) Status of corrective and preventive actions; and
(v) Follow-up actions from earlier management reviews planned changes that could affect the QMS, and recommendations for improvement.

During the management reviews, the improvements in the QMS and its processes, improvement in the product standard and resource needs are identified. Besides, once in a week, performance review of the Works Division is also carried out by the ED (Works) along with HODs. The Chief

Management Representative maintains the records of management reviews and weekly performance reviews.

STRUCTURE AND FUNCTIONS OF TQM–ISO CELL

Structure of TQM-ISO Cell

The TQM-ISO Cell was set up on January 1997. At present, it comprises 5 members, viz., Chief Superintendent (TQM), Manager (TQM), Deputy Chief Manager (ISO), Manager (ISO) and Assistant General Manager (TQM-ISO). The AGM (TQM-ISO) heads the TQM-ISO Cell and reports directly to the General Manager (Services), who in turn is accountable to the Executive Director (Works). The organisational chart of the TQM-ISO Cell is presented in Figure 3.3.

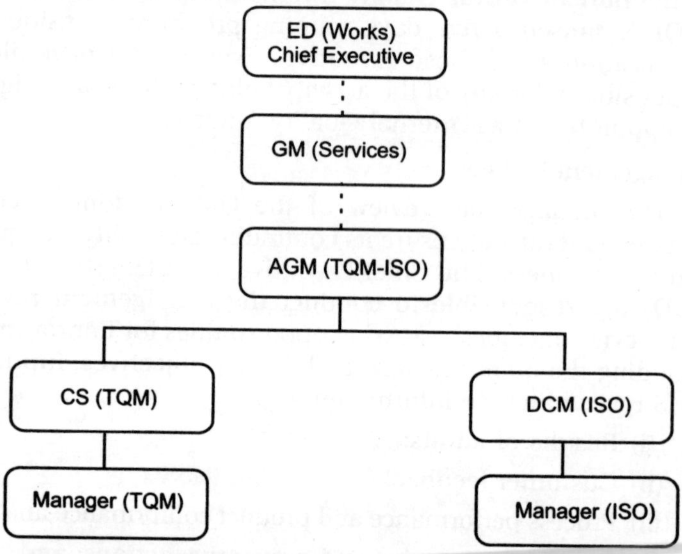

Notes:
ED - Executive Director
GM - General Manager
AGM - Assistant General Manager
CS - Chief Superintendent
DCM - Deputy Chief Manager

Figure 3.3. Organisational Structure of TQM-ISO Cell

Functional Responsibilities of TQM-ISO Cell

The TQM-ISO Cell performs several quality related functions that include:

- Identification of Quality Improvement Projects (QIPs) in different departments.

- Coordination of various QIPs; and
- Monitor and coordination of the functions of Memorandum of Understandings.

CORPORATE QUALITY POLICY AND OBJECTIVES

The corporate quality policy and objectives have been defined and documented keeping in view the needs of the organisation as well as of customers. The quality policy envisages, "commitment to meeting the requirements of the customers as well as continual improvement". It also provides framework for establishing and reviewing quality objectives.

Corporate Quality Policy

The Quality Policy of RINL/VSP provides for:

- Supplying quality goods and services to achieve customers' delight;
- Achieving quality of the products by following systematic approach through planning, documented procedures and timely review of quality objectives;
- Continuously improving the quality of all materials, processes and products; and
- Maintaining an enabling environment, which encourages teamwork and active involvement of all employees with total commitment.

Corporate Quality Objectives

The quality objectives of RINL/VSP focus on:

- Promoting awareness of customer requirements throughout the organisation in order to achieve customer satisfaction;
- Meeting statutory and regulatory requirements as applicable to the products and processes;
- Maintaining an effective QMS, demonstrating adherence to the same, and striving for continual improvement;
- Developing a competent, well trained and motivated workforce; and
- Determining yearly measurable quality objectives needed for meeting the requirements of the processes and products at organisational as well as departmental level and review then periodically.

The corporate quality policy and objectives provide the broad framework within which departmental quality objectives are determined annually by the HODs. These are subject to the approval of the CE.

PILLARS OF TQM IN RINL/VSP

Tom Peters wrote, 'most quality programmes fail for one of the two reasons. They have system without passion, or passion without system. You must have the both'. RINL/VSP has both the system as well as passion for TQM. TQM in the company stands on the pillars of customer focus, continuous improvement, teamwork, measurement, and systematic support. These pillars are based on organisational values such as honesty, commitment to customer satisfaction, and commitment to create an environment in which employees can do their best in work. These five pillars constitute the foundation of RINL/VSP as a quality organisation.

Customer Focus (Meeting Requirements)

RINL/VSP always follows the 'voice of the customer' in its quality management practices. This voice comes from both external and internal customers. In order to enhance customer satisfaction, it ensures that the requirements of customers, whether stated or not, but is necessary for their specified or intended use are fulfilled.

Regarding external Customers the Regional Managers, Branch Managers and HODs are responsible to deal with external customers. Customer needs are periodically assessed so as to determine their actual requirements. Product requirements specified by the customers including the requirements for availability, delivery and support and not specified by the customers, but necessary for intended or specified use as well as obligations related to product including statutory and regulatory requirements are determined while finalising enquiry specifications for a tender/contract/orders. The enquiry specifications for a tender/contract/order are reviewed with the customer so as to ensure that the product requirements are adequately defined and documented before the acceptance of the contract/order. The contract with customer is finalised only after ensuring that the capabilities to meet the contractual requirements does exist in the company. In case of any change in the product requirements by the customers, the contract is accordingly amended and the concerned personnel are made aware of the changed requirements. The Marketing department monitors the fulfilment of customer's orders and this is also reviewed in various management review meetings. Communication with the customer is always maintained with respect to product information, contracts, order handling including amendment in the orders, and to receive feedback and customer complaints.

Regarding internal customers, each customer department identifies its supplier/customer department and they enter into Memorandum of Understanding (MoU). The progress with respect to MoU is reviewed through departmental quality meetings. Thus, RINL/VSP always strives towards satisfying its customers and bringing an alignment between customers' needs and suppliers' capabilities (Figure 3.4).

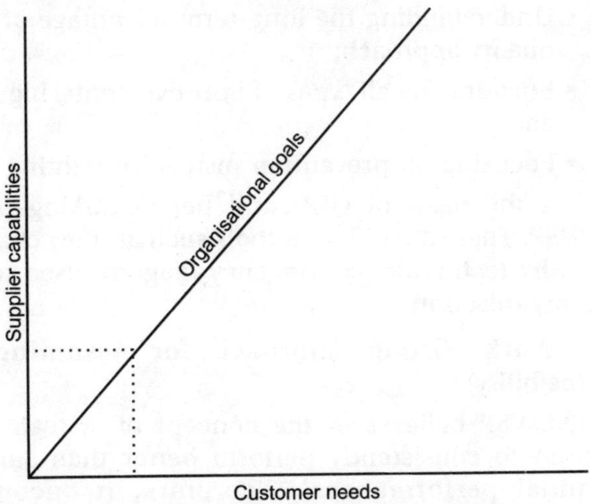

Figure 3.4. Alignment between Supplier's Capabilities and Customers' Needs

There are two important points about alignment upon which the company always emphasizes:

- Alignment is the process of matching supplier capabilities (what is deliverable) with customer needs (what is expected); and

- Alignment must occur both vertically and horizontally. It is essential not only between work groups that are connected in a horizontal chain, but also between organisational levels that are connected in a vertical chain. Similarly, if the employees perform their work without taking into consideration the policy and objectives of the organisation, it will also result in misalignment.

To improve and evaluate the alignment with the customers, RINL/VSP takes care of the six key points (details of which are given in Table 3.2).

Continuous Improvement (Preventing and Innovating)

Continuous Improvement (CI) is central to the quality efforts of RINL/VSP. It is achieved by:

- Applying the quality blueprint to every aspect of work;
- Understanding the long-term advantage of a cost-of-quality approach;
- Encouraging all types of improvements, big and small; and
- Focusing on prevention instead of fighting fires.

CI is the basis of QIPs and benchmarking projects in RINL/VSP. There are different tools such as, flow chart, control chart, why technique, contingency diagram used to bring CI in the organisation.

Team Work (Group Approach for Assuming Quality Responsibility)

RINL/VSP believes in the concept of 'a team, which is supposed to consistently perform better than sum total of individual performances'. Therefore, it encourages all employees to participate in teams by providing them necessary stimulus and creating continuous learning environment.

QIPs, QATs, and Quality Circles demonstrate different forms of teamwork created for different purposes in the organisation. For instance, a QIP normally comprises of 5 to 6 members, is created in order to improve the quality of activities in a particular area/department. Similarly, Quality Circles are set up in different departments to resolve different work-related

TABLE 3.2: Six Key Points followed By RINL/VSP to Build Alignment between Customers and Suppliers

Steps	Description
I. Identification of customers	Identify the customers and understand their expectation which are influenced by both wants and needs.
II. Understanding customers' needs	Through discussion understand their expectations and set them out as requirements.
III. Determining all quality elements	• Product or service: • Is it what our customer needs ? ■ Does it do what our customer wants? • Relationship: • Do we trust each other? • Have we talked about, how we will work together? • Integrity: • Can we provide that support which our customer needs? • If requirements are not met, what we will do? • Delivery: ■ Do we ensure that the product/service is delivered on time to the right person or location? ■ Do we see that it arrives ready to use? • Expense: ■ Does the customer believe that the product/service provide good value?
IV. Helping the customers	• What would you like from us, to define their needs that you are not getting? • Are you getting information from us, which you do not need? • What happens to you, if you do not get what you need from us ?
V. Ensuring that customers' expectations are consistent with the product it offers	–
VI. Ensuring that it can fulfil its customers' expectations completely and concisely	–

Note: '–' indicates no description in that stage.
Source: Complied and collated from RINL/VSP.

problems. Besides, a number of work teams such as, production teams, advise teams and action teams have also been constituted in the company with a view to achieve total quality.

Measurement (Monitoring Quality)

RINL/VSP uses various measurement tools to track its progress as it believes, 'we do not know where we stand without any measurement of what we have done'. In order to meet quality goals, it has established baselines and chart progress against them. Customer requirements always influence its decision about what to measure and the measurement is done only by those, who are doing the actual work. Accordingly, using facts and data rather than relying on intuition decisions relating to quality are taken.

Systematic Support (Leading and Reinforcing)

All the systems in the organisation such as planning, budgeting, scheduling and performance management are concocted in order to aid its quality effort. The quality efforts of employees are recognized and accordingly rewarded.

IMPLEMENTATION OF TQM TOOLS

In RINL/VSP, the following TQM tools are implemented with a view to bring continuous improvement in the quality of work, process and products:

(a) Quality Improvement Projects
(b) Memorandum of Understanding
(c) ISO Certification
(d) Benchmarking
(e) Employee Involvement Schemes
(f) Housekeeping

QUALITY IMPROVEMENT PROJECTS

Quality Improvement Projects (QIPs) cover the activities related to the improvement in current status of a project through constitution of Quality Action Teams (QATs) for different areas of the QMS. The responsibility of QIPs lies with various HODs including the HOD, TQM-ISO Cell.

Every year, Heads of different departments with the assistance of the HOD, TQM-ISO Cell identifies QIPs in their respective departments. These projects are identified with quantifiable and measurable targets. The identified projects are then sent to the ED (Works) for approval. After the approval of QIPs, the team leaders and the members are selected. Generally, each QIP comprises five to six team members including team leader and a facilitator. As far as possible, the team leader who heads the project is an executive of E-5/E-6 grade, i.e., in the rank of DCM/CS or AGM. Each project is numbered and provided with a facilitator by the HOD, TQM-ISO Cell.

After the selection of a project for improvement, the respective HOD submits a format along with the proposed names of team leader and team members. The team leader establishes a system for measuring and monitoring the performance of the QIP. HOD of the concerned department supports and sponsors the project. A monthly progress report is submitted by the team leader though the concerned HOD to the HOD, TQM-ISO Cell, who in turn presents the summary of all these reports in the management review meeting. After the completion of the project, the implementation status is monitored and observed for a period of six months to know whether the desired results are achieved or not. Then, the status report is submitted by the respective HOD to the HOD, TQM-ISO Cell.

Generally, the duration of QIPs is one year. However, in certain cases it may be extended. In case, any QIP fails to achieve the desired result within the stipulated time, then it may get some favour with regard to time or other facilities on citing genuine reasons in the management review meeting. Sometimes many QIPs are dropped if they are not tenable, which of course happens in rare cases. In this case, the project is presented to the ED (Works) and General Manager and if they are convinced, they may allow to drop that particular QIP.

FADE CYCLE

In RINL/VSP, quality improvement is an enduring part of everyone's job and everyone is required to have the skills and knowledge essential with regard to FADE cycle. The steps involved in the cycle are:

TABLE 3.3: Phases of FADE Cycle

Phases	Steps		
Phase I : Focus	**Generate a list of problems**	**Select one problem**	**Verify and define the problem**
Defining a problem	Make a list of all the different problems that members might like to solve. In this way, the team can see the range of problems and can also see at a glance whether some problems are widespread or especially important.	From the list, one problem must be selected to begin with. (Others can be taken up later.)	Is the problem really important enough to be worth the effort? How does it affect people. How extensive is it? It is important to answer those questions as best you can with the information already available in the team. You can verify that you really do have a worthwhile project and can get a better idea of what the problem is about.
Phase II: Analyze	**Decide what you need to know**	**Collect data-baselines and patterns**	**Determine the most influential factors**
Gathering and analyzing data	Consider what data might help you understand the problem. Typically, people want to know the incidence of the problem (where, when, and how often it happens) or they want to look at the work process (how people are organized to do the job).	Collect data that will give you baseline measure and will help you identify key factors or root causes. When these are controlled, the problem will also be controlled.	If the data collected do not give you this information, you need to ask more questions and perhaps collect more data. Once you understand the problem and its contributing factors it is enough to develop solutions, you can move to the next phase.

TABLE 3.3 (Contd.)

Phases	Steps		
Phase III: Develop	**Generate a list of promising solutions**	**Select one Solution**	**Develop an Implementation Plan**
Developing a Solution	This can be done through brainstorming or by using methods that are more creative.	If there is more than one promising solution, one of them must be selected or further defined.	Start planning by assessing what obstacles stand in the way of solution and what forces will support it. Then do a trial run of the solution. Once it works, a new or changed standard operating procedure may be needed to let people know how to do their jobs when implementation begins. Finally, an action plan ensures that all of the solutions will be correctly implemented
Phase IV: Execute	**Gain Commitment**	**Execute the Plan**	**Monitor the Impact**
Implementing and Monitoring the Plan	As you now approach individuals or groups, do more than just give them the facts. Listen carefully to their concerns and ideas. Your plan may be improved by their suggestions.	Once responsibilities have been delegated, they need to be carried out. Someone needs to coordinate and make it sure that the timetable is followed. When possible, pretest the solution before full implementation. If the plan is complex or involves potential snags, then contingency plans and other preventive actions may be necessary.	You will probably reuse your original reference measures for this purpose, but you may also want to add some other measure now that you know what your solution entails. Monitoring techniques may be simple or complex, but need to have some indication of how well your solution is working.

- Phase I: Focus-Focus on the right problems to solve;
- Phase II: Analyse-Analyse those problems;
- Phase III: Develop-Develop realistic and worthwhile solutions; and
- Phase IV: Execute-Evaluate how well new procedures and systems are working.

The details of these phases are outlined in Table 3.3.

Quality Action Teams (QATs) are based on the premise that 'every employee holds the key to organisational excellence and quality improvement'. They use the FADE cycle and various tools involved in that for implementation of QIP. QATs use different tools in each phase of FADE cycle, the details of which are given in Table 3.4.

Evaluation of QIP Performance

During the last four years, as many as 292 QIPs were taken up for improvement in RINL/VSP. The total number of QIPs taken up since 1997-98, and their outcome measured in terms of net financial savings for the company have been presented in Table 3.5.

A figurative presentation of the performance of QIPs during the period 1997-98 to 2001-02 is delineated in Figure 3.5., which is self-explanatory.

Recognition for Successful QIPs

At present, the CMD along with the top management of RINL/VSP are planning to recognise and award merit certificates to those selected projects, which have really contributed to the process of continuous improvement. They have proposed to constitute one committee to select the three best QIPs in each year from the first, second and third cycle projects, which stand completed.

MEMORANDUM OF UNDERSTANDING

RINL/VSP uses Memorandum of Understanding (MoU) in the place of Internal Customer Satisfaction (ICS) model (this linkage is outlined in Figure 3.6). The MoUs are being monitored and coordinated by the TQM-ISO Cell.

TABLE 3.4: Tools used in the FADE Cycle

Phase	Tools	Description
Focus	• Brain Storming	A technique for generating a list of ideas about an issue.
	• Multivoting	A technique for narrowing down a list of options.
	• Selection Grid	A technique for selecting one option from several possibilities.
	• Impact Analysis	A procedure for discovering what impact a situation has on people and their environment.
	• Problem Statement	A technique for describing a problem, its impact and the desired state.
Anaylse	• Checklist	A list of things to be done or items to be obtained.
	• Data-Gathering Plan	Technique for collecting data, including check sheets, sampling and surveys.
	• Checksheet	A method of data-recording form that tells how many times something has happened.
	• Sampling	The process of selecting a small group of individuals or items that represent the whole population in which you are interested.
	• Fishbone Diagram	A diagram showing a large or possible causes of a problem.
	• Survey	The process of asking people for their options, knowledge by using face to face interviews, questionnaires or both.
	• Flowchart	A drawing that shows the steps of a work process in the sequence in which they occur.
Develop	• Innovation Transfer	The use of solutions to other problems to generate possible solution to problem.
	• Force Field Analysis	A method for listing, discussing and dealing with the forces that make possible or obstruct a change you want.
	• Cost-benefit Analysis	A way to compare the costs and benefits of plans.

(Contd.)

TABLE 3.4 (Contd.)

Phase	Tools	Description
	• Standard Operating	Procedure A set of explicit instructions dealing with the action necessary to do things on an ongoing basis.
	• Action Plan	An outline of who will do what, when and by what methods.
Execute	• Building Individual Support	A process of communicating with other individuals to inform them and gain their commitment.
	• Basic Descriptive Charts	A way to describe what is happening by summarizing data in simple visual displays.
	• Presentation	A method of formal communication, usually conducted for groups.
	• Specifications	These are indicators of the level of performance you need.
	• Control Limits	These are indicators of how the process usually performs.
	• Measuring	It is the means of keeping track of how close you are to where you want to be or how far from it.
	• Monitoring	It is the means of keeping track of how close you are to where you want to be—or how far from it.

TABLE 3.5: QIP Implementation and their Outcome

Year	No. of Projects	Savings (Rs. in crores)	Savings per project (Rs. in crores)
1997-98 (First Cycle)	62	32.5	0.52
1998-99 (Second Cycle)	60	18.5	0.30
1999-2000 (Third Cycle)	58	26	0.44
2000-2001 (Fourth Cycle)	49	29	0.59
2001-2002 (Fifth Cycle)	63	50*	0.79
Total	292	156.0	2.64
(Average)	(58)	(31.2)	(0.52)

Note: '*' Indicates expected savings.
(Figures in parenthesis indicate the average number per year.)
Source: Data collect from RINL/VSP.

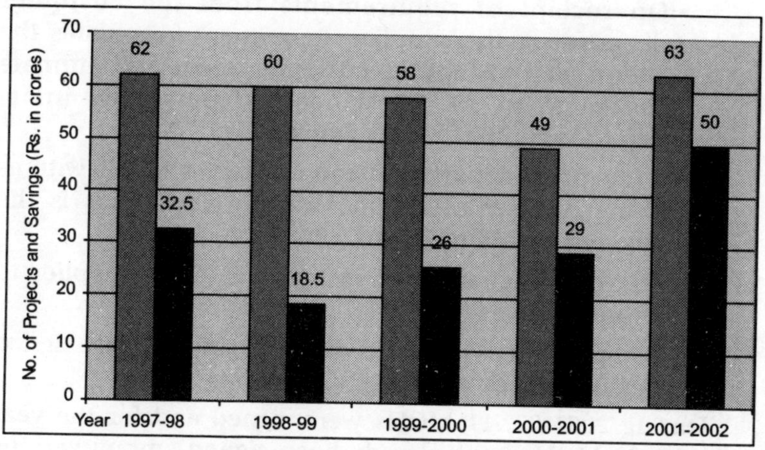

Figure 3.5. Performance of QIPs

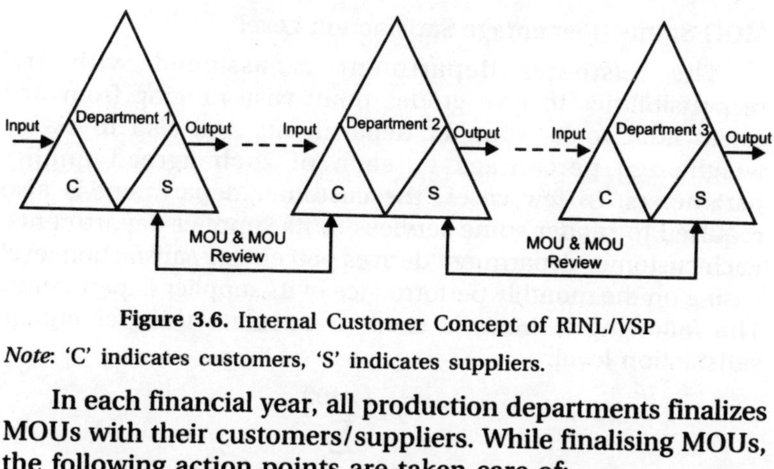

Figure 3.6. Internal Customer Concept of RINL/VSP

Note: 'C' indicates customers, 'S' indicates suppliers.

In each financial year, all production departments finalizes MOUs with their customers/suppliers. While finalising MOUs, the following action points are taken care of:

- **Each department (customer) identifies its supplier departments.**
- **Each customer department will indicate the key parameters to all its suppliers, which it expects from them to fulfil to improve efficiency and cost reduction.**
- **While entering the MOUs, all the MOUs points are to be graded as per their importance in a 'five point' scale by the customer department.**

- On receipt of requirements from the customer department, the supplier department formulates the action plan to fulfil its customer needs and intimate the same to all the concerned personnel in its department upto Junior Officer level.
- A customer department can enter into MOUs with as many number of supplier departments. This is the sole responsibility of the concerned HODs.
- The customer department can also be a supplier to another department.
- A copy of the MOU thus entered and mutually signed has to be sent to TQM-ISO Cell.

During 2001-02, 11 MOUs were signed and for the year 2002-03, 22 MOUs have already been signed among various departments.

MOU Status (Percentage Satisfaction Level)

The customer department is assigned with the responsibilities to give grades point-wise ranging from one to no limit to its supplier departments and also to assign weight age percentage to each of such agreed quality parameters. In few cases, the customer department is also required to render some services to its supplier departments. Each customer department derives percentage satisfaction level basing on the monthly performance of its supplier departments. The following formula is used to calculate this percentage satisfaction level.

$$I = \frac{i \times 100}{\sum i}$$

Where, I : Percentage

i. : Grading given to a particular MOU point on 5-point scale

$\sum i$: Summation of grades assigned to all the points

The percentage satisfaction level as certified by the customers for the year 2001-02 for the wire rod mill has been presented in Table 3.6 as a case example.

TABLE 3.6: Wire Rod Mill MOU Ratings in 2001-2002

Sl. No.	Depart-ments	MOU Points	Apr-01	May-01	June-01	July-01	Aug-01	Sept-01	Oct-01	Nov-01	Dec-01	Jan-02	Feb-02	Avg.
1	ACVS	6	-	-	90	90	95	95	90	95	95	95	95	93.3
2.	CME	6	-	-	95	95	96	95	96	97	97	97	97	96.1
3.	CMM	3	95	95	95	96	96	95	95	95	95	95	95	96.2
4.	DNW	3	-	-	90	95	95	90	90	95	95	95	95	93.3
5.	EMD	7	90	90	90	90	94	90	94	95	95	95	95	92.6
6.	ETL	5	85	90	90	90	90	90	90	90	85	90	95	88.6
7.	INSTN	3	90	95	96	96	96	96	96	96	96	96	96	96.4
8.	LMMM	8	93	93	95	95	95	95	95	95	95	95	97	94.8
9.	MMD	3	85	85	90	90	90	90	90	90	90	96	96	90.2
10.	PPM	4	95	95	95	96	96	96	96	96	96	96	95	95.6
11.	QATD	9	90	95	96	96	96	96	95	95	96	96	95	95.1
12.	RED	4	90	95	85	90	90	90	95	95	96	96	96	92.6
13.	RS & RS	7	95	95	93	96	95	96	95	95	96	96	96	95.3
14.	SYSTEMS	5	90	90	95	95	95	96	95	95	95	95	100	94.5
15.	STORES	4	95	95	95	98	95	95	96	96	96	96	100	95.9
16.	TRAFFIC	6	95	95	95	95	95	95	95	95	95	95	95	95.0
17.	TELCOM	5	-	-	90	95	95	95	95	95	95	95	95	94.4
18.	T & DC	5	-	-	90	90	90	90	95	95	95	95	95	92.8
19.	WMD	7	90	80	90	90	90	90	95	95	95	95	95	91.4

Source: Data Compiled and collated from the TQM-ISO Cell, RINL/VSP.

Customer-Supplier Meeting

Customer-Supplier meetings are held once in a month to monitor and review the progress made on the MOUs entered. In these meetings, discussions are held regarding:

- Status of MOU fulfilment for the previous month;
- Comparative rating of supplier by customer departments for each month (a sample of comparative rating is given in Table 3.7);
- Cost reduction effectiveness over commitments given; and
- Efforts made on reducing cycle time for the areas mentioned.

The monthly performance report of each customer department is sent to the TQM-ISO Cell through the Chief Management Representative. The TQM-ISO Cell in turn compiles all the reports and represents the same in the monthly management representative meeting. In these meetings, they discuss the progress and shortfalls, if any, of the entered MOUs. If any problem arises with regard to the satisfaction level, the ED (Works) interferes and asks for an explanation from the concerned HOD of the supplier department for the low performance and he is asked to take corrective measures.

Benchmarking

In RINL/VSP, the existing parameter with similar conditions is taken into consideration while benchmarking and it is determined as a benchmark basing on which the improvement is planned. Through benchmarking, the company expects to gain the following benefits:

- Eliminating defects.
- Eliminating failure/work stoppages.
- Increasing productivity.
- Delivering quality products.
- Becoming a global market leader.

TABLE 3.7: Comparative MoU Ratings Given to Supplier Departments by Various Customer Departments for the Month of April 2002

Sl. No.	Service	Customer Departments							
		CCDD	BF	SMS	LMMM	MMSM	WRM	SP	TPP
1.	Qatd	95	98	94	98	97	97	93	95
2.	Instn.	93	97	95	98	95	97	92	95
3.	FMD	93	98	96	N.R.	N.R.	N.R.	94	N.R.
4.	Telecom	97	97	97	90	95	95	93	95
5.	WMD	92	96	96	95	95	95	93	95
6.	ETL	100	96	94	95	94	95	93	N.R.
7.	ACVS	95	94	96	94	94	95	94	N.R.
8.	DNW	93	90	94	95	95	90	92	95
9.	CMM	95	96	97	94	97	97	95	N.R
10.	CME	94	95	94	95	96	97	93	N.R.
11.	Traffic	N.R.	98	97	95	95	95	N.R.	N.R.
12.	EMD	92	96	97	97	95	95	92	95
13.	RMHP	95	96	96	N.A.	N.A.	N.A.	94	95
14.	PPM	N.R.	98	97	93	95	97	94	N.R.
15.	T&DC	95	95	95	93	95	95	94	100

Note: N.R.= Not required
N.A.= Not applicable

Source: Data compiled and collated from the TQM-ISO Cell, RINL/VSP.

RINL/VSP embarks on both external and internal benchmarking. It benchmarks with British Steel Co. to reduce the rejection rate, South Korean Steel Plant, POSCO for afforestation, i.e., planting of trees to cut down pollution, and with SAIL and TATA Steel for improving manpower productivity.

The company also undertakes internal benchmarking in its various departments. Internal benchmarking is done mostly in Works area and it is the responsibility of senior officers of the plant. They prepare the list of benchmarking projects in different work units and ED (Works) approves the benchmarking projects, which ultimately works as QIPs. Various benchmarking projects for the year 2002-03 submitted to the ED (Works) for approval are enlisted in Table 3.8.

TABLE 3.8: List of benchmarking projects for the year 2002-03

Sl. No.	Depart- ment	No. of Projects	Project Description
1.	C & CCD	1	To increase yield of Crude Benzol to 0.75% by 2003-04
2.	TPP	3	1. Reduction in Auxiliary Power consumption from present 29.3 KWH/t of steams 27.9 KWH/t by 2002-03. 2. SPM level of TPP Stacks from the present level of 145-150 mg /cm to 100 mg/cm by 2003-04. 3. To achieve 96.5% (for no capital overhaul) and 95% (one machine overhaul) operational availability of Main Turbo-generators.
3.	SP	3	1. To reduce the specific coke consumption for sinter to 62 kg by September 2002. 2. To reduce specific heat consumption for sinter to 47 Mcal/t.Gr. sinter by 2001-02. 3. To increase LD Slag Consumption to 22 kd/T.ch. sinter by 2002-03.
4.	BF	6	1. To reduce BF fuel rate to 500 kg/THM. 2. To achieve taping duration of 20 hours. 3. To achieve standard deviation of S_i in HM to less than 0.1. 4. To achieve Productivity (w.r.t.W.V.) of 2 OT/ m^3/day. 5. To conduct scheduled Mechanical Maintenance on quarterly basis. 6. To conduct scheduled Electrical Maintenance on quarterly basis.
5.	SMS	2	1. Reduction in Refractory consumption to 9.0 kg/tis by 2004-05. 2. Improvement in Average heats/sequence in CCD to 20 by 2003-04.
6.	LMMM	1	Improvement of Production rate of 16 mm Rebars in Bar Mill to 220 t/day by 2003-04.
7.	WRM	1	Improvement of Production of Wire Ro Mill to 10,00,000 t/ann by 2004-2005.
8.	MMSM	1	Improvement of rolling hours of capital MMSM to 18 hours-day/2003-04.

TABLE 3.8 (Contd.)

Sl. No.	Department	No. of Projects	Project Description
9.	PEM	1	To reduce the vibration levels of all blower and exhauster of SP from the present level of 6 mm/sec to 4 mm/sec.
10.	CMM	1	To reduce the Consumption of conveyor belt per Tls from present level of Rs. 23.11/Tls to Rs. 14.00/Tls by 31.03.2002.
11.	FMD+ Traffic	1	To reduce the diesel of oil consumption in FMD/Traffic deptt from the present level of 0.341/0.40 lt/tls to 0.324/0.39 lts/tls by September '02.
12.	ES&F	2	1. To improve the life of coke crusher side assemblies and reduce the present annual consumption of 45 nos. to 40 nos. by August 2002. 2. To improve the life of Bullhead hammers from the present level of 40 hrs. to 75 hrs. by May 2002.
13.	Hyd & LC	1	To reduce the lubrication consumption per ton of Liquid steel from present level of 0.58 kg Tls to 0.53 kg/Tls by March 2003.
14.	Total	24	

Note: '00' indicates improvement in Rolling hours of MMSM to 18 hrs/day by 2003-04.

Source: Data compiled and collated from TQM-ISO Cell, RINL/VSP.

ISO Certification

RINL/VSP has started manufacturing products of international standard within a very short span of its commissioning. Capitalizing on this and also to maintain itself as a leading international steel player, it has gone for ISO-9001:2000 version certifications in a phased manner. Additionally, the company has also been certified with ISO-14001:1996 (Environmental) and ISO-18001: 1999 (Occupational Health and Safety). Table 3.9 provides the details of ISO certifications to different departments of the company. The Bureau Veritus Quality International (BVQI), USK, has issued all these certification to RINL/VSP.

TABLE 3.9: ISO Certification Details of RINL/VSP

	Certification	Date
A.	ISO-9002 Certification	
	• For WRM in Phase I	7-10-1994
	• For LMM, MMSM, SMS in Phase II	21-12-1995
	• For all 38 departments	30-09-1999
	• For the entire Plant	09-05-2000
B.	ISO-9002 Certification Upgraded to ISO-9001:2000 version	04-01-2001
C.	ISO-14001:1996 Certification	18-05-2002
D.	ISO-18001:1999 Certification	29-01-2002 (Issued on 14-02-02)

Source: Data compiled and collated from the TQM-ISO Cell, RINL/VSP.

Steps taken to Obtain ISO Certification

Following steps were taken by RINL/VSP to obtain ISO-9001:2000 certification:

- Arranging talks with key persons from ISO-9002 certified organisations and deciding on the phases for obtaining certification for different units and ultimately the entire plant.
- Appointing Management Representative and Chief Executive for the QMS.
- Formation of Steering Committee.
- Preparing a battery of 80 qualified and experienced Internal Quality Auditors after imparting training by BVQI.
- Training for writing work procedures and work instructions to the identified persons (both executives and non-executives) in each department.
- Training on ISO-9002: awareness to all employees.
- Systematic monitoring by internal auditors and organising regular review meetings by the CMD.

- Monthly review programmes conducted by Management Representative and Chief Executive nominated by the management.
- Acquiring relevant literature books, films relating to ISO procedures.
- Defining clearly the objectives and policies of individual department.
- Following different SQC techniques.
- Developing a film on ISO-9000 series in Telugu.

Internal Quality Audit

Internal quality audit is carried out to verify and determine the effective implementation and maintenance of the QMS in various departments and also to identify potential opportunities for improvement. The responsibility for quality audit lies with the Chief Management Representatives and Internal Quality Auditors.

Internal quality audit are based on the status and importance of the activities and areas to be audited as well as the results of the previous audits. Internal quality auditors audit each department at least four times a year. However, the frequency of audit for any particular area in a department may be increased at the discretion of the Chief Management Representative on the basis of the status and importance of the activity being carried out in that area. The audit result is recorded in the internal quality system audit reports. These reports are distributed to the Auditee/the HOD of the area audited and the Chief Management Representative. The Auditee, in consultation with the HOD, takes necessary corrective actions on the deficiencies pointed out during the audit. Follow-up audit is also carried out to verify and record the implementation and effectiveness of the corrective action taken. Records of the internal quality audits are maintained both with the CMR and with the respective HOD. The results of the internal quality audits form an integral part of the agenda for the management review meeting.

Benefits

Benefits accrued to the company after ISO-9001:2000 certification are as follows:

- Minimized defects.
- Systematic way of working.
- Improvement in production and profitability.
- Promotion in systematic record keeping.

Employee Involvement Schemes

Employee Involvement (EI) refers to the degree that employees share information, knowledge, rewards, and power throughout the organisation. The level of participation ranges from an employee providing information without knowing the problem to a work team having control over all the phases of the decision process.

RINL/VSP has adopted a formal procedure to encourage EI in the quality improvement process. It has introduced a number of EI schemes, which are initiated even before the TQM practice was launched in the company. Various EI schemes which are in operation in RINL/VSP at present are:

(a) Quality Circles; and

(b) Suggestion Schemes.

All these EI schemes are monitored and coordinated by the Management Services Department. At the beginning stage, initiatives taken for employees' involvement were made mandatory and gradually it was followed by the willing commitment of employees. Now, all the employees of the company participate very enthusiastically in the administration of the EI schemes.

(a) *Quality Circles in RINL/VSP*

QC Model at Vizag Steel: In RINL/VSP, Quality Circle (QC) activity was started in April 1990 along with the commissioning of the major units of the plant. The QC implementation model in the company is shown in Figure 3.7.

The Structure of a Typical Quality Circle in RINL/VSP

Success of any organisation largely depends on its structure and functional support. A Quality Circle is an integrated system made up of several parts:

(a) Circle Leaders and Deputy Leaders
(b) Circle Members
(c) Facilitators
(d) Coordinators
(e) Steering Committee

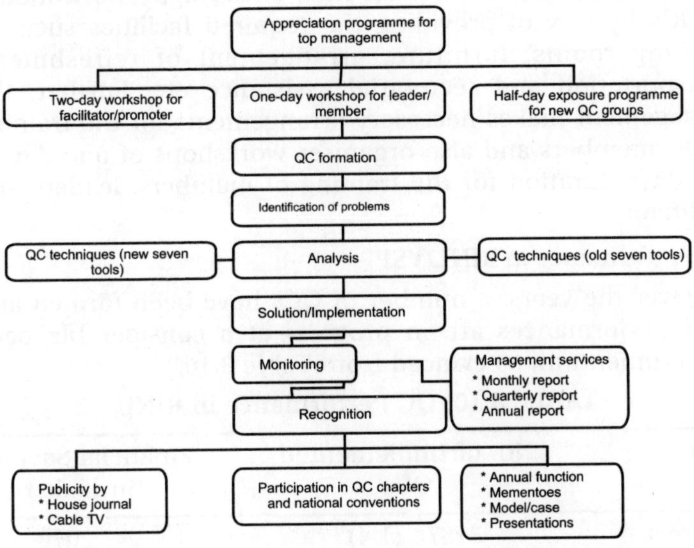

Figure 3.7. QC Implementation Model at Vizag Steel

Operation of a Quality Circle

QC operations in RINL/VSP are carried out in various steps, namely,

Steps

1. Identification of problems
2. Analysis of problems
3. Solution of problems by Quality Circle Members
4. Arriving at best solutions.
5. Presentation of the solution before the management
6. Review and approval by the management

7. Implementation
8. Monitoring the progress
9. Recognition.

While analyzing different problems, QCs use different tools and techniques like brainstorming, data collection, pareto analysis, fish-bone diagram, cause-effect diagram, line-graphs, frequency distributions, scatter diagram, and histograms.[2]

In RINL/VSP, the management encourages the workings of QCs by way of providing the required facilities such as, meeting rooms, furniture, arrangement of refreshment, transportation and secretarial assistance etc. Further, the management makes necessary arrangements for the training of QC members and also organises workshops of one-day or two-days duration for the training of members, leaders and facilitators.

QC Performance in RINL/VSP

Over the years, a number of QCs have been formed and their performances are in progress at a considerable pace and momentum, as evinced from Table 3.10.

TABLE 3.10: QC Performance in RINL

Year	No. of Implemented QCs	Financial Savings (in lakhs)
1997-98	3187 (1.4)	2018
1998-99	3250 (1.9)	1200
1999-00	3350 (3.07)	900
2000-01	3400 (1.49)	850
2001-02	3450 (1.47)	900

Note: Figures in parenthesis denote percentage growth of QCs in relation to the previous year.

Source: Data collected from RINL/VSP.

Table 3.10 indicates that there is a 8.25% growth of QCs over the year 1997-98 to 2001-2002, which has resulted in significant financial savings of Rs. 58.68 crores of the company.

2. The description of techniques is given in Chapter 1 supra.

Rewards/Awards to QCs in RINL/VSP

Since the QCs relate to improving work place situation, all employees participate freely in their operations. Every year, best operating QCs are rewarded in the annual recognition functions. Rewards to the successful QCs include the following:

(a) **Mementos:** Mementos are presented to all the members of the implemented QC projects by management every year.

(b) **QC Dinner:** A dinner is arranged once in a year for all QC members.

(c) **Annual Recognition Function:** QC projects case studies are displayed in the annual recognition function, where the CMD, Directors and senior officer remain present.

(d) **Presentation of Director's Shield:** The QC group that exhibits best performance receives the running shield from the Director (Personnel) in the annual recognition function.

Benefits of QCs to RINL/VSP

The company has derived the following benefits from the implementation of QC Projects. To enumerate some of them:

- Improved production and productivity.
- Improved quality of products.
- Reduction in wastage.
- Inspiration for harmonious employee relations.
- Development of coherent problem-solving approach.
- Contribution to evolve a productive work culture.

Suggestion Reward Scheme—*'Srujan Vikas 1996'* of RINL/VSP

In order to increase efficiency, productivity and bring about all-round progress, a Suggestion Scheme named Suggestion Reward Scheme—***'Srujan Vikas 1996'*** has been introduced in the company with effect from 1 April, 1996. The objectives of the scheme are as follows:

- To encourage creative thinking.
- To recognise positive contribution.

- To provide a forum for collective initiative and mutual cooperation.

Eligibility: All employees in the grade of E-6 and below (including trainees who are in the regular employment, their family members, spouse and unmarried children), customers, and suppliers are eligible to be covered under the scheme.

Suggestion Receipt/Collection: The following provisions are made in the company in regard to receipt/collection of suggestions from employees:

- Employees may drop their suggestions in the prescribed proforma in form of necessary documents, drawings etc. in suggestion boxes placed at different places like Area Shop offices, shop floors, market complexes etc. The respective Zonal Personnel Executives collect these suggestions weekly.
- Employees may also give their suggestions in the prescribed proforma directly to the Zonal Personnel Executives or through the department coordinator of suggestion scheme.
- After recording the details of the suggestion, the Zonal Personnel Executive shall send acknowledge slip to the suggestor indicating his suggestion number.

Evaluation of Suggestions: It is done in the following ways:

I. *Prima facie* Evaluation

- The suggestion is evaluated for *prima facie* in the preliminary screening by the respective HOD/sub-committee consisting of Sectional-in-Charge (not below the rank of E-4).
- Once the suggestion is accepted for prima-facie, a gift worth of Rs. 25 will be given to the suggestor and the suggestion goes to Zonal Suggestion Evaluation Committee (ZSEC) for further evaluation.
- If the suggestion is rejected, a communication will be sent to the suggestor indicating the reason for rejection.

II. ZSEC Evaluation

- 28 ZSECS are constituted in the company, which are headed by the respective HODs. The respective Zonal personnel Executives are member conveners and executives of Finance and MS department as members of the committee.
- The ZSEC scrutinizes the suggestion thoroughly for feasibility of its implementation and decides the rewards depending upon the usefulness and the benefits to the organisation arising out of implementation of the suggestion.
- For any suggestion, if ZSEC feels that it is worth to be awarded more, it recommends the same to the Apex Level Suggestion Evaluation Committee (ALSEC).
- If the suggestion is rejected, a communication will be sent to the suggestor mentioning the reasons for rejection.

III. ALSEC Evaluation

- There are 6 ALSECs headed by the respective General Managers.
- The ALSEC examines the suggestions referred to it by the ZSEC, which deserves higher rewards. The suggestors may be called wherever necessary to understand his views on his suggestions.
- In case the suggestion merits still higher rewards, the ALSEC will submit its recommendations for consideration and approval of CMD. The convener will intimate the decision of ALSEC to the suggestor.

The details of the suggestion evaluation schedule of the company are given in Table 3.11.

Implementation of Suggestions

Suggestions accepted for implementation are forwarded to the concerned HOD for implementation. The person/group of persons who are assigned the responsibility of implementing a suggestion are the 'implementer' under the scheme. The HODs constitute a 'Task Force' in their respective departments to monitor the implementation of the accepted suggestions.

TABLE 3.11: Suggestion Evaluation Schedule of RINL/VSP

Phases	Week	Day
Collection/Receipt of suggestion	Every Thursday	
• Date of entry and send to a *prima facie* evaluation	Every Saturday	2nd day
• PF Evaluation	Every Monday	4th day
• Cash/gift/rejection intimation	Every Thursday	7th day
• ZSEC evaluation	Every Monday	11th day
• Cheque issue/rejection	Every Thursday	14th day
• ALSEC evaluation/sending to CMD	Every Monday	32nd day
• Cheque issue	Every Thursday	35th day
• Evaluation by CMD	Every Monday	39th day
• Cheque issue	Every Thursday	42nd day

Source: Data collected from RINL/VSP.

Rewards and Awards for Suggestions

Those suggestions, which are evaluated as the best by the ALSEC are both rewarded and awarded by the company. Award/reward is given to both individual employees and departments. The details of reward/award scheme is presented in Table 3.12.

Review of Implemented Suggestions

The Monitoring Cell of Management Services department monitors and reviews the functioning of the scheme and organises different programmes to propagate the scheme.

Srujan Vikas Performance in RINL/VSP

The performance of *Srujan Vikas* Suggestion Schemes in terms of number of suggestions received, accepted, implemented,

TABLE 3.12 (a): Rewards for Suggestion Schemes in RINL/VSP

Individual Reward	Amount of Reward	Empowered Authority
• *Prima facie* acceptable suggestion	Gift article worth Rs. 25	Member convener of ZSES in consultation with Head of ZSEC.
• Volunteers who have collected 25 suggestions from the employees	-do-	do-
• For every 5 or 10 *prima facie* accepted suggestions	Gift article worth Rs. 100 or Rs. 200	-do-
• Suggestion resulting in one time saving	10% of actual saving subject to a maximum of Rs. 18,000 and a minimum of Rs. 200	Upto Rs. 2,500 by ZSEC. Above Rs. 2,500 and upto Rs. 5,000 by ALSEC. Above Rs. 5,000 by CMD.
• Suggestion resulting in savings of recurring nature	20% of actual saving for the next 5 years subject to a maximum of Rs. 18,000 and a minimum of Rs. 200	-do-

Source: Data collected from RINL/VSP.

TABLE 3.12 (b): Awards given for Suggestions by RINL/VSP

Award	To whom	When
• Gold medal	Best Suggestor of the year	Every year
• Silver medal	Second best Suggestor of the year	-do-
• Three rolling trophies (Basing on generating highest no. of rewards)	• To the main production units • To the services departments • To the non-works departments	
• Momentoes	• To the best ZSEC	-do-
	• To three best suggestors who have given highest number of prima-facie accepted suggestion	-do-
• Special Industrial tour, Specialized Training etc. (In addition to cash rewards)	For rewardees in deserving cases	-do-

Source: Data collected from RINL/VSP.

and rewarded is outlined in Table 3.13. The table indicates that there has been a constant increase in the number of suggestions received, implemented and also savings of the company due to the implementation of the scheme. On an average, every year approximately 23,962 suggestions are received, of which 18,528 (77.38%) were rejected and 5434 (22.68%) were accepted by the management. Of the accepted suggestions, only 2654 (48.84%) suggestions were implemented in the company. Every year, approximately, Rs. 13.35 lakhs are rewarded to the suggestors. Implementation of the suggestions has cumulatively saved Rs. 6,783 lakh of the company.

TABLE 3.13: *Surjan Vikas* Performance in RINL/VSP during 1997-98 to 2001-02

Suggestions	Year					Average
	1997-1998	1998-1999	1999-2000	2000-2001	2001-2002	
1. Received	19,480	22,110	23,263	25,005	29,953	23,962
2. Rejected	13,869 (71.19)	18,255 (82.56)	17,254 (74.17)	21,520 (86.07)	21,740 (72.59)	18,528 (77.32)
3. Accepted	5,611 (28.18)	3,855 (17.43)	6,009 (25.83)	3,485 (13.93)	8,213 (27.41)	5,434 (22.68)
4. Implemented	2,711 (48.31)	1,806 (46.84)	1,465 (24.38)	3,291 (94.43)	4,001 (48.71)	2,654 (48.84)
5. Rewarded	4,927	1,925	1,677	3,291	4,001	3,164
6. Rewarded amount (Rs. in lakhs)	16.75	14.24	8.38	13.48	13.93	13.35
7. Estimated Savings (Rs. in lakhs)	1,900	1,905	792	982	1,204	1,356

Notes: 1. Figures in parenthesis indicate percentage of suggestions accepted to the receipts during the year.
2. Figures in parenthesis indicate percentage of suggestions implemented to the acceptance of suggestions during the year.

Source: Data compiled and collated from RINL/VSP.

Housekeeping

The importance of housekeeping in the perspective of achieving total quality cannot be underrated. Indian corporate sector has started recognising its significance through method-engineering and other techniques. Japanese companies follow simple tools of 5s to improve quality and productivity on a continual basis.[3]

Housekeeping implies an orderly arrangement of operations, tools, equipment, storage facility and supplies. It should not be mistaken as floor cleanliness or broomstick operations. Bad housekeeping affects the productive efforts at every stage of the industrial activities. It affects the man, his tools, his job, his fellow workers and his health. Many of the accidents are caused due to poor housekeeping. The following simple facts establish the worth of good housekeeping.

In RINL/VSP, good housekeeping is always a matter of concern, because of the benefits that it accrues. These benefits are as follows:

- (i) Control of production becomes easier because materials and parts do not get lost or mixed.
- (ii) Little or no production time is lost through the need to search for tools.
- (iii) Easy access to machines during maintenance.
- (iv) If tools are well placed and easy to find, the job runs much more smoothly and produces better results.
- (v) Protection of health.
- (vi) Promotion of safety and low accident rates.
- (vii) Elimination of fire hazards.
- (viii) Protection of equipments.
- (ix) Improvement of productivity.
- (x) Better flow of work.

Ultimately, good housekeeping would lead to happier employees with high morale, greater involvement, and low employee turnover. In RINL/VSP a check-sheet is used for

3. The 5s' approach is a people as well as a practice-oriented approach for good housekeeping. The 5s are: SEIRI—To sort out unnecessary items in the work place and discard them; SEITON—To arrange necessary items in good order, so that they can be easily picked for use; SEISO—To clean one's work place thoroughly; SEIKETSU—To maintain high standard of housekeeping at all the times; SHITSUKE—To train people to follow good housekeeping to become disciplined automatically.

good housekeeping, the details of which is given in Table 3.14. This check-sheet is prepared very carefully and a copy of it has been distributed among all employees with an instruction to strictly adhere to the check-points.

EFFECT OF TQM INITIATIVES IN RINL/VSP

The company took the TQM initiatives after a series of brainstorming sessions held by the management. As a result of its implementation, the performance of the company has been improved in several dimensions. Successful Japanese companies use 13 Quality Performance Indicators (QPIs) to track their progress (Fenwick, 1991). These indicators are also used in this study to measure the quality progress in RINL/VSP. Table 3.15 provides the details of the same.

Besides, a comparative analysis of the performance of the company is also made in-between the Pre-TQM (1994-95 to 1996-97) and Post-TQM (1997-98 to 2001-02) period. Table 3.16 provides the detailed comparative picture from which it is revealed that on an average, it has increased the sales per year from Rs. 3263.66 crores to Rs. 7867.6 crores, reduced the manufacturing expenses from Rs. 3947, 06.6 crores to Rs. 3961, 58.86 crores, reduced the net loss incurred by the company from Rs. 6975, 25.90 crores to Rs. 400, 94.58 crores, reduced the percentage of the defective blooms from 5.76 to 1.2, reduced the accident rates (both fatal and non-fatal) from 113 to 107, declined the customer complaint rates from 0.27 to 0.13 (of total sales), and increased the productivity rates (tonnes per man year) from 176 to 204 from the Pre-TQM period to Post-TQM period.

Thus, it may be concluded that TQM has improved the overall performance of the company.

FUTURE CONCERNS FOR TQM IN RINL/VSP

RINL/VSP has proposed to undertake the following activities for further enrichment of its quality initiatives:

1. Re-introducing value-engineering; and
2. Introduction of six-sigma strategy.[4]

---

4. 'Six-Sigma quality' is a term used generally to indicate that a process is well controlled, i.e., process limits ± 3 sigma from the centerline in a control chart and requirements/tolerance limits 6 from the centerline.

TABLE 3.14: Housekeeping Check-Sheet in RINL/VSP

Sl. No.	Category	Check Points
1	Putting away unnecessary items	No unnecessary items lying around.
2	Storage of cleaning equipments	To be handy, yet out of the way.
3.	Floor cleaning	No garbage, dirt or oil on the floor. No danger of slipping. No trash on the floor like cigarette butts, scraps of paper, used hand gloves, cotton waste etc.
4.	Display board	No, outdated, torn or soiled announcements displayed. Papers straight and neat. No torn corners or tape marks left over from old displays.
5.	Emergency access	Nothing obstructing access to fire extinguishers and houses. Nothing in front of emergency exists and corridors. Location and use of switches and breakers are pasted. Zebra marks are painted on safety risk areas.
6.	Items on floor	Work-in-process, tools, previously used items, papers and documents etc. Large items are carefully moved.
7.	Walkway maintenance	Walk ways can be found with a glance and are aligned at right angles. The lines marking the walkways are not chipped off and not soiled. Nothing is placed on the walkways and lines. Layout of walkways should be appropriate.
8.	Storage and stacking methods.	Storage is well organised in straight-lines and right angles. Stack contents are clearly marked. Retrieval is simple and items can be quickly transformed to the next process.
9.	Cleaning of machines, structures and fixtures	The factory equipment is pained. There are no places in the factory less than 2 m up that are not painted. Machinery, platform, equipment etc. are not soiled. Glass in the window is regularly polished. Nothing leans against the walls, pillars or

(Contd.)

The term was initiated by Motorola management. Adoption of a six-sigma quality objective is intended to convey continuous process improvement and the achievement of very high quality in internal processes as well as in their products and services.

TABLE 3.14 (Contd.)

Sl. No.	Category	Check Points
		equipment. Nothing is placed on top of machines or cabinets.
10.	Surrounding area cleanliness	Surrounding area is clear of any garbage.
11.	Organizing inventory and stored documents	Inventory and documents are stores so that they are easy to use and to retrieve. Each group of stored inventory or documents has identification, storage period, and name of the responsible persons is indicated on it.
12.	Arrangement of tools	Commonly used jigs and tools are stored and displayed rationally. Tools and inputs are located convenient to machines, equipment and workbenches so that work can be done by a single person.
13.	Organizing of shelves and desks	All shelves and desks are divided and labeled so that it is clear where things are and where things should be returned. There are no unused files or documents on top of the desks. Drawers in desk are systematically organised.

Source: Data collected from RINL/VSP.

TABLE 3.15: Performance Indicators for the TQM Programme in RINL/SP

Sl. No.	Performance Indicators
1.	Number of TQM projects completed: 292
2.	Management attendance at Quality Council Meetings: #
3.	Number of TQM projects linked strategic goals: All the OIPs
4.	Number of quality related standard operating procedures: 3@
5.	Percentage of employees in TQM Team: 12%
6.	Number of quality goals mutually established by managers/ employees: All
7.	Number of formal quality service agreements established with customer: Nil
8.	Percentage of TQM projects initiated at suggestion of customers: Nil
9.	Number of internal customer supplier agreements: 33

TABLE 3.15 (Contd.)

Sl. No.	Performance Indicators
10.	Percentage of quality solutions applying to multiple departments/ functions: more than 50%
11.	Hours of TQM training per employee: 20 hours per year.
12.	Number of TQM teams with members from more than one department: All the QIPs
13.	Number of customer complaints: 0.13 to total sales (during 1997-98 to 2001-02)

Note: "#"-Quality councils had been dissolved with the commencement of QIPs in the company.

"@"-ISO-9001:2000 version, ISO-14001:1996 version and ISO-18001:1999 version.

Source: Data compiled and collated from concerned departments of RINL/VSP.

SUMMARY

With a view to bring continuous improvement in the quality of work process and product, the company has implemented a number of TQM tools such as, QIPs, MOUs, ISO certification, benchmarking, employee involvement schemes, and house keeping.The company embarks on both external and internal benchmarking for improving its production, commercial as well as financial performance. The Bureau Veritus Quality International, U.K. has issued ISO 9001: 2000, ISO 14001: 1996, and ISO 18001: 1999 certificates for manufacturing products in conformity with the international standard, environmental protection as well as for occupational health and safety respectively.

The implementation of all the TQM tools have enabled the company to improve its performance in several dimensions such as, increase in sales, reduction in customer complaints, reduction in net loss incurred by the company, increase in labor productivity, and decrease in the customers' complaint rate etc.

TABLE 3.16: Effect of TQM Initiatives in RINL/VSP

Parameters	Before TQM			Average	After TQM					Average
	1994-95	1995-96	1996-97		1997-98	1998-99	1999-2000	2000-2001	2001-2002	
Manufacturing	2982	3400	5457	3947	1860	3430	3792	4005	4218	3461
Expenses (in crores)	81.69	77.63	60.52	06.6	21.32	34.29	91.57	52.81	94.44	58.86
Sales (in crores)	2209	3039	4543	3263.66	1664	3071	27612	2973	4018	7867.6
Profit/Loss	10,424	10,296	204	6975	452	206	776	561	751.502	400
(in crores)	84.5	66.78	26.53	25.90	19.99	31.61	91.88	77.93		94.58
Rejection Rate (%)	Nil	Nil	Nil	Nil	Nil	Nil	Nil	Nil	Nil	Nil
% of Defective Blooms	6.[illegible]3	6.02	5.12	5.76	2.13	1.90	1.40	0.25	0.32	1.2
Customer satis-	352	340	323	338	303	227	249	349	122	250
faction (no. of	(0.[illegible]9)	(0.28)	(0.26)	(0.27)	(0.20)	(0.17)	(0.15)	(0.14)	(0.0)	(0.13)
complaints)										
Safety (Fatal/	08	04	02	4.66	02	04	04	03	NA	2.6
Injured Cases)	104	101	59	88	51	125	150	120	78	104
Tonnes per man-year	156	183	191	176	197	201	205*	208*	213*	204

Note: Figures in brackets indicates total sales vs. the complaints received in that year.

* indicates approximate figures.

Source: Compiled from data collected from RINL/VSP.

APPENDIX 3.1: Responsibility Matrix of QMS

Title	Key responsibility	Supporting Responsibility
Management Responsibility	CE Chief MR	HODs
Quality management system	CE Chief MR	HODs
Customer related processes	HODs Regional Managers Branch Managers	NIL
Design and development	HOD of respective Production department	HOD of QATD
Control of documents	Chief MR Document controlling authorities	Nil
Purchasing	Head of MMD Head of Workmen's Compensation	Heads of all the concerned departments.
Customer Property	Not applicable	Not applicable
Product identification and traceability	HODs of Production departments HOD of RMD HOD of RMHP HOD of MMD HOD of Marketing HOD of Branch Managers	Nil
Process control	Heads of all the concerned departments	Heads of QA & TD, Head of Institution.
Inspection & testing	Head of Heads of QA & TD, TPP, RMD, ERS, CED, EMD, RED, RMHP, ES&F, WMD, Hyd & Lub, receipt inspection, Head of MMD	Head of MMD
Control of monitoring and measuring devices	Head of Institution Head of QA & TD Head of all concerned departments	Branch Managers
Inspection and test status	Heads of the Production departments Head of QA & TD Head of receipt inspection	HODs of concerned departments.

(Contd.)

APPENDIX 3.1 (Contd.)

Title	Key responsibility	Supporting Responsibility
Control of nonconforming Product	Heads of production departments Branch Managers	Head of QA & TD
Corrective and preventive action	Chief MR, HODs	Nil
Handling, storage packaging, preservation & delivery	Heads of the production departments, HODs of EMD, SSD, MMD, CME, ERS, Plant design, Branch Managers	Head of QA & TD
Control of quality records	Chief MR, HODs	Nil
Internal quality audits	Chief MR	HODs, Internal Quality Auditors
Training	Head of Training Head of HRD Head of SED Head of OHS&RC Head of CISF	HODs of the other departments
Servicing	Head of MKT Regional Managers Branch Managers	HODs of related Departments
Measurement analysis and improvement	HODs of all concerned departments	Nil
Customer satisfaction	Head of Marketing Regional Managers Branch managers HODs of all other departments	Nil
Factored items	HOD of Marketing Regional managers Branch managers	Nil
Standards and codes	Head of Training Head of QA &TD	Heads of other departments Branch Managers
Statutory and regulatory requirements	Chief Executive Chief MR, HODs	Nil

Note: Wherever two or more persons are mentioned, each of them is responsible in his respective area.

Source: Compiled and collated from the data collected from TQM-ISO Cell, RINL/VSP.

4

The Human Dimension of TQM

INTRODUCTION

People are the building blocks of an organisation. No system/strategy in an organisation would ever succeed, unless people are passionate about it. TQM as a people-driven management system aims at continual increase in customer satisfaction, by involving all employees across the departments, functions and positions. Involvement of employees is an integral part of quality management as quality is the responsibility of all in everything they do. Quality is quite personal. If employees do not 'buy-into' the quality philosophy, learn the quality tools and techniques, develop the spirit to work together in teams in order to improve business processes and work designs, and use new abilities, skills and knowledge (ASK) in their daily work, then nothing will happen.

However, the personal commitment to quality will not develop by default, it must be properly nurtured by the management. As Deming said, quality problems are the fault of the system 85 to 90% of the time, which can be corrected only by the management. Therefore, the bottom-line is that, if the management fails to show the required commitment and involvement, and if managers and workers do not work as both individuals and teams to remove barriers to quality, quality will never be achieved.

TQM is just like a tripod based on customer focus, continuous improvement, and team work. Absence of anyone would destabilize the entire system (Figure 4.1).

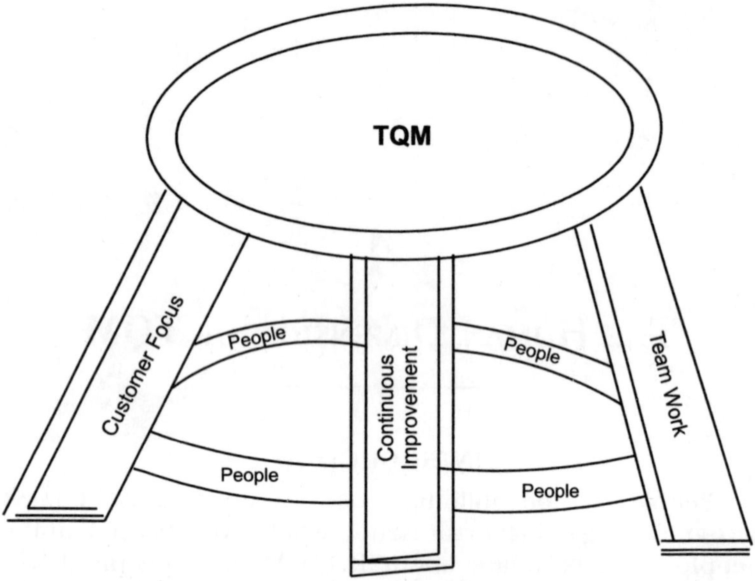

Figure 4.1. TQM as a Tripod

The first and most important principle is customer focus. The goal of satisfying customer is fundamental to TQM and is expressed by the organisation's attempt to design and deliver products/services to fulfil customer needs. The second principle is continuous improvement, which means commitment to constant examination of technical and administrative processes in search of better methods. Teamwork, that is collaboration between managers and non-managers, between functions, and between customers and supplier is the third principle of TQM process (Dean and Bowen, 1994).

Each of these principles, although stated as distinct, is inextricably linked to one another. The ultimate aim is for fulfilment of customer's needs by using the most effective and efficient methods. Customer focus is driven by the desire of an organisation to identify customer needs and acquire feedback on his/her satisfaction with the organisation's current efforts to meet those needs. Continuous improvement is the next logical step that requires organisation to act based on the acquired information. In order to achieve and maintain customer satisfaction, organisations may need to continuously develop better products and services and improve methods of producing and delivering them. Finally, for an organisation to experience continuous improvement everyone involved with producing and delivering a good or service must try to identify opportunities for improvement and works together to implement the necessary changes. This requires the collaboration across levels, functions and other organisational boundaries, making teamwork essential.

Other distinctive features of TQM like leadership, process management, individual and organisations learning, internal and external cooperation, employee empowerment and fulfilment (Anderson *et al.*, 1994) are all related to these principles. Visionary leadership, which refers to the ability of management to provide a long-term vision for the organisation based on changing customer needs rather than on internal control, is a derivative of the first principle that is customer focus. Top management has to develop and champion a vision for the organisation that facilitates the transition to TQM and maintains customer orientation after the transition.

Continuous improvement underlies the shift towards process management and the need to facilitate learning at the individual, group and organisational level. Process management focuses on managing the means rather than the ends. It requires people to understand the organisational processes and seek newer and better ways of their execution. However, employees in a non-TQM environment were not required to examine organisational processes, and often lack the necessary skills to do so. Therefore, process management necessitates the creation of learning environment in the organisations. The learning environment is exemplified by a company's training, or external and internal educational as well as developmental opportunities that enhance the ability of everyone to participate in process management leading to continuous improvement.

Teamwork leads to internal and external cooperation and the need for employee empowerment and fulfilment. It requires members of the team to indulge in non-competitive activities to achieve better collective goals. If properly implemented, this results in cooperation with in an organisation and with other organisations with which it interacts. Finally, in order to make teamwork more successful, employees must be provided with decision-making authority and organisational support to make real changes happen to improve the processes. It is also essential to see that they receive monetary and non-monetary rewards for their efforts, leading to initiative and commitment to the organisation.

The above discussion clearly elucidates that TQM centres around people. People, if suitably oriented and involved act as the most effective instruments in achieving total quality. By the same token, people who are disinterested or do not share the collective values supportive of a transformation to Total Quality can be the biggest impediments in the process. Against this background, the present study was carried out to examine the interface between TQM, KHFs and HRM in RINL/VSP. The discussion made in this chapter has been divided into three parts. The first part discusses the interface between Human Resource Policy and Quality Policy of the organisation. The second part highlights upon the role of HR professionals in successful implementation of TQM in the company. Under this part various issues such as, the role of HRD professionals at various stages of TQM implementation, various human resource challenges associated with TQM implementation, and above all the role the HRD professionals as internal consultants have been covered. Moreover, in the concluding part, an attempt has been made to find out the exact interface between TQM and KHFs and accordingly hypothetical interrelationships among the relevant KHFs (that have been identified from the literature review) are stipulated. The stipulated hypothetical interrelationships are subject to empirical verification in the following chapter.

INTERFACE BETWEEN HR POLICY AND QUALITY POLICY

In RINL/VSP, it is largely believed that people make things happen and they give strength and direction to the organisation. Therefore, the organisation has always considered the human resources as its greatest and most valuable assets. The Human Resource Plan of company aims at developing the wholehearted commitment, creativity, competence and initiative of the personnel in meeting its business challenges.

(a) Human Resource Policy

The Human Resource policy of the organisation revolves around the basic tenet of creating a highly motivated, vibrant and self-driven work force. It lays thrust on the following aspects:

- Continued upgradation of skills.
- Competence building.
- Developing motivational climate.
- Improving internal communication.
- Building productive business culture.
- Discipline as a part of work life.

(b) Quality Policy

RINL/VSP is committed to supply to its customers quality products and services. To accomplish this, the company ensures that it will:

- Manufacture products as per specifications and standards agreed to with the customers.
- Follow clearly documented procedures for achieving expected quality standards of products and services.
- Continuously strive to improve quality of all materials, processes and products.
- Maintain an enabling environment, which encourages active involvement of all employees to pursue continuous improvements in quality.

As it is seen from the above, Quality policy of the company emphasises on adherence to the laid down specifications and standards agreed to by customers and to follow the documented procedures. To achieve this, HR plan lays emphasis on continued upgradation of skills, competence building and internal communication. Quality policy stipulates an enabling environment, which encourages active involvement of all employees to pursue continuous improvements in quality. This can be achieved by the HR Plan, which provides for the development of motivational climate and building productive business culture.

HR plan of the company has also envisaged an action plan to promote activities like, multi-skilling, job flexibility, broad banding of designations, team working, optimization of attendance, accelerated learning curve, overlapping shifts, optimum utilization of manpower, stabilizing good work practices, flattening the organisation structure etc. This action plan has been supplemented by combining HR plan and Employees Development Plan.

ROLE OF HR PROFESSIONALS IN SUCCESSFUL TQM IMPLEMENTATION

TQM is a management philosophy as well as a management programme. TQM was introduced in RINL/VSP in the year 1996-97 and started spreading across the organisations during the ensuing years. It gathered momentum in the company during the first year of its implementation itself. Various TQM initiatives/measures like employees' suggestion scheme, quality circles, value engineering, ISO certification for the company's products and processes are already afoot from quite nascent stage. Efforts are made in the company to integrate all these initiatives in its march towards Total Quality and further initiatives are likely to be taken by the management to make it a more successful movement in the organisation. The HR professionals have played a key role at various stages of TQM implementation. They have squarely shouldered the responsibility starting from envisioning to implementing and to sustaining the momentum in the company. Figure 4.2 provides a blueprint of the role of HR professionals at various stages of TQM implementation.

Phase I: Envisioning

The HR professionals played a crucial role in creating and communicating the TQM vision of the company, which reads as, "RINL shall be a self-supporting and growing company, with continuous improvement in productivity, quality, and customer satisfaction".

Phase II: Preparing

Just as a table must be set before we eat, an organisation must also make itself ready prior to the implementation of TQM. The preparation stage is very crucial as it paves the way for future of TQM activities and sets the tempo. In RINL/VSP, at the outset the top executives tried to make themselves

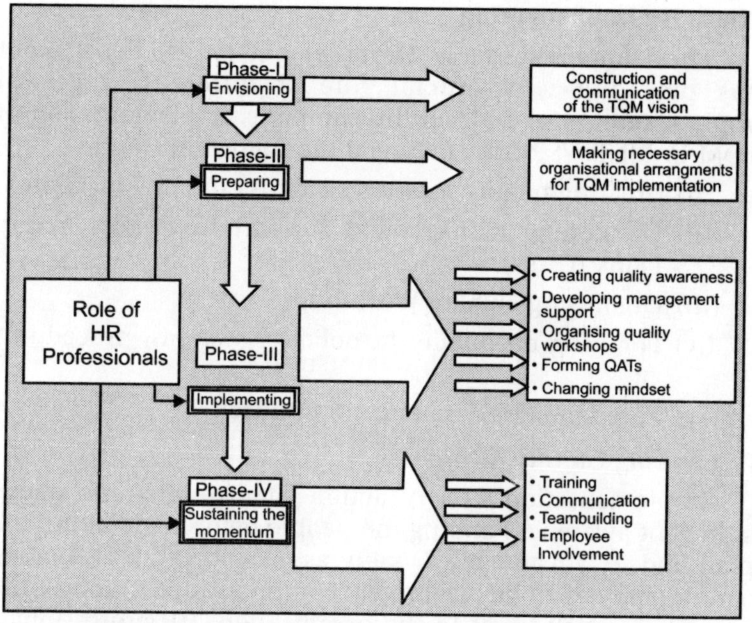

Figure 4.2. Blueprint of Role of HR Professionals in TQM Implementation in RINL/VSP

ready and were motivated to look into the need for and the benefits of TQM. During this stage, the HRD department played a pivotal role in close collaboration with the TQM-ISO Cell. They tried to create the right ambience in the company by assisting the top executives while formulating the draft quality policy, system and procedure.

The major activities undertaken by HRD department at this stage are listed below:

- Assisting the top executives to draft quality friendly policies, plans, systems, and procedures.
- Hiring a consultant.
- Development of quality statement, TQM goals, and objectives.
- Communication to employees, customers, suppliers and others.
- Decision to proceed and obtain the commitment from the top management to provide resources to implement TQM.

Phase III: Implementing

The Human Resource Development (HRD) department has played a very crucial role at different stages of implementation of TQM in the company. Implementation of TQM in RINL/VSP has envisaged the following steps:

(i) Creating quality awareness across the organisation.

(ii) Developing management support to Quality Action Plans (QAPs).

(iii) Organising Quality Workshops.

(iv) Focusing on quality in policies, systems, procedures etc.

(v) Paradigm Shift—change in mindset.

(i) *Creating Quality Awareness*

Implementation of any action plan/programme needs sufficient awareness among the people beforehand about the plan and its advantages. Quality as a concept as well as an action plan has to be extensively communicated amongst the employees at all levels in the organisation. HR professionals in RINL/VSP have taken up the responsibility to create TQM awareness among employees by carrying out different communication exercise through Briefing Groups, Shop-floor Communication Programmes, Work Place Communication, Participative fora etc. in consultation and collaboration with line executives. Besides, they have also prepared a variety of literature on quality in forms of Pamphlets, Posters, Slogans, Wall Boards, Quality Policy Statement etc., which have gone a long way in creating the knowledge repertoire in the organisation. So far, 35 quality awareness programmes have been organised in the company with the active assistance of HR professionals.

(ii) *Developing Management Support*

Successful implementation of TQM also greatly depends on acceptance of TQM as a philosophy of management. Towards this end, HR professionals in RINL/VSP have worked by organizing TQM appreciation workshops by inviting internationally famous consultants viz., ODI, Singapore for providing training to top management as well as key executives in the organisation. They have succeeded in spreading the message that TQM is a Management Programme to the top management and garnering their support which is evident from the fact that Executive Directors, Directors and Chairman-cum-Managing Director of the company invariably attended inauguration and valedictory programmes of Quality Workshops.

(iii) *Organising Quality Workshops*

HRD department of RINL/VSP has organised a series of workshops for TQM facilitators and key executives to appreciate TQM and spread the message of total quality at all levels. The details of the programmes conducted since the inception of TQM in the company are given in Table 4.1.

TABLE 4.1: Quality Workshops Organised by HRD Department of RINL/VSP during 1996-97 to 1999-2000

Year	No. of Programmes conducted	Number of Employees covered	
		Executives	Non-Executives
1996-97	120	850 (7.08)	2000 (16.66)
1997-98	115	750 (6.52)	1750 (15.21)
1998-99	135	1000 (7.41)	2500 (18.5)
1999-2000	140	1200 (8.57)	2700 (19.28)

Note: Figures in the parenthesis denote average number of participants per quality workshops.

Source: Data collected from the HRD Department RINL/VSP.

In all these workshops, pocket books and literature on quality were supplied to the participants. They were also given clear ideas on concepts like QAT, FADE Cycle etc.

(iv) *Formation of Quality Advantage/Action Teams (QATs)*

With a view to piloting the implementation of TQM in its "Nuts & Bolts", a number of QATs have been constituted in RINL/VSP to streamline the systems and procedures. These teams have taken up various projects and developed solutions for implementation, which have created what many of the analysts call as "Waves of TQM". So far, 292 QATs have been formed in the company for various projects.

(v) *Focusing on Quality in Policies, Systems, and Procedures*

The HRD department also assisted in the formulation of new quality friendly policies, systems and procedures as well as updation and rationalization of the existing ones in order to create the right kind of ambience for effective implementation of TQM.

(vi) *Paradigm Shift—Change in Mindset*

All efforts for promotion and implementation of TQM may not yield the desired result unless and until quality becomes the attitudinal propensity of all the employees. Towards this, HR professionals have laid emphasis on what may be called a PARADIGM SHIFT i.e. change in mindset of people. Prior to the implementation of TQM, the attitude of people was to give emphasis on production and sales. After implementation of TQM, emphasis was put on total quality in the processes so as to make the end result qualitative. The slogan "Quality first time and every time" has become the buzzword among all the employees of RINL/VSP. Quality awareness, experiences of successful implementation of TQM in other organisations, formation of QATs and feedback for corrective measures, have all led to an imperceptible, but steady change in the attitudinal dimension of the employees. Today, each employee of RINL/VSP is committed to TQM not as a programme, but as a means for his own survival. TQM has been linked to the survival of the business enterprise and articulation of such a need has made TQM a functional system in the organisation. Thus, the attitudinal transformations coupled with TQM being functional system have speeded up its implementation with success. Thus, HR professionals have played a pivotal role in the company at all stages of implementation of TQM.

Phase IV: Sustaining the Momentum

Implementation of TQM sounds like a 'well-executed' strategy in RINL/VSP, but it was not totally a happy and easy experience on the part of the top management. The discussion made at the beginning of this chapter reveals how the company brought about TQM awareness by putting a cross-section of executives through awareness programmes. These weeklong programmes not only generated urgency for TQM, but also taught employees valuable skills for its effective implementation.

When a company introduces a new programme, employees need to learn how to modify behaviour patterns to benefit from the new programmes. In this context, training is of paramount importance since it helps them learn the required skill and knowledge to make the programme successful as well as to sustain the momentum. Besides training, communication is another strategy required for sustaining the TQM implementation. Through effective communication, the company keeps its employees informed about what is expected of them and what they can expect from the TQM effort. Although time consuming and costly, communication can potentially reduce fear of the employees associated with new role patterns, make them feel more comfortable with breaking previous routines, and develop performance consistent with TQM effort. In RINL/VSP, through proper training and communication all the employees are convinced to accept TQM, and through employee involvement and team-building activities, the implementation process has achieved a momentum.

A. Training

In RINL/VSP, a well-thought out training programme has been designed to provide training to employees (both executive and non-executives) on TQM. The training needs of each employee are identified and assessed regularly and thereafter training is provided to fill up the skill and knowledge gap. The details of the identification and assessment of training needs as well as training methods have been discussed below.

(i) *Systematic Identification and Assessment of Training Needs*

Identification and assessment of training needs of employees are made in the following manner:

(a) Annual Confidential Reports (ACRs) in case of non-executive employees.

(b) Appraisal Reports in case of executive employees.

(c) Periodic survey by Training Department/HRD Department.

(d) Feedback of Reporting Officers and Reviewing Officers.

(e) Recommendations of HODs.

(f) MOU with Training Department.

(a) **Annual Confidential Reports (ACRs) in Case of Non-executives:** In Annual Confidential Reports (ACRs) of non-executive employees, there are provisions for Reporting Officer and Reviewing Officer to recommend the training needs of the employees. Such recommendations are compiled grade-wise, and discipline-wise. Further, they are scrutinized based on the type of training programme recommended. Thus, Personnel Department gets the data on training needs of employees in various grades and departments in their respective areas such as Welding, Managerial skills, leadership etc.

(b) **Appraisal Reports in Case of Executive Employees:** Annual Appraisal System for Executive employees provides for development plans in Part 'E' of the Appraisal System, which include: strengths, weaknesses, and development needs of the executives.

In the Development Plan, the Reporting Officer identifies the strengths and weaknesses of the concerned executive and recommends development needs. Keeping in view the development needs, training programmes are recommended by the Reporting Officer. All training programmes have been codified and code list of development programmes are given along with the appraisal report. The HRD department through computer consolidates training programmes recommended in the Appraisal Reports, and accordingly various training programmes are organised to improve the quality of work of executives.

(c) **Periodic Survey by Training Department/HRD Department:** Training/HRD Department conducts periodic survey in the plant department-wise, grade-wise or position-wise with a view to identify training needs for the concerned employees. In such exercise, they circulate questionnaires amongst the employees for self-assessment of training needs, amongst Reporting Officers and Reviewing Officers for identification of training needs of employees working under them as well as amongst all concerned to assess training requirements to discharge the functions effectively. Such assessments of training needs are then compiled, codified and pursued.

(d) Feedback of Reporting Officers and Reviewing Officers: This system of identification of training needs is used as booster dose of training or follow-up measures. In this exercise, employees after the completion of training get back to their respective jobs. Reporting and Reviewing Officers are then asked to give feedback on improvement in their performance in the aftermath of the training. Depending on the feedback, refresher courses and follow-up measures are taken to help them for effective functioning.

(e) **Recommendations of HODs:** The HODs are responsible for smooth and effective functioning of their respective departments. With a view to ensure optimum efficiency of the employees working in their departments, HODs are very often asked about the training needs of various categories of employees. Recommendations of HODs, if any, are processed and training needs are identified.

(f) **MOUs with Training Department:** This system of identification of training needs has proved to be quite effective. Departments identify their training requirements and enter into MOUs with Training Department with target and time frame fixed for achievement.

(ii) *Organising Training Programmes*

The training programmes are organised regularly by both the Training and Development Centre (T&DC) and Centre for HRD. The details of the programme with regard to TQM and ISO conducted at the Centre for HRD during the last 6 years have been presented in Table 4.2, which is self-explanatory. Similarly, a number of training programmes have also been organised at T&DC for both executives and non-executives relating to TQM & ISO. The details of these programmes organised during the period 1997-98 to May, 2002 have been presented in Table 4.3.

TABLE 4.2: Training Programme Conducted at Centre for HRD during the Period 1996-97 to 2001-02

Programmes/year	1996-1997		1997-1998		1998-1999		1999-2000		2000-2001		2001-2002	
	E	NE	E	NE	E	NE	E	NE	E	NE	E	NE
Workshop on SPC & SQC Technique for ISO-9002	20	1	-	-	-	-	-	-	-	-	-	-
Total Quality Advantage	36	-	2769	-	22	-	-	-	-	-	-	-
Total Quality Advantage for facilitators	17	-	32	-	-	-	-	-	-	-	-	-
ISO-9002 for internal quality auditors	102	-	20	-	-	-	-	-	-	-	-	-
ISO-9002 Documentation	177	-	-	-	-	-	-	-	-	-	-	-
ISO Procedures and Instructions	38	29	-	-	-	-	-	-	-	-	-	-
Quality Action Tea (QAT) facilitator	-	-	40	-	-	-	-	-	-	-	-	-
QAT Leaders	-	-	82	-	204	-	-	-	-	-	-	-
QAT Members	-	-	332	-	-	-	-	-	-	-	-	-
FADE Cycle	-	-	64	-	-	-	-	-	-	-	-	-
ISO-14000 Awareness	-	-	-	-	23	-	-					
ISO For Key Executives	-	-	-	-	-	-	26	-	-	-	-	-
ISO Procedures	-	-	-	-	-	-	27	-	-	-	-	-
Intricacies of audit	-	-	-	-	-	-	47	-	-	-	-	-
ISO systems	-	-	-	-	-	-	67	-	-	-	-	-
Teamwork for SMS etc.	-	-	-	-	-	-	-	-	-	-	-	307
Technology & Teamwork	-	-	-	-	-	-	-	-	-	-	-	247
Teamwork for FMD etc.	-	-	-	-	-	-	-	-	-	-	59	252

TABLE 4.2 (Contd.)

Programmes/year	1996-1997		1997-1998		1998-1999		1999-2000		2000-2001		2001-2002	
	E	NE	E	NE	E	NE	E	NE	E	NE	E	NE
Teamwork & BF & SMS	-	-	-	-	-	-	-	-	-	263	-	-
Technology & Teamwork	-	-	-	-	-	-	-	-	-	292	-	-
Teamwork for Mills	-	-	31	396	27	255	-	-	-	-	-	-
Teamwork for C & CCD	-	-	12	116	19	227	-	-	-	-	-	-
Teamwork for RMHP & SP	-	-	2	50	35	376	-	-	-		-	-

Note: 'E' indicates Executives, 'NE' - Non-executives, '-' indicates nil.

Source: Data compiled and collated from RINL/VSP.

TABLE 4.3: Number of Trainees Attended the Training Programmes Conducted at T&DC on TQM during the Period 1997-98 to May, 2002

Programmes/year	1997-1998	1998-1999	1999-2000	2000-2001	2001-2002	April, '02-May, '02
Concept of Total Quality	-	-	-	270	1,093	189
ISO-9001:1994	770	505	164	-	-	-
ISO-9001:2000	-	-	-	12,534	317	-
ISO-14001	-	-	-	12,158	524	-
ISO-18001	-	-	-	185	14,185	-
Quality Circle	-	-	352	347	449	58

Note: '-' indicates nil.

Source: Complied from the data collated from RINL/VSP.

B. Communication

Communication is considered as an indispensable tool for effective TQM implementation. The quality of organisational communication has found to play a significant role in employees' acceptance of a new system/strategy. Besides, effective interpersonal communication also helps to reduce cost and improve quality. Realising the importance of the quality of organisational communication in successful implementation of TQM, the HR professionals in RINL/VSP have introduced a number of schemes for improving interpersonal communication within the organisation. These schemes *inter alia* include viz., Workplace Communication Scheme wherein the Personnel Executive/Shift in-charge communicate directly with the workers within the workshop, Shop-floor Interaction Sessions, Participative Forum of unions, *Samalochana* Session within the department etc. All these communication exercises have enabled continuous dialogue between individual employee and management and have made the organisation a learning organisation. Figure 4.3 denotes the number of employees covered under various communication exercises conducted by the HRD department.

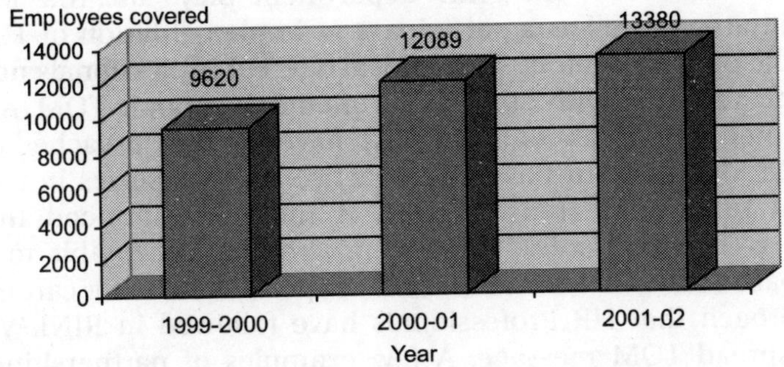

Figure 4.3. Employees covered under various Communication Exercises during the period 1999-2000 to 2001-02

C. Team Building

The Directorate of Personnel has organised many synergetic teams to effectively handle matters relating to TQM. Team building is facilitated in various areas of functioning by tailor-made workshops on team building viz., technology and team work, team working, enhancing management effectiveness etc. which were organised to impart training on 'Team Building' and 'Team Working' as an attitude and skill across the organisation. In the multi-union setting of RINL/VSP, team building is targeted towards managing the plural diversity of unions and facilitating evaluation of commonality of perceptions of unions on vital issues affecting the organisation.

D. Employees' Involvement

Employee participation is promoted at all levels to cultivate commitment and involvement of employees through small group activities like Suggestion Scheme, Quality Circle and other participative fora. Apart from the above, power is delegated in different degree at all levels across the organisation so that the individual responsibility is discharged in commensurate with authority.

INTERFACE BETWEEN HRD DEPARTMENT *VIS-À-VIS* OTHER DEPARTMENTS TO SUPPORT TQM

Partnership of HRD with other departments is a must to support TQM progress. Because, TQM does not confine itself to any functional specification, instead it spreads to the entire business of the company.

In RINL/VSP, the HRD department plays the role of a facilitator as well as a participant in implementation of TQM in the organisation. In such endeavour, HR professionals need to be a partner with other departments to support TQM. As a partner, HR Professionals in RINL have not only preached the TQM Mantras, but have also practised it themselves in their own functional areas. 'Action is more pronounced than words' is what made TQM as a programme acceptable to all departments. Collaboration and cooperation are the cardinal approach that HR Professionals have followed in RINL/VSP to spread TQM message. A few examples of partnership of HRD with the line departments would make it more elucidative. Quality Action/Advantage Teams (QATs) have been constituted with managerial personnel from cross-functional disciplines as well as HRD. TQM facilitators have been chosen not only from HR Department, but also from all other departments to conduct Quality workshops. Similarly, at the outset Quality Policy of the organisation had been discussed amongst all the managers, which was facilitated by the HR professionals and then they were formulated and practised. In all activities of TQM, partnership between HR and other departments is clearly evident.

ROLE OF HR PROFESSIONALS AS INTERNAL CONSULTANTS

HR Professionals have also acted as internal consultants to other departments for better implementation of TQM. The following action points taken by the HR Professionals substantiate their role as internal consultants:

(i) HR Professionals acted as felicitators and trainers in conducting Quality Workshops.

(ii) At the time of entering into MOU by different departments with their customer/supplier departments, HR Professionals act as internal consultants and advise the departments with regard to formulation of draft MOU and points for discussion and resolutions etc.

(iii) HR Professional act as internal consultant in the area of cost reduction and reduction of activity cycle.

(iv) HR Professionals also suggest ways and means to improve work climate index as obtained from "Voice of Employees" survey conducted every year.

HR CHALLENGES ASSOCIATED WITH TQM

Implementation of TQM in RINL/VSP has posed several unique human resource challenges to HRM practitioners. These challenges are as follows:

(i) Motivating Knowledge Workers

(ii) Mobilizing Key Managerial Personnel

(iii) Obtaining Employees' Satisfaction

(iv) Overcoming Communication Barriers

(v) PSU Trappings

(vi) Vastness of the Organisation

(i) Motivating Knowledge Workers

Employees of RINL/VSP are well educated as compared to the employees of the sister steel plants. For instance, in the non-executive category, Charge men are holding Diploma in engineering and Technicians are having Matriculation with ITI. These workers are well informed and their need in terms of Maslow's (1943) hierarchy of need is not confined to physical and security needs. Instead, they have enlarged need for recognition.

Motivating workers with high recognition need in the direction of TQM require special efforts on the part of HR Professionals. The strategy being adopted by the HR Professionals to motivate these employees for implementation of TQM can be broadly discussed under:

(a) Involvement

(b) Empowerment

Briefing Groups, Quality Circles, Value Engineering and Suggestion Schemes can achieve involvement and provide empowerment to these employees. In the areas of Quality Circles, the following initiatives have been taken up during the year 1997-98, wherein preparatory works were made for implementation of TQM:

- Conducted 12 workshops on QC techniques for the members and leaders.
- Organised 120 exposure programmes on QC concepts in different departments.

- Annual Quality Circle Recognition function was held to felicitate the QC members for implementing the projects. A compendium on 3187 QC implemented projects was released during the above function.
- Department-wise QC functions were held during the year to recognize and motivate the employees by distributing the mementos to the eligible QC members.
- Four teams, one each from Utilities, Blast Furnace, Coke and Coal Chemicals Department, and Energy Management Department were sent to QCFI chapter convention at Bokaro in October, 1997.

In the matter of Suggestion Schemes, massive effort was also made by the HRD department to generate more number of suggestions from employees, which is evident from the increasing number of suggestions received over the period 1997-98 to 2001-2002.[1] Figure 4.4 provides support to this fact.

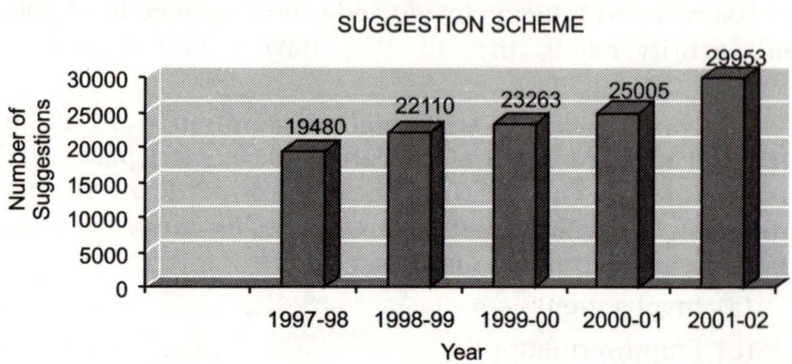

Figure 4.4. Number of suggestions received during 1997-98 to 2001-02

(ii) Mobilising Key Managerial Personnel

Another challenge faced by the HR Professionals was with regard to mobilisation of key managerial personnel. The key managerial personnel were mobilised for speedy TQM implementation by undertaking the following activities:

- Two presentations by EICHER Consultancy Team on implementing TQM in RINL/VSP were organised for senior managers.

1. For details refer Table 3.13 of Chapter 3.

- Two presentations for senior managers and 10 days assessment study were organised with the help of M/s. Xerox Quality Solutions regarding implementing TQM in the company.
- M/s. Qualteam Consultants conducted assessment study in connection with implementing TQM in the company.
- The competent authority approved TQM implementation through M/s. Qualteam Consultants.
- M/s. Qualteam covering conducted two Workshops on "The Quality Advantage" for 36 executives senior executives.

(iii) Obtaining Employees' Satisfaction

Satisfaction of employees is most important to achieve total quality. A good quality of work life is a major component of obtaining employees' satisfaction. In RINL/VSP, employees' satisfaction is pushed up through various measures such as, reward and recognition scheme, open door policy, fair and non-discriminatory grievance handling scheme, suggestion schemes, incentive schemes to enhance productivity, group incentives, maintenance of good working and environmental condition etc. Besides, attempts are being made to build up confidence in every employee to perform the work efficiently and achieve excellent results. Every employee must have a hope that the job he/she is doing is worth the effort and leads to achieve total quality. In this context, the HRD department has to create an environment in the organisation, where every one derives satisfaction, develops confidence and hope.

In order to find out the level of employees' satisfaction with their work life, an organisation-wide survey was conducted by the HRD department in November 2002. From this survey, the overall satisfaction index in each division in the company was estimated separately for both executives and the non-executives, which is presented in Figure 4.5. It was presumed that if the index were less than 49, it would show pronounced dissatisfaction; between 50-69, it would show no pronounced satisfaction or dissatisfaction. However, the figure indicates that the employees' satisfaction indexes in all the cases are more than 70, which reveals the pronounced satisfaction of employees with their work life.

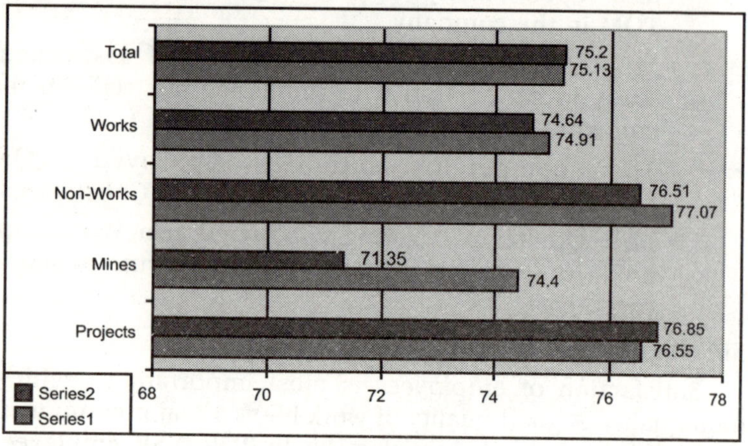

Figure 4.5. Employees' Satisfaction Index for Quality of Work Life in RINL/VSP

Note: Series 1 indicates Executives and Series 2 indicates Non-Executives.

(iv) Overcoming Communication Barriers

In a large organisation like RINL/VSP with a vast network of marketing offices across the country, the success of implementation of TQM critically hinges on a successful communication exercise. HR Professionals took this as a serious challenge and developed some communication exercises to communicate the TQM message to the farthest person of the organisation. The specific measures undertaken in the area of communication which are enumerated below:

- Introduction of a number of schemes for improving communication within the organisation viz. work place communication wherein Personnel Executive/Shift in-charge communicate on the shop floor itself with the workgroups.
- Shop floor interactions sessions.
- Participative forum of unions.
- 'Samalochana Session' within the department.
- Open House Session with CEO etc.

Provision of formal as well as information channels of communication with all unions and associations has ensured effective communication at all levels of personnel functionaries. This has ushered in a culture of dialogues and discussions with unions to sort out issues instead of conflict and confrontation.

(v) PSU Trappings

RINL/VSP is a PSU under the Ministry of Steel. Its Policies, Rules and Regulations are approved by the Board of Directors, which comprises of two Government nominees also. Some of the policy decisions are even taken at the Ministry level. Besides this, directives of the Department of Public Enterprises, Ministry of HRD, and Cabinet Secretariat etc. also guide the activities of the company. Sometimes these plethora of rules and regulations have posed hindrance in communication and implementation of novel concepts like TQM. The HR Professionals have found ways and means to introduce and operate TQM within the framework of these rules and regulations.

(vi) Vastness of the Organisation

TQM is the responsibility of every employee and it has to be achieved in every thing that is done in the organisation. If any employee fails to achieve total quality or total quality has not been achieved in any activity or process, it has to be averred that TQM is a failure in the organisation. This poses the challenge for the managers including the HR professionals. RINL/VSP is a large public sector undertaking employing nearly 17,006 numbers of employees, who hail from different socio-economic and educational backgrounds. This is indeed a formidable task for the HR professionals to conceptualise, communicate, and convince all the employees to accept, internalise and implement TQM, not only as a better management technique, but also as a survival kit.

ROLE OF KEY HUMAN FACTORS AND THEIR INTERRELATIONSHIPS

I. Awareness

Creating awareness among people is an absolute necessity before implementing TQM. People must understand the need for implementing TQM as well as the way it has to be implemented. And moreover, awareness about the programme beforehand would help to reduce their stress level that may develop due to the organisational changes associated with TQM and to encourage them to find out or recommend strategies for its effective implementation.

In RINL/VSP, a well-designed awareness programme was organised to make the people familiar with TQM concepts and tools. At the outset, training was provided to senior executives, which gradually cascaded downwards to cover all the employees (both executives and non-executives).

Hypothesis[1]: There will be a positive relationship between awareness among people about TQM and training provided to them.

Hypothesis[2]: There will be a positive relationship between awareness about TQM and innovation.

Hypothesis[3]: The more the employees are aware of TQM beforehand, the lesser would be their stress level.

II. Vision

Vision represents a long-term goal that describes 'what' an organisation wants to become. A well-articulated vision engages people emotionally to pursue the over-arching purpose of the organisation. However, a vision held only by leaders is not enough to create any real change. The management must continuously and creatively articulate the company's vision and share it with the employees. This can be achieved only through open communication system that facilitates a two-way flow of information. As the company's alternate goal is to satisfy the customer, therefore, it is imperative that employees must understand what is expected of them as well as their responsibility for achieving results.

TQM was implemented in RINL/VSP with a vision that it will 'help the company to become a self-supporting and growing company, with continuous improvement in productivity, quality and customer satisfaction'. However, mere articulation of the vision is not sufficient; it must be well communicated to all the employees. If the vision is well communicated, it will help the programme to acquire a momentum that will sustain the implementation, even if it runs into difficulties.

A well-communicated vision makes the people more innovative. It creates the feeling of delight and encouragement to overcome organisational as well as professional barriers to effective TQM implementation.

Hypothesis[1]: A well-articulated and communicated vision will have a positive influence upon innovativeness.

Hypothesis[2]: A well-articulated and communicated vision will make the people more delighted and excited about their work.

Hypothesis[3]: A clear vision has a positive impact on teamwork in the company.

III. Leadership

Quality is leadership (Kandula, 1997). The top management of the organisation is the main driver of TQM. Therefore, the key factor for successful implementation of TQM is his leadership style (Zairi, 1992). TQM requires a particular type of leader and particular style of leadership. A TQM leader should be both transactional and transformational in his approach. Transactional leadership is about 'managing and helping' people to achieve their current objectives more efficiently through practices such as, linking job performance to valued rewards, and ensuring that employees have the resources to get their job done etc. On the contrary, transformational leadership is about 'leading and changing' the organisation's strategies and culture so that people have a better fit with the surrounding environment. Transformational leaders are the brokers of dreams. They shape a strategic vision of a realistic and attractive future that bonds employees together and focuses their energy towards a superordinate organisational goal. In nutshell, while transactional leadership improves efficiency of people, transformational leadership steers people onto a better course of action. Thus, both the kinds of leadership styles are equally essential to implement Total Quality Management more successfully.

TQM was implemented in RINL/VSP in the year 1997, when Mr. J. Mehra was the CMD of the company. Mr. Mehra spent a lot of time in meeting and convincing people about various operational matters. His dynamic leadership and persuasive style and belief in not yielding to adversity, has succeeded in getting the best out of employees. "Mehra convinced people who may not agree but do not say so. As a result, they agree to do something, but not everybody implements it. It is this constant setting of stretch goals that are higher than what may be achievable that motivates employees towards superior performance. His energetic demeanour permeates down the line and this had created a performance enhancing culture in RINL/VSP. History is replete with examples of how only leaders who are both driven and driving, are able to make a difference in adverse situations under complex environments" (Ghosal, 2001).

Management leadership in the company is evident from the allocation of resources to support TQM. More often than not, TQM was implemented in the company in an environment, when the company was already facing resource constraints. In that context, leadership means, being able to explicitly provide resources both financial and non-financial in the face of severe constraints. Leadership also means developing vision, encouraging teamwork, and establishing ethics at workplace.

Hypothesis[1]: There will be a positive relationship between leadership and vision for TQM.

Hypothesis[2]: There will be a positive relationship between leadership and resources allocated.

Hypothesis[3]: There will be a positive relationship between leadership and teamwork during TQM implementation.

Hypothesis[4]: There will be a positive relationship between leadership and workplace ethics.

IV. Innovation

Innovation means junking conventional wisdom, destroying old advantage, violating established norms, reengineering business practices, and behaving in counter intuitive and indeed unpredictable ways (Mehra, 1999). An innovative organisation is one, where people are allowed to do something new and potentially useful without being directly shown or talked (Robinson & Stern, 1977).

Innovation requires a new paradigm and above all people involvement. It has to be constantly fostered and nurtured in the organisation. Innovation is fueled by an organisation's culture and goals (Dougherty, 1996; and Gundri, Kickul and Prather, 1994); organisational characteristics such as, its structure, strategy, technology, resources and rewards (Sternberg & Lubart, 1996; Woodman, Sawyer and Griffin, 1993); and, the amount of creative behaviours that occur within workgroup as well as the creative behavioural performance of its members (Kreitner and Kinicki, 1998).

Innovation requires an organisation culture, where failure is treated not only as a feedback, but a badge of honour. It is an anti-thesis of 'Doing it right first time'. It encourages mistakes, experimentation and prototyping. This demands trust in the ability of people and instilling in them a sense of ownership. Unless everyone in the company feels he has a stake in it, the spirit of innovation cannot be unleashed. All this requires entirely new leadership skills.

According to Brina Quinn (who has spent decades studying innovation), the process of managing innovation is 'controlled chaos'. At the heart of this process, successful managers make use of power of vision, innovative managements whether technical or not, project clear long term visions for their organisation that go beyond simple economic measures. Such vision attracts quality people to the company and gives focus to their creative and entrepreneurial drives.

In RINL/VSP, people are constantly motivated to innovate ideas and ways to achieve total quality. To achieve this end, the company has followed a quite simple procedure. It has placed a number of suggestion boxes have been placed at different places in the company, and the employees are encouraged to contribute their ideas in the prescribed proforma of the Suggestions Reward Scheme.[2]

2. The details of the Suggestion Reward Scheme are presented in Chapter 3.

It is assumed that creativity always flourishes at the moderate level of stress. Higher level of occupational stress kills creativity and very low level of occupational stress does not stimulate creativity. This is also assumed that an organisation having flexible structure (called organic organisations) bolsters creativity as compared to an organisation having a rigid and tight structure (called mechanic organisations).

Hypothesis[1]: There will be a significant relationship between innovation and stress level.

Hypothesis[2]: There will be a positive relationship between innovation and organisational structure and processes.

Hypothesis[3]: There will be a positive relationship between innovation and leadership style.

Hypothesis[4]: There will be a positive relationship between innovation and quality culture of the organisation.

V. Ethics

Ethics has been defined as the philosophy/science of ethical and moral values. Values often have the character of rules of conduct, Rules of conduct serve partly the objective of realising a good life for the individual and partly to strengthen and encourage the sense of solidarity. Thus, ethics must have a two pronged philosophy. On one side, a philosophy about values or rules, and on the other, a philosophy about how these values or rules can be made to be binding. In this latter sense, ethics must become a project for commitment to values, or a project for the development of the community (Floistad, 1995).

Ethics at workplace does play a very crucial role in successful implementation of TQM. Bill Creech (1994) made an extensive study of TQM practices in US based companies and concluded that work ethics, savings ethics and company loyalty are the major reasons for Japan's success in TQM. People are more involved in the TQM implementation process, when they feel that they are getting fair treatment at the workplace and their organisation maintains a high ethical standard.

Hypothesis[1]: There will be a significant relationship between ethics and leadership.

Hypothesis[2]: There will be a positive relationship between ethics and rewards and recognition are provided to employees. In other words, more equitably rewards and recognitions are provided to employees based on their competence not favouritism, more reasonably people feel that they are being fairly treated at the work place.

Hypothesis[3]: There will be a positive relationship between ethics and employees empowerment.

Hypothesis[4]: There will be a positive relationship between innovation and quality culture of the organisation.

VI. Perception

Long ago, the Greek philosopher Plato wrote, "we see reality only as shadows reflecting against the rough wall of a cave" (Plato, 1955). In other words, reality is always filtered through an imperfect perceptual process. Perceptual process means receiving information about and making sense of the world around us. It involves deciding which information to notice, how to categorize this information, and how to interpret it within the framework of our existing knowledge.

Perception, specifically social perception (otherwise known as social cognition, or social information processing system) affects each decision and action of an individual. There is a powerful perceptual process called self-fulfilling prophecy (also known as Pygmalion effect) that plays a vital role in causing the action of a person consistent with his expectation. According to the self-fulfilling prophecy, people first form expectations about the organisation, its strategies, culture and processes etc. and accordingly they direct their work behaviour. Effective coaching, training and communication have a great bearing on their perceptual schemata.

It is assumed that people would be more inclined to get themselves involved in the TQM process depending upon their perception to organisational culture, personal performance, and peer performance. Perception to personal performance depends upon how a person perceives his job, which in turn depends upon what he expects from his job. Thus, expectations of a person always influence his perception to TQM. This fact should be the major consideration while designing the training programmes for TQM.

Hypothesis[1]: There will be a significant relationship between people's perception to quality culture and personal performance.

Hypothesis[2]: There will be a positive relationship between people's perception to quality culture and peer performance.

Hypothesis[3]: There will be a positive relationship between personal performance perception and peer performance perception.

Hypothesis[4]: There will be a positive relationship between perception and training.

VII. Communication

Effective communication is a critical factor for the success of TQM. The delicate nature of the quality improvement process, which needs engaging each and every employee personally to focus on improved performance in the job he or she has hired to do, requires an atmosphere of open and honest communications throughout the entire organisation. Quality improvement is impossible without this atmosphere, where mistakes are not made simply because people are afraid to ask. Not are uninformed supervisors who more concerned with office politics than the quality of work manipulating it ever likely to be attained by unhappy employees. For, in fact, quality improvement is not as much about standards as it is about winning the hearts and minds of all the people.

Every company develops its own communication systems—some formal and rigidly controlled, other informal and uncontrolled. While too much emphasis at either of these extremes might cause problems for a company, a more important consideration is, whether the communications are open and honest, or restrained and manipulative. Only an open and honest atmosphere has the potential to prevent or overcome serious credibility gaps between the company and its employees. This kind of honest relations also has the power to release the energies needed to overcome and change the *status quo*, primarily by driving fear out of the workplace. This will make the employees feel free to become highly creative, and productive. They may even begin to take pleasure in their work.

In order to be effective from an overall company point of view, communications must take place both horizontally and vertically. Vertical communication usually means there is a network in place to push communications downward but in the spirit of quality improvement, there must also be a guarantee of an open, honest, and responsive formal system for the upward flow of communications. The horizontal communications take place between peers, especially inter-functional peers. Increased horizontal communication can help employees to understand their jobs better, by helping them to see how their work fits in with the broader operations of the company.

Besides, management experts also note that effective communication is a cornerstone of ethical work behaviour. Communication by the top executives keep the firm in its ethical course. The top executives must ensure that the ethical climate is consistent with the company's overall objectives. Communication is important in providing guidance for ethical standards and activities that provide integration between the functional areas of the business (Ferrell & Fraedrich, 1991).

Before embarking upon a formal quality improvement programme, a company has to open up all these positive channels of communication, especially to give all employees the opportunity and encouragement to use the upward channel. The quality policy must be clearly communicated to them and the company should also gather inputs from them relating to its successful implementation. Because employees represent a reservoir of the most intimate knowledge about how the business really works. Management cannot afford to be without their inputs, if there is to be any hope for its true success. Do not leave communications to chance. Understand its intrinsic value to the achievement of quality improvement and build its effectiveness throughout the company, right from the beginning (Hagan, 1997).

Hypothesis[1]: There will be a positive correlation between communication and quality policy.

Hypothesis[2]: There will be a positive relationship between communication and employees' empowerment.

Hypothesis[3]: There will be a positive relationship between communication and ethical work behaviour.

VIII. Mental State (Stress and Delight)

Mental state of a person plays a pivotal role in regulating his work performance. It is normally assumed that the more a person is delighted with his work, the better would be his work performance and *vice versa*. However, life in this competitive era has become hectic and occupational stress is on the rise for several reasons. First, the biggest contributor to work stress revolves around fundamental changes occurring in work organisations. As a result of increasingly competition, people are being asked to deliver a better quality and a greater quantity of work in lesser time with scarce resources. Second, technological advancements make it harder for employees to adapt themselves to new technologies. And, finally, the dynamics of modern life make it difficult to balance the demands between work and home. Research demonstrates that work stress spills over into one's personal life and *vice versa* (Jones & Fletcher, 1996).

In RINL/VSP, a number of stress management techniques have been adopted by the company to reduce and manage occupational stress. Recognition for accomplishments, support from top management at the time of crisis, time-off for personal development or rest, provision of payment of equitable rewards, better promotional avenues, opportunity for interpersonal contact through team building, encouragement to employees to contribute ideas through suggestion scheme, and arrangements for entertainment programmes beyond the working hours are some of the steps taken by the organisation to prevent burn-out. Besides, a number of other measures have also been undertaken to enrich the quality of life of the employees, which has a great bearing on the quality of their work life.

Hypothesis[1]: There will be a positive relationship between people's delight and leadership style.

Hypothesis[2]: There will be a positive relationship between people's delight and teamwork.

Hypothesis[3]: Better is the reward and recognition system in the organisation, lesser would be the occupational stress level of people.

Hypothesis[4]: More the people are empowered in the organisation, lesser would be their occupational stress level.

IX. Rewards and Recognition

Equitable rewards and recognition for accomplishment play a vital role in stimulating positive work performance. Recognition is the heart of quality improvement programme. Recognition that is honest, deserving, and sincere forms the base of good management and provides management with a tool that truly integrates people into the quality improvement system. Once quality measurements are in place and specific improvements are verified, then formal recognition should be accorded to individuals and groups in a manner that they can appreciate and their associates can understand. This is one of the best methods for sustaining personal interest and individual effort for continued quality progress. Spontaneous recognition from supervisors and managers to employees is the most effective and inexpensive type available, especially if done in front of as many employees' peers as possible. Their bosses as well as peers for doing a good job have pointed out many quality surveys that a primary desire of most employees is to be recognised. Failure to take advantage of this tactics by the management is a business blender of the first order (Hagon, 1997).

In RINL/VSP, an elaborate reward and recognition system has been designed to motivate employees as well as to increase their efficiency and productivity. Every year, merit certificates are awarded to the best quality circles (QC), which have really contributed to the company in terms of financial savings. The best QC of the year receives the Director's Shield in the Annual Recognition Function and a memento is presented to all the QC members as a token of appreciation for their work. Similarly, individual employees are also rewarded for their best suggestions. Which are accepted for implementation, by the company.[3]

Reward and recognition for accomplishment delight the people, and motivate them to be more involved in the TQM process as well as to be more innovative and creative.

Hypothesis[1]: There will be a positive relationship between rewards and recognition and people's delight.

Hypothesis[2]: There will be a positive relationship between rewards and recognition and innovation.

X. Maturity and Breadth

Maturity and breadth represents the social, moral and emotional maturity of people and their broad range of interest in different activities. Maturity level influences the degree of involvement of people in TQM implementation. It largely determines whether people demonstrate cooperative behaviour, treat others fairly and respectfully at the work place etc. It is assumed that the higher the social/moral maturity level of people, the more they do believe that their work is important to the success of the organisation and accordingly they share responsibility for its success or failure. Such people also demonstrate high ethical work behaviour and they are likely to be more creative than others.

XI. Attitude and Morale

Attitude is defined as 'a learned pre-dispositions to respond in a consistently favourable or unfavourable manner with

3. During the opinion survey, nearly 70% of the sample respondents opined that, they are satisfied with the rewards and recognition system of the organisation. Nearly 20% of the sample respondents expressed that they are highly satisfied with the rewards and recognition system, only 2% expressed their dissatisfaction, and the rest remained neutral.

respect to a given object' (Fishbein and Ajzen, 1975). Total quality needs an organisation-wide adherence to new values and principles. It indicates that the starting point for Total Quality has to be the creation of a new collective paradigm or mindset, and development of positive attitude in all the members of the organisation, so that all in concert makes the movement to the point where the organisation has to be.

Quality comes mainly from people as a result of attitudes and values, not by technology alone. Unless the TQM drive aims at attitudinal change, divorcing stereotype beliefs, it may not be feasible to introduce it (Singh, 1991; and Chakraborti, 1997). Thus, changing attitude that is supportive to total quality is an absolute necessity for its effective implementation. There are many tactics to change and develop employees' attitudes towards TQM. Some of these tactics include: clear and credible communication, creating total quality organisational climate etc. Although attitudes often are resistant to change, they can be influenced through proper education and training that may help to change underline beliefs. Regular employee-attitude surveys can also let managers know, if their ideas and changes go with or against the grain of popular sentiment.

In RINL/VSP, employee attitude surveys are conducted regularly to assess employees' attitude and opinion towards various organisational systems and processes. Before the introduction of TQM, the HRD department conducted one employees' voice index survey to assess the employees of attitude towards this novel concept.

Hypothesis[1]: There will be a positive relationship between attitude and morale of people and organisation structure and processes.

Hypothesis[2]: There will be a positive relationship between attitude and morale of people and peerteam support.

Hypothesis[3]: There will be a positive relationship between attitude and morale of people and system feedback coordination.

Hypothesis[4]: There will be a positive relationship between attitude of employees and training provided.

XII. Customer Satisfaction Sensitivity

TQM is a customer-centred management approach. It recognizes that continuously satisfying the customers is the root to the success in the market place (Thiagarajan and Zairi, 1997).

In RINL/VSP, the voice of the customers (both external and internal) is always followed in its quality management practices. In order to enhance customer satisfaction, it always ensures that the requirements of the customers, whether stated or not, but are necessary for specified or intended use, are fulfilled. Regular contact is maintained with customers to get product information as well as to receive feedback and complaints. Attempt is always made to bring a proper alignment between customer's needs and suppliers capabilities.

Hypothesis[1]: There will be a positive relationship between customer satisfaction sensitivity and organisation structure and processes.

Hypothesis[2]: There will be a positive relationship between customer satisfaction sensitivity and system feedback coordination.

XIII. Resources

Proper allocation of resources play a major role in the successful implementation of any programme. TQM was launched in RINL/VSP at the time, when it was incurring heavy losses. Therefore, allocation of resources (both monetary and other resources) to the TQM programme became a crucial decision for the top management. If the company expects each of its production, non-production, and supporting unit to implement TQM based on normal resources budgeted to it, then the implementation of the programme will definitely suffer. Low budgetary allocation will also lead to little or no formal training on TQM related issues. This is quite imperative for the employees in the company to get themselves acquainted with various tools used in the TQM programme. They need to be taught how to design and implement quality improvement projects as well as quality circles. Proper allocation of resources such as, supply of right tools, equipments, and materials also facilitate performance of people.

Hypothesis[1]: There will be a significant relationship between quantum of resource allocation and performance of people.

Hypothesis[2]: There will be a positive relationship between quantum of resource allocation and training provided to people.

XIV. System Feedback Coordination

Total quality experts say, in order to improve quality of work one has to work smarter, not harder. In order to work smarter, needless to say one needs not only sound education and appropriate skill training, but also constant instructive and supportive feedback. Feedback exerts a powerful influence on work behaviour and job performance by improving role perceptions, ability and motivation. A well-administered feedback system improves employee ability by frequently providing information to correct performance problems. It also let people know what behaviours are appropriate or necessary in a particular situation. Besides, feedback is also a great source of motivation. Positive feedback fulfils personal needs and makes people more confident that they are able to accomplish certain tasks. Employees receive objective feedback from various sources such as, superiors, subordinates, peers, and outsiders (customers). Another major source of feedback is oneself.

In RINL/VSP, in addition to traditional top-down feedback (performance appraisal system), non-traditional feedback (feedback from other multiple sources such as, upward-feedback, group evaluation, etc.) is also provided to employees. Non-traditional feedback is gaining popularity in the company in recent years for the following reasons:

(i) Traditional performance appraisal system has its own limitations (such as appraiser's bias, favouritism, and incompetence act as inhibitors for effective feedback) have created widepread dissatisfaction among employees.

(ii) After the introduction of TQM programme, many of the activities are required to be performed through teams. This trend requires employees to have good inter-personal skills, which are best evaluated by team members.

(iii) Multiple-rater system is supposed to provide more valid feedback than single-source feedback.

(iv) Bottom-up feedback meshes nicely with the trend of the company toward employee empowerment and participative management.

(v) Co-workers and subordinates do know more about the strengths and weaknesses of an employee than his boss.

Hypothesis[1]: There will be a significant relationship between feedback system and structure and processes of an organisation.

Hypothesis[2]: There will be a positive relationship between feedback system and employee empowerment.

Hypothesis[3]: There will be a positive relationship between feedback system and peoples' perception to personal performance.

XV. Empowerment

"Empowerment is moving decision-making down to the lowest level, where a competent decision can be made" (Hodgettes, 1996). The highest degree of empowerment is delegation, the process of granting decision-making authority to lower-level employees, which amounts to power distribution. As it has been rightly pointed out by Stephen R. Covey (1989) that, "Management must empower its people in the deepest sense and remove the barriers and obstacles it has created that crush and defeat the inherent commitment, creativity, and quality service that people are otherwise prepared to offer. To receive joy and pride in one's work is the right of all and it is the management practices that prevent it. To achieve total quality, managers must become leaders, drawing from their people their greatest capacity to contribute ideas, creativity, innovative thinking, attention to detail and analysis of process and product to the workplace. In other words, management must become empowering leaders."

The keys to 'empowerment' are sharing information with

employees, building organisational structure that will provide more freedom of action to people, and involving people in the decision-making process. These may be easy to understand, but are really hard to implement. It requires tremendous courage of the company to share sensitive information. It takes real growth to allow teams to take over the management decision-making processes. And above all, it takes perseverance to complete the empowerment process (Rahdolph, 1995).

In RINL/VSP, employee empowerment is confined to information sharing (but not the sensitive information) and encouraging employees to suggest new solutions and ideas that will helpful during the decision-making process. It is assumed that this process will reduce the cost, improve the quality, and contribute to employee's job satisfaction.

Hypothesis[1]: There will be a significant relationship between empowerment and organisational structure and processes.

Hypothesis[2]: There will be a positive relationship between empowerment and innovation.

Hypothesis[3]: There will be a positive relationship between empowerment and attitude and morale of people.

XVI. Training

Training is a process of updating the knowledge, developing skills, bringing attitudinal and behavioural changes, and improving the trainees' ability to perform efficiently and effectively. Every company has a basic responsibility to educate and train its employees and this responsibility is magnified when quality management programme is launched in the company. Whether TQM is a new system or a newly renovated old system for a company, it is essential that all participants, that is all employees must have knowledge of its principles, values, objectives, tools and techniques and the company's plan for its implementation. This implies that employees must be educated why TQM is being done and trained how well it has to be done. Besides, when employees learn new role patterns essential for TQM implementation through training, they are likely to experience less stress and feel more comfortable with breaking previous routines. This is evident from the Japanese experience. One of the significant facts responsible for the present world leadership in quality attained by Japan is its emphasis laid upon training of personnel in Quality Control. According to different estimates, about 7 million industrial personnel have already been trained and currently 10,000 engineers are trained every year in design of experiments alone (Sreenivasan and Narayana, 1996).

In RINL/VSP, training programmes are organised regularly on Total Quality Advantage (TQA), TQM concepts and tools, quality audit, ISO series, various statistical techniques, teamwork and other quality related topics to both executives and non-executives. On an average, each employee is provided 20 hours training annually on TQM and allied activities.

Hypothesis[1]: There will be a positive relationship between training efforts and teamwork.

Hypothesis[2]: There will be a positive relationship between training efforts and feedback system.

Hypothesis[3]: There will be a positive relationship between training and communication.

Hypothesis[4]: There will be a positive relationship between training and occupational stress.

XVII. Quality Policy and Guidance

Quality policy of an organisation is a documented outcome of the process of strategic quality planning. It serves to provide internal consistency between the goals and the procedures of a company, by aligning each member, division, and element of the organisation towards its long-term objectives. In order to be effective, such policy documents have to possess the following characteristics: the statements has to be clear, brief and unambiguous; it must be widely circulated; it must focus on a meaningful and attainable specifics, rather than vague generalities; the policy must communicate the values and beliefs on the basis of which the overall plan has been framed, while simultaneously specifying the approaches that are to be used in the attainment of goals; and, it must be signed by the CEO, and/or his team, and then faithfully adhered to by them, all others in the organisation too must abide by it (Wakhlu, 1994).

RINL/VSP has a well-documented quality policy which envisages upon 'commitment to meeting the requirements of the customer as well as achieving continual improvement'. The present quality policy of the company has been printed and issued to each and every employee in form of pocket diary. It has also been pasted at all the prominent places of the organisation. There are three basic tenets of the quality policy that serve as guideline for the actions of everyone in the organisation. These tenets are:

(i) Every individual must be respected and given an opportunity for continuous improvement;

(ii) The requirements of the customer must be fulfilled; and

(iii) Excellence and superior performance must be pursued.

Hypothesis[1]: There will be a significant relationship between quality policy and attitude and morale of employees.

Hypothesis[2]: There will be a positive relationship between quality policy and meeting customer's requirements.

Hypothesis[3]: There will be a positive relationship between quality policy and training.

Hypothesis[4]: There will be a positive relationship between quality policy and empowerment.

Hypothesis[5]: There will be a positive relationship between quality policy and feedback system.

XVIII. Organisational Structure and Processes

Organisational structure refers to the division of labour as well as the patterns of coordination, communication, workflow, and formal power that direct organisational activities. An organisation with a narrow span of control and high degree of formalisation and centralisation is called a mechanic organisation. On the contrary, an organisation with a wide span of control, little formalisation, and highly decentralised decision-making is called an organic organisation. Whether an organisation will adopt an organic or mechanic structure, it largely depends upon its quality policy.

In RINL/VSP, like the other Indian public sector undertakings, the structure of the organisation is based on the traditional form of pyramid structure. Those at the top of the organisational hierarchy hold the formal decision-making authority. However, after implementation of TQM that requires the formation of quality improvement projects and quality circles, the organisation has taken some steps towards lateral structure (team-based), but it exists within or in conjunction with the traditional structure. At present, a number of free floating teams are operating in the organisation, which are typically organised around work processes such as, identifying work-related problems, quality-related problems, customer-related problems, and finding out solutions for them. These teams have relatively a flat structure with a little formalisation, and centralisation in decision-making process. They are given relatively few rules about how to organise their work. Instead, output goals such as, the volume and quality of products/services, or productivity improvement targets for the work process are assigned to these teams and they are encouraged to use available resources and their own initiative to achieve those objectives.

Hypothesis[1]: There will be a significant relationship between organisation structure and processes and employees' attitude towards TQM.

Hypothesis[2]: There will be a positive relationship between organisation structure and processes and quality policy.

Hypothesis[3]: There will be a positive relationship between organisation structure and processes and innovation.

XIX. Total Quality Ecological Sustainability

The TQM organisations must show a lot of concern for environment, society, and ecology. In fact, this has become the necessity with the development of the ISO-14000 series of generic environmental management system by the International Organisation for Standardisation. The components of ISO-14000 include: the general categories of environmental management systems, environmental auditing, environmental labeling, environmental performance evaluations, and life-cycle assessments.

RINL/VSP has adopted a number of policies and practices to promote ecological sustainability of the company. Sustainable development, rather than unmanaged growth or stagnation is a typical approach of the organisation towards nature. VSP has gained nation-wide popularity for its afforestation programmes. This is evident from the certification of the company with the ISO-140001:1996 (Environmental) on 18 May, 2002 by the International Organisation for Standardisation.

Hypothesis[1]: There will be a positive relationship between total quality ecological sustainability and people's delight.

XX. Peer Team Support

Good teamwork constitutes the base of TQM. Teamwork requires the spirit of cooperation, complementation, and synergetic relationship among members. Work teams have a much greater chance of being effective, if they are nurtured and facilitated by the organisation. In order to be more effective, teams must be led by leaders who exhibit both transactional and transformational leadership style. The team, which is operating with a higher degree of empowerment, is more likely to make good decisions and stimulate innovation.

In RINL/VSP, a number of work teams have been formed for various purposes. For instance, advise teams such as quality circles have been formed to provide suggestions for quality-improvement. A number of small production teams have been formed to facilitate the performance of day-to-day operations. Action teams such as quality Action Teams (QATs) have been formed to identify and solve work, related and quality–related problems. Members of these teams mostly exhibit good interpersonal skills and chemistry and display cooperation and trust upon each other. Team leaders are trying to be both transactional and transformational in their leadership approach. In order to make teamwork TQM oriented, the company is striving towards taking the following measures:

- Creating purpose of the team in concert with the organisation's strategy.

- Creating a culture in the organisation that values team participation and autonomy.
- Providing appropriate technological resources and training to team members.
- Reinforcing teamwork by the reward system of the organisation.

Hypothesis[1]: There will be a positive relationship between teamwork and employee empowerment.

Hypothesis[2]: There will be a positive relationship between teamwork and innovation.

A model representing the stipulated hypothetical interrelationships among the relevant KHFs is presented in Figure 4.6.

AN OVERVIEW

Of course, TQM is management strategy, but it is quite personal. If employees do not 'buy-into' the quality philosophy, learn the quality tools and techniques, develop the spirit to work together in teams, and use new skills and knowledge in their daily work, TQM will never succeed.

Realising the potential of human factors, RINL/VSP has formulated quality policy and plans in alliance with HR policy and plans and specifically involved its HR professionals in effective implementation of TQM in the company. The HR professionals have also taken keen interest in the matter and involved themselves at all stages of TQM implementation starting from envisioning to preparing to implementing and sustaining the TQM movement in the company. In particular, they have helped in spreading the TQM message in the company, creating quality awareness among the employees, organizing quality workshops, forming QATs, providing training on TQM advantage and other related matters, developing communication exercises and above all, bringing about a change in the conventional mindset of the employees.

There are several HR challenges associated with the effective implementation of TQM, which act as stumbling blocks for the HR professionals in the performance of their roles as TQM implementor and facilitators. Motivating the employees who are mostly knowledge workers, mobilising managers who

are hardly prepared to share with their power and delegate it, plethora of rules, regulations and directives by the Government, too much emphasis on formal communication system, and above all, the vastness of the organisation act as major barriers and pose real challenges to the HR professionals.

The HRD department in the company acts in collaboration with other departments for successful TQM implementation. HR professionals act as internal consultants, to other departments in the context of TQM. Specifically, they provide consultancy to other departments at the time when they enter into MOUs with their customer/supplier departments.

Various human factors play a crucial role in effective TQM implementation. Some of the human factors which are worth mentioning are awareness, vision, leadership, innovation, ethics, perception, mental state, maturity and breadth, attitude, empowerment, peer support etc. All these actors are interrelated with each other and have a cumulative effect on successful TQM implementation in the company.

REFERENCES

- Anderson, John C., Rungtusaratham, Manus, and Schroeder, Roger G. (1994). "Theoretical Model of Total Quality Management", *Academy of Management Review,* Vol. 19, No. 3, July, pp. 472-509.
- Chakraborti, T. (1997). "TQM – A Hard Climb", *The Economic Times Supplement,* March 28 – April 3.
- Covey, S.R. (1989). *The Seven Habits of Highly Effective People,* Simon & Schuster K. Ltd., London.
- Creech, B. (1994). *The Five Pillars of TQM: How to Make TQM Work for You,* Trauman Tally Books, New York.
- Dean Jr., J.W. and Bowen, D.E. (1994). "Management Theory and Total Quality."
- Dougherty (1996). "Organising for Innovation", in *Hand Book of Organisation Studies,* SAGE Publications, London, pp. 424-39.
- Ferrell, O.C. and Fraedrich, J. (1991). *Business Ethics: Ethical Decision Making and Cases,* Houghton Mifflin, Boston, p. 143.
- Fishbein, M. and Ajzen, I. (1975). *Belief, Attitude, Intention and Behaviour: An Introduction to Theory and Research,* Addison-Wesley Publishing, p. 6.
- Floistad, G. (1995). "Community Culture, Ethics, Professionalism and Human Values : A View from Norway", *Journal of Human Values,* p. 16.

- Ghosal, S., Pirmal, G. and Budhiraja, S. (2001). *World Class Organisations in India,* Penguin Books, New Delhi, p. 473.
- Gundry, L.K., Kickul, J.R., and Prather, C.W. (1994). "Building the Creative Organisation", *Organisational Dynamics,* Spring, pp. 22-36.
- Hagan, J. (1997). *Management of Quality: Strategies to Improve Quality and the Bottom Line,* Oxford University Press, New Delhi, p. 87.
- Hodgettes, R.M. (1996). "A Conversation with Steve Kerr", *Organisational Dynamics,* Spring, p. 71.
- Jones, F. and Fletcher, B.C. (1996). "Taking Work Home: A Study of Daily Fluctuations in work Stressors, Effects on Moods and Impacts on Marital Partners", *Journal of Occupational and Organisational Psychology,* March, pp. 89-106.
- Kandula, S. (1997). "Critical Appraisal of TQM as an OD Intervention", *Indian Journal of Training and Development,* January—March.
- Kreitner, R. and Kinicki, A. (1998). *Organisational Behaviour,* Irwin McGraw Hill, North America.
- Maslow, A.H. (1954). *Motivation and Personality,* Harper and Row, New York.
- Mehra, M. (1999). "Competing through Innovation", *Quality for Business Transformation* (ed.), Institute of Directors, New Delhi, p. 2.
- Plato (1955). *The Replubic,* Translated by Lee, D., Penguin, U.K., Part XII, Sec. 7.
- "Quality: Improving Research and Practice through Theory Development", *Academy of Management Review,* Vol. 1, No. 3, pp. 392-418.
- Rahdolph, W.A. (1995). "Navigating the Journey to Empowerment", *Organisational Dynamics,* Spring, pp. 53-60.
- Robinson, A.G. and Stern, S. (1997). *Corporate Creativity: How Innovation and Improvement Actually Happen,* Beret-Koehler Publishes Inc., San Francisco, p. 11.
- Singh, A. (1991). "TQM: Concept and Practice in India", *Productivity,* Vol. 32, No. 3, October-December.
- Sreenivasan, N.S. and Narayana, V. (1996). *Managing Quality: The Concepts and Tasks,* New Age International Ltd., p. 240.
- Sternberg, R.J. and Lubart, T.I. (1996). "Investing in Creativity", *American Psychologist,* July, pp. 677-88.
- Thiagarajan, T. and Zairi, M. (1997). "Understanding the Fundamentals of TQM", *Productivity,* No. 3.
- Wakhlu, B. (1994). *Total Quality Excellence through Organisation-wide Transformation,* Wheeler Publishing, New Delhi, pp. 11-13.

- Woodman, R.W., Sawyer, J.E. and Griffin, R.W. (1993). "Toward a Theory of Organisational Creativity", *Academy of Management Review,* April, pp. 293-321.
- Zairi, M. (1992). *Total Quality Management for Engineers,* Woodland Publishing Ltd., UK.

5

Results of Opinion Survey

The human dimension of TQM has been analysed in the previous chapter based on the information provided by the management of RINL/VSP. The thrust is laid upon the role of Human Resource Professionals as well as Key Human Factors (KHFs) in effective TQM implementation. Besides, hypothetical interrelationships among the relevant KHFs have also been formulated for empirical verification.

In order to make a more objective assessment of TQM–HR interface and verify the stipulated hypothetical interrelationships among KHFs, the researcher in the company conducted an opinion survey. During the opinion survey, subjective data relating to various human dimensions of TQM such as, employees' perception to the quality profile of the organisation as well as to the organisational process climate, identification of the most crucial KHF for effective TQM implementation, assessment of leadership style, identification of the motivating factors for employee involvement in the TQM process etc. were collected from the sample respondents, which are analysed and interpreted in the present chapter.

SAMPLING

The opinion survey covered 372 sample respondents (124 executives and 248 non-executives) from different departments and sections of RINL/VSP.[1] The sample respondents were selected on the basis of stratified random sampling method. All the sample respondents were requested to fill in a structured questionnaire and that was followed by both structured and unstructured interviews as well as information discussion.

1. The details of the sampling design is given in Chapter 2.

The questionnaire had six parts and each part contained some items relating to different human dimensions of TQM.

Part A of the questionnaire[2] included basic information about the demographic profile of the sample respondents. The sample group constituted around 2 per cent of the total population (17,006) of the company. The mean age of the sample respondents was 37.6 years and length of service (total work experience including the organisational tenure) ranged from 4 to 22 years. The male and female ratio was around 2:1.

RESULTS OF THE OPINION SURVEY

The Quality Profile Survey

The survey of the quality profile of the organisation was made on the basis of the questionnaire developed by Philip, B. Crosby (1987). Crosby has developed five sets of questions that include five crucial aspects of quality, namely:

- Deviations in outgoing products/services.
- 'Fix it' orientation.
- Clarity of employees on management's expectations from them concerning quality.
- Management's awareness of the price of non-conformance.
- Belief of management relating to the cause of quality problems.

This part of the questionnaire[3] was meant only for the executive sample respondents. The summary of the results obtained from the survey is presented in Table 5.1.

Discussion and Results

From Table 5.1 it is revealed that highest percentage i.e., 38.71 per cent of the sample respondents assigned score in the 6-10 range and the average score obtained is 8.39, which according to Crosby's interpretation the organisation is in the **'Healing'** stage. This indicates that the organisation needs regular check-up and care in order to become a 'whole' or 'total quality' organisation.

---

2. For details, see Part-A of the Questionnaire given in Annexure II.
3. For details, see Part-B of the Questionnaire given in Annexure II.

TABLE 5.1: Results of the Quality Profile Survey of RINL/VSP

Sl. No.	Range of scores	Status of organisation (Crosby)	Crosby's remark	No. of respondents in the score range	Percentage of respondents
1.	21-25	Critical	Needs intensive care immediately	0	0
2.	16-20	Guarded	Needs life support system hookup	4	3.22
3.	11-15	Resting	Needs medication and attention	26	20.97
4.	6-10	Healing	Needs regular check-up	48	38.71
5.	<5	Whole	Needs counselling	46	37.10

Average score is 8.39—"Needs regular check-up."

Source: Compiled from the data collected during the opinion survey.

Organisational Process Climate Survey

The process climate of an organisation adduces evidence in support of/against TQM implementation. The process climate may be exploitative, impoverished, supportive or total quality. Although the total quality climate is the most desirable one, the supportive climate also nourishes the TQM effort.

In order to assess the process climate of RINL/VSP a survey was made by administrating a well-structured questionnaire (Petrik and Quinn, 1996)[4] containing seventeen dimensions to the executive sample respondents. The sample respondents were requested to encircle a number on a 1-20 point scale against each dimension. The summary of the survey findings have been given in Table 5.2.

Discussion and Results

Table 5.2 indicates that maximum number of sample respondents i.e., 53.22% of the sample assigned scores between 11-15.9 and the average score obtained is 14.7. This depicts that RINL/VSP has a **'Supportive'** organisational process climate.

4. For details, see Part-C of the Questionnaire appended in Annexure II.

TABLE 5.2: Results of the Organisational Process Climate Survey of RINL/VSP

Sl. No.	Range of scores	Status of organisation	No. of respondents in the score range	Percentage of respondents
1.	1-5.9	Exploitive	0	0
2.	6-10.9	Impoverished	12	9.67
3.	11-15.9	Supportive	66	53.22
4.	16-20	Total Quality	46	37.11

Average score is 14.7 –**'Supportive'** organisational process climate.
Source: Compiled from the data collected during the opinion survey.

Supportive organisational process climate maintains power in the hands of managers, but there is good communication, encouragement and participation throughout the organisation. Employees understand the goals of the organisation, rarely hesitate to discuss job-related problems with their managers, and are committed to achieve organisation goals as long as the external reward and recognition system compensates them adequately. There is no sense of employee ownership of process and/or product improvement. Supportive process climate creates productive, but dependent followers and underutilises the intellectual capital of an organisation relative to the total quality organisations.

Verification of Hypothetical Interrelationships Among Key Human Factors (KHFs)

For an empirical verification of the hypothetical statements concerning interrelationships among the KHFs stipulated in the preceding chapter, Pearson's Correlation Coefficient (PCC) measure and its significance level (2–tailed) have been used in this section. PCC is considered to be highly significant at the 0.01 level and significant at the 0.05 level. The statistical properties of the interrelationships are presented in a series of tables.

Descriptive, Reliability and Factor Analysis of KHFs

Part-D of the questionnaire[5] contained 81 TQM and HR related statements on a six-point interval scale. All these items

5. For details, see Part-D of the questionnaire given in Annexure II.

are grouped into 23 headings. Table 5.3 provides the descriptive reliability and factor analysis of these factors.

TABLE 5.3: Descriptive, Reliability and Factor Analysis of KHFs

Sl. No.	KHFs	No. of Items	Mean	Standard Deviation	Cronbach Alpha	KMO Value
1.	Awareness	3	4.62	0.94	0.7672	0.769
2.	Vision	3	4.38	1.06	0.8464	0.692
3.	Leadership	12	4.54	0.98	0.8871	0.8071
4.	Innovation	2	4.44	1.08	0.6644	0.5
5.	Ethics	3	4.22	1.02	0.8391	0.718
6.	Quality culture	3	4.51	0.92	0.7986	0.686
7.	Personal performance	3	4.98	0.75	0.8686	0.727
8.	Peer performance	3	4.73	0.64	0.8664	0.716
9.	Communication	2	4.52	0.89	0.8841	0.5
10.	Stress	2	4.38	0.94	0.8086	0.5
11.	Delight	3	4.30	0.88	0.9094	0.758
12.	Rewards & recognition	5	4.38	1.04	0.8151	0.888
13.	Maturity & breadth	2	4.50	0.81	0.8058	0.5
14.	Attitude and morale	3	4.50	0.88	0.8647	0.722
15.	Customer satisfaction	4	4.61	0.88	0.896	0.827
16.	Quality task resources	3	4.58	0.95	0.79	0.699
17.	System feedback	3	4.61	0.93	0.826	0.694
18.	Empowerment	4	4.38	0.99	0.326	0.753
19.	Training	3	4.19	1.22	0.176	0.46
20.	Quality policy	3	4.68	0.95	0.8799	0.735
21.	Organisational structure & processes	5	4.55	0.89	0.8169	0.725
22.	Total quality ecological sustainability	3	4.94	0.83	0.823	0.693
23.	Peer team support	2	4.53	0.89	0.8882	0.5

Note: KMO indicates Kaiser–Moyer–Olkin Measure (Kim & Mueller, 1978).

Source: Compiled and calculated from the data collected during the opinion survey.

Discussion and Results

The Table 5.3 provides the descriptive analysis of 23 KHFs. Columns 4 and 5 of the table show the mean value and standard deviation for each factor. Column 4 indicates that the mean values of all the factors are greater than 4.00, which reveals that the sample respondents almost agreed to the statements. The standard deviation depicts the reliability of the collected data. Co-efficient alpha in column 6 shows reliability (internal consistency) measures for the factors. Nunnally (1967) suggests that reliability co-efficient of 0.6 is sufficient. The value of Cronbach alpha in all cases except factor number 19, which has value less than 0.6, indicate that each factor is sufficiently reliable. Column 7 provides KMO value for sampling adequacy. Kim and Mueller (1978) suggest that KMO values of 0.7s to 0.8s range are considered 'meritorious' and those in the 0.6s to 0.7s range are being 'middling'. KMOs of 0.5 are considered 'poor', although not unacceptable. In the present case, KMO values of factor numbers 1, 3, 5, 7, 8, 11, 12, 14, 15, 18, 20 and 21 range between 0.7 to 0.8, which indicate high sampling adequacy of the factors. KMO values for the factor numbers 2, 6, 16, 17 and 22 range between 0.6 to 0.7, which indicate middling sampling adequacy and for the other factors (except factor no. 19 of which KMO value is 0.46) KMOs are 0.5.

Discussion and Results of Hypothetical Interrelationships Among KHFs

I. Awareness

The interrelationships between awareness and each of the selected KHFs such as training, innovation and stress level of people are laid out in Table 5.4.

TABLE 5.4: Relationship of Awareness with Selected KHFs

Sl. No.	Statistical Property	Training	Innovation	Stress level
1.	PCC	0.335**	.394**	.258*
2.	Significance Level (2-tailed)	.008	.002	.043

Note: '**' and '*' indicate significance level at 0.01 and 0.05 level respectively (** $P < 0.01$ & * $P < 0.05$) in all the Tables of this section.

The Table 5.4 indicates that the relationship between awareness and training is highly significant ($P < 0.01$) and moderate (0.335). It implies that a well-organised training programme does have a direct and significant influence on creating awareness among people.

There is a highly significant (P< 0.01) and moderate (.394) relationship between awareness and innovation. This implies that creating awareness is crucial to enable the people to understand the rationale behind introducing TQM, and also to encourage them to innovate novel ways for its implementation. Thus, the hypothesis that people become innovative when they are made aware of the programme beforehand is found to be true from the collected data. Hence, the hypothesis is established.

There is a significant (P<0.05) and moderate (.258) relationship between awareness and stress level of people. It suggests that when people are made aware of TQM programme before its actual implementation, it has definitely a positive impact on reducing their stress-level, although the actual effect may not be very high.

II. Vision

Table 5.5 marks the interrelationships between vision and some KHFs, such as, people's delight and excitement about their work, innovation and teamwork.

TABLE 5.5: Relationship of Vision with Selected KHFs

Sl. No.	Statistical Property	Innovation	Delight	Teamwork
1.	PCC	.335**	-.022	.039
2.	Significance Level (2-tailed)	.008	.884	.761

There is a highly significant (P < 0.01) and moderate (.335) relationship between vision and innovation. This implies that a well-articulated and communicated vision definitely has a positive impact on people's innovativeness.

Vision and delight are found to be not well related. The PCC measure of -.022 indicates that there is a small and negative correlation between them. Moreover, the relationship is loose as it is not significant (P>0.05). Thus the hypothesis that well-articulated vision makes people more delighted and excited is not tenable/acceptable as verified from the collected data.

There is an insignificant (P>0.05) and small (.039) relationship between vision and teamwork. It suggests that, through a well-defined vision has a positive impact on teamwork, it does not sufficiently ensure effective functioning of team. There are several other components such as, cooperation, trust and cohesiveness among team members, which make significant contribution to achieve effective teamwork.

III. Leadership

Table 5.6 records the relationship between leadership and resources allocated, teamwork, and maintenance of ethics at workplace.

TABLE 5.6: Relationship of Leadership with Selected KHFs

Sl. No.	Statistical Property	Resources	Teamwork	Ethics
1.	PCC	-.081	.152	.332**
2.	Significance Level (2-tailed)	.531	.240	.008

There is an insignificant (P>0.05) and small (.152) relationship between leadership and teamwork. It suggests that, direct participation of the senior management does not ensure good teamwork in the organisation. A probable explanation for this may be that, in RINL/VSP all the departments have been provided the autonomy to form the QATs and QCs in order to identify and solve various work related problems. These teams have been provided autonomy to decide what would be the nature of interaction among themselves, rather than be prodded by senior executives.

There is a highly significant (P<0.01) and moderate (.332) relationship between leadership and workplace ethics. It suggests that the words and deeds of managers have a highly significant impact on maintenance of a high ethical standard in the organisation. Thus the hypothesis that there will be a positive relationship between leadership and ethics is well established from the collected data.

There is a small (-.081) negative and insignificant (P>0.05) relationship between leadership and resources allocated. It suggests that leadership does not have any impact on the resources allocated for the implementation of TQM programme. Ironically, the relationship between the two has been just the opposite of what was being predicted. Implementation of TQM requires adequate resources and it is definitely the responsibility of the senior managers to ensure that sufficient resources are allocated for this purpose.

IV. Innovation

Table 5.7 brings out the interrelationships between innovation and stress level of people, structure and processes of an Organisation, leadership, and quality culture.

TABLE 5.7: Relationship of Innovation with Selected KHFs

Sl. No.	Statistical Property	Stress level	Organisational structure and processes	Leadership	Quality Culture
1.	PCC	.313*	.029	.037	.059
2.	Significance Level (2-tailed)	.013	.821	.774	.648

There is a significant ($P<0.05$) and moderate (0.313) relationship between innovation and stress level of people. It suggests that the stress people experience in their day-to-day life has a significant impact on their creativeness. Therefore the hypothesis that stress and innovativeness go hand in hand is tenable. It is commonly believed that the higher is the stress level, lower would be the creative ability of people. However, experiencing low stress does not guarantee a corresponding increase in their creativeness. Rather, creativeness flourishes at the moderate stress level.

Organisational structure and processes have an insignificant ($P>0.05$) and small (0.029) influence on innovation. The magnitude of influence and lack of significance of their relationship is quite surprising. It contradicts the findings of the previous research studies which suggest that bureaucratic organisations i.e. organisations having a tight and mechanic structure act as a barrier to innovation and on the contrary, organic organisations i.e., organisations having a fluid and flexible structure stimulate creativity. From the collected data, it may be concluded that the present bureaucratic structure of the organisation has a little impact on the creativity of its people.

There is a small (0.37) and insignificant (P>0.05) relationship between innovation and the leadership style of the top management. It shows that although leadership skills of the top management in the company has a positive impact on the innovativeness of people; their contribution is very marginal.

The relationship between innovation and quality culture of the organisation is also found to be small (0.059) and insignificant (P>0.05). It shows that the present culture of the organisation does not act as a great stimulator for innovation.

V. Ethics

The relationship between ethics and rewards and recognition provided to people for their accomplishment as well as employees' empowerment have been presented in Table 5.8.

TABLE 5.8: Relationship of Ethics with Selected KHFs

Sl. No.	Statistical Property	Rewards & recognition	Empowerment
1.	PCC	.213	.161
2.	Significance Level (2-tailed)	.096	.216

Both the correlation coefficient (.213) and its significance level (.096) are relatively low so far as rewards and recognition and ethics are concerned. The relationship is however significant at 10% level, which is often accepted in social science research. This implies that rewards and recognition have a role to promote the ethics of the people in the organisation.

There is insignificant (P>0.05) and small (.161) relationship between ethics and employee empowerment. It suggests that sharing power with people (non-executives) through participative management does not ensure that people will exhibit ethical behaviour at workplace. A probable explanation for this may be that RINL/VSP as a young and vibrant Public Sector Unit of the country has been equipped with many highly qualified professionals, who have the ability to distinguish between the right and wrong and to make decisions, and for this, they may not truly need to be empowered.

VI. Perception (People's Perception to Quality Culture, Personal Performance and Peer Performance)

The interrelationships between people's perception to quality culture, personal performance and peer performance have been enumerated in Table 5.9.

TABLE 5.9: Relationship of Perception with Selected KHFs

Sl. No.	Statistical Property	Quality Culture & Personal Performance	Quality Culture & Peer Performance	Personal Performance & Peer Performance
1.	PCC	-.096	-.107	.088
2.	Significance Level (2-tailed)	.458	.407	.498

The Table 5.9 reveals that there is a negative (-.096) and insignificant (P>0.05) relationship between people's perception to quality culture and their performance level. This finding again contradicts our perception that the quality of performance of a person is significantly influenced by his perception to the quality culture of the organisation. It probably suggests that the company has excessively focused an improving the work performance of people without providing adequate attention to improving its quality culture.

There is also an insignificant (P>0.005) and negative relationship (-.107) between people's perception to the quality culture of the organisation and performance of their peer, which again disproves our hypothesis.

There is an insignificant (P>0.05) and small (.000) relationship between people's perception to personal performance and performance of their peer. This means that how people perceive the performance of their peer at work place has a little bearing on their own performance level. The magnitude of the relationship and its significance level again contradicts our prediction, that activities of the peers have a profound impact on the activities of a person at the work place.

VII. Communication

Table 5.10 depicts the interrelationships between communication and some selected KHFs such as quality policy, employee empowerment and ethical behaviour.

TABLE 5.10: Relationship of Communication with Selected KHFs

Sl. No.	Statistical Property	Quality Policy	Ethics	Empowerment
1.	PCC	.302*	.025	.287*
2.	Significance Level (2-tailed)	.017	.846	.025

The relationship between communication and quality policy has been significant (P<0.05) and moderate (.302). It indicates that the quality policy has been well communicated to all the employees. Besides, the company has also tried to gather necessary inputs from its employees relating to successful implementation of TQM.

The relationship between communication and empowerment of employees has been small (.287), but significant (P<0.05), as is evident from Table 6.10. It suggests that before the implementation of the quality improvement programme, if the company communicates its decision to people and specially provide them opportunities to share their knowledge and ideas for its better implementation, it will definitely exert a positive impact on their involvement and participation in the progress of TQM.

There is an insignificant (P>0.05) and small (0.025) relationship between communication and ethical work behaviour. The relationship, which has been drawn from the collected data, denotes that although top executives are trying to enforce ethical standards within the organisation, the role of communication in this direction is not quite effective.

VIII. Mental State (Stress and Delight)

Table 5.11 reveals the interrelationships between mental condition and the three selected KHFs such as reward and recognition, empowerment, leadership, and teamwork.

TABLE 5.11: Relationship between Mental State and Selected KHFs

Sl. No.	Statistical Property	Delight & Leadership	Delight & Teamwork	Stress & Reward and Recognition	Stress and Empowerment
1.	PCC	.015	-.242	-.202	.067
2.	Significance Level (2-tailed)	.908	.058	.116	.606

There is a very small (0.15) and insignificant (P>0.05) relationship between people's delight and excitement about work and leadership style of managers. It shows that leadership styles of managers definitely have a positive impact on people's delight with their jobs, but not in the magnitude as it was predicted.

People's delight and teamwork are not found to be well related. The PCC measure of -.242 depicts that there is a small and negative correlation between these two factors. Moreover, the relationship is also loose as it is not significant (P>0.05). Thus, the hypothesis that people feel delighted when they are allowed and encouraged to work as a team is not acceptable. People do not derive great pleasure from their association with co-workers in the organisation.

Occupational stress of people and reward and recognition system of the organisation are negatively (-.202) related. The relationship is also not significant (P>0.05). It can be inferred that the present reward and recognition system in the organisation has not been able to reduce the occupational stress of people.

Stress and empowerment are positively correlated. However, the PCC measure of .067 indicates that there is a small and insignificant (P>0.05) relationship between them. It implies that when people in the organisation are encouraged to make free and frank exchange of information and allowed to participate in decision-making, it definitely affects their stress level, but to some extent.

IX. Rewards and Recognition

The interrelationships between rewards and recognition

and the selected KHFs such as delight and innovation have been presented in Table 5.12.

TABLE 5.12: Relationship between Rewards & Recognition and Selected KHFs

Sl. No.	Statistical Property	Delight	Innovation
1.	PCC	-.332**	.021
2.	Significance Level (2-tailed)	.008	.873

The Table indicates that there is a moderate (-.332) negative and significant ($P<0.01$) correlation between rewards and recognition and people's delight. The probable reason for this may be due to lack of satisfaction of people with the present reward and recognition system of the organisation.

The correlations between reward and recognition and innovation have found to be very small (.021) and insignificant ($P>0.05$). This again indicates a little impact of the present reward and recognition system on the innovativeness of people. In other words, the present reward structure of the company hardly motivates the people to innovate novel ways and ideas for more effective implementation of TQM.

X. Maturity and Breadth

The interrelationships between people's social/morale maturity level and some selected KHFs such as attitude towards the work place, ethics, innovation, and perception of people to peer performance have been given in Table 5.13.

TABLE 5.13: Relationship between Maturity and Breadth Selected KHFs

Sl. No.	Statistical Property	Ethics	Attitude	Innovation	Perception
1.	PCC	.133	-.054	-.205	.151
2.	Significance Level (2-tailed)	.304	.677	.110	.241

The Table 5.13 indicates that there is a small (.133) and insignificant (P>.0.05) relationship between social and morale maturity level of people and ethics at workplace. It implies that although social/morale maturity level of an individual does have a positive impact on the maintenance of a work place ethics, it is not a significant factor. There are some other factors, which must be taken care of in order to maintain high ethical standards.

There is an insignificant (P>0.05) and small (-.054), but negative relationship between social/morale maturity level and attitude of people. It conveys that maturity level of a person does not have any impact on his attitude towards TQM. This is probably because before the implementation of TQM sufficient care was taken by the management to train and teach employees the context, content and relevance of TQM for the success and survival of the company. Through periodic surveys, the attitude of people towards the programme was ascertained and accordingly measures were taken to motivate them. During the opinion survey, it was found that all the sample respondents showed their positive attitude towards the programme. It implies that the other factors such as, leadership, training, awareness programmes organised by the company had a great bearing on their attitude towards TQM, rather than their social morale maturity level.

Similarly, social/morale maturity level of people and their innovativeness are found to be negatively correlated. Their interrelationship is small (-.205) as well as insignificant (P>0.05). Thus, the hypothesis that social/morale maturity level of people has a positive bearing on their innovativeness is not tenable. The people having a low social/morale maturity level may become more innovative than others.

People's social/morale maturity level and their perception to peer performance are found to be positively but weakly correlated. The PCC is very small (.151)) and insignificant (P>0.05). It means that maturity level of a person has a very marginal direct impact on his perception to the performance of peers. It is definitely not the sole factor that helps to make accurate perception.

XI. Attitude and Morale

Table 5.14 enumerates the interrelationships between attitude and morale with selected KHFs such as, organisational structure and processes, peer team support, system feedback coordination, and training.

TABLE 5.14: Relationship between Attitude and Morale with Selected KHFs

Sl. No.	Statistical Property	Training	Organisational structure & processes	Peer team support	System feedback coordination
1.	PCC	.223	.538**	.562	.294**
2.	Significance Level (2-tailed)	.082	.000	.000	.020

The Table 5.14 reveals that there is a strong (.583) and highly significant (P<0.01) relationship between attitude and morale of people with organisational structure and processes. The significance and strength of the relationship suggest that the structures and processes of an organisation significantly influence the attitude of a person towards TQM. Thus, the hypothesis that a well structure organisation and processes have a positive impact on the attitude of people is established.

Similarly, attitude and peer team support are also found to be strongly (.562) related. The significance level is also very high (P<0.01). It suggests that the greater the support received from the peer, the greater the chances that people will develop positive attitude towards TQM. Thus in order to ensure a positive attitude towards TQM programme necessary social support must be generated from the peers.

Attitude and morale have a highly significant (P<0.01) and good (.294) relationship with system feedback coordination. It suggests that the greater the focus on system feedback coordination, the greater the chances that there will be a noticeable improvement in the attitude of people towards TQM.

However, the relationship between attitude and morale and training has been found to be insignificant (P>0.05) and moderate (.223). It indicates that unlike organisational structure and processes, peer team support and system feedback coordination, training does have a moderate impact on attitude and morale of people. The magnitude and significance level of this relationship is not in line with our prediction. It may reflect a weakness of the study in not being able to separate the effect of attitudinal training in general from training on TQM programme.

XII. Customer Satisfaction Sensitivity

Table 5.15 propounds the interrelationships between customer satisfaction sensitivity and organisational structure and processes as well as system feedback coordination.

TABLE 5.15: Relationship between Customer Satisfaction Selected KHFs

Sl. No.	Statistical Property	Organisational structure & processes	System feedback coordination
1.	PCC	.313*	.428**
2.	Significance Level (2-tailed)	.013	.001

As the Table indicates, the relationship between customer satisfaction sensitivity and organisational structure and processes is significant (P<0.05) and moderate (.313). Hence, the hypothesis that there will be a positive relationship between these two KHFs has been proved.

The interrelationship between customer satisfaction sensitivity and system feedback coordination has been highly significant (P<0.01) and good (.428). It suggests that the greater the focus of the company on customer satisfaction sensitivity, the greater will be the need for making necessary arrangements to get objective feedback from the customer relations to product/services and performance of the company.

XIII. Resources

The interrelationships between quality task resources and the two selected KHFs such as performance of people and training is shown in Table 5.16.

TABLE 5.16: Relationship between Quality Task Resources and Selected KHFs

Sl. No.	Statistical Property	Performance	Training
1.	PCC	.227	.319*
2.	Significance Level (2-tailed)	.076	.010

The Table 5.16 reveals that allocation of resources and performance of people are well related. The PCC measure is .227 and the significance level is low (P<0.10). It indicates that though proper allocation of resources does have a positive influence on the performance of people, it does not always ensure good performance. In addition to proper allocation of resources, other variable need to be in place to ensure that people achieve and develop total quality.

The influence of resources on training is significant (P<0.05) and good (.319). The significance of the relationship suggests that adequate resources are essential for everyone to get the required amount of training for the TQM programme. In the absence of abundant resource, there is a tendency to neglect resources for training, which can have a drastic impact on the implementation of the programme.

XIV. System Feedback Coordination

Table 5.17 puts across the interrelationships between system feedback coordination and selected KHFs such as, Organisational structure and processes, employee empowerment, and people's perception to personal performance.

TABLE 5.17: Relationship between System Feedback Coordination and Selected KHFs

Sl. No.	Statistical Property	Organisational Structure & Processes	Empowerment	Perception
1.	PCC	.485**	.360**	.005
2.	Significance Level (2-tailed)	.000	.004	.972

The Table 5.17 indicates that there is a highly significant (P<0.01) and strong (.485) correlation between system feedback coordination and organisational structure and processes. It suggests that the greater the focus on system feedback coordination, the greater the chances that there will be a noticeable improvement in the structure and processes of the organisation.

Similarly there is also a highly significant ($P<0.01$) and good (.360) relationship between system feedback coordination and employees empowerment. This may be due to the reason that, as the customers (internal) of other departments, employees have to continuously and consistently provide feedback to their supplier departments relating to the quality of product/service, which requires greater involvement and participation of employees.

From the collected data it is revealed that there is a small (.005) and insignificant ($P>0.05$) relationship between feedback and performance perception. The magnitude and significance of their relationship is not as per our expectation. This indicates that employees in the company are not receiving regular and meaningful feedback about their performance.

XV. Empowerment

The interrelationships between empowerment and selected KHFs such as, organisational structure and processes, innovation, and attitudes and morale have been demonstrated in Table 5.18.

TABLE 5.18: Relationship between Empowerment and Selected KHFs

Sl. No.	Statistical property	Organisational structure & processes	Innovation	Attitude & Morale
1.	PCC	.515**	.032	.294**
2.	Significance Level (2-tailed)	.000	.806	.020

The Table points out that there is a highly significant ($P<0.01$) and strong (.515) relationship between empowerment and organisational structure processes. It reveals that more the emphasis is laid on empowering employees, the greater is the need to build an organisational structure that will provide more freedom of action and decision to people.

Employee empowerment has an insignificant ($P>0.05$) and small (.032) relationship with innovation. In other words, the present employee empowerment scheme itself does not have much of a role on employees' innovativeness. This probably may be due to the reason that at present employee empowerment in RINL/VSP is confined only to information sharing that too not the sensitive information. They are hardly delegated any power to make decisions.

The impact of empowerment on attitude and morale of people is significant (P<0.05) and small (.294). It suggests that empowerment is essential to ensure development of right attitude of people for the implementation of TQM programme.

XVI. Training

Table 5.19 brings out the interrelationships between training and selected KHFs such as, peer team support, system feedback coordination, communication and occupational stress.

TABLE 5.19: Relationship between Training and Selected KHFs

Sl. No.	Statistical Property	Stress	Peer team support	System feedback coordination	Communication
1.	PCC	-.243	.269*	.376**	-.095
2.	Significance Level (2-tailed)	.057	.035	.003	.461

Training has a significant (P<0.05) and moderate (.269) relationship with peer team support. It suggests that when proper training is provided to people, it definitely has a positive impact on teamwork.

There is a highly significant (P<0.01) and good (.376) relationship between training and system feedback coordination. It suggests that training definitely has a positive impact on the way people provide objective information their own performance as well as of others, although its actual contribution may not be very large.

The relationship between training and communication has been found to be insignificant (P>0.05) and negative (-.095). It shows that sufficient training is not provided to the employees to manage their communication competence.

Training has an insignificant (P>0.05), small (-.243) and negative relationship with occupational stress. It shows that training which was provided to employees on TQM has not been able to reduce the stress level associated with it.

XVII. Quality Policy and Guidance

Table 5.20 shows the interrelationships between quality policy and guidance with selected KHFs such as, attitude and morale, customer satisfaction sensitivity, training, empowerment, and system feedback coordination.

TABLE 5.20: Relationship between Quality and Guidance with Selected KHFs

Sl. No.	Statistical Property	Attitude & Morale	Customer satisfaction sensitivity	Training	Empowerment	System feedback coordination
1.	PCC	.555**	.295*	.281*	.585**	.357**
2.	Significance Level (2-tailed)	.000	.020	.022	.000	.004

Quality policy and guidance have a very significant (P<0.01) and strong (.555) direct relationship with attitude and morale. The significance and strength of the relationship suggest that a well documented quality policy and procedures are absolutely essential for developing positive attitude towards TQM.

Quality policy and guidance and customer satisfaction sensitivity are found to be well related. The PCC measure of .295 indicates that there is a moderate and significant (P<0.05) correlation between them. Thus, the hypothesis that a well-documented quality policy helps to obtain customer satisfaction is found to be true from the collated data.

Similarly the impact of quality policy and guidance on training is significant (P<0.05) and moderate (.281). It indicates that the greater the focus of quality policy and guidance on organisational commitment, the greater the chances that there will be a significant improvement in the method and content of training programme.

Quality policy and guidance have also a highly significant (P<0.01) and strong (.585) relationship with employee empowerment. It again shows that greater the focus of quality policy and guidance on organisational commitment, the greater the possibility that people will be more encouraged to get involved and participate in decision-making and other quality related activities.

There is a highly significant (P<0.01) and good (.357) relationship between quality policy and guidance and system feedback coordination. Thus, the hypothesis that there will be a positive correlationship between these two KHFs has been proved.

XVIII. Organisational Structure and Processes

The interrelationships between organisational structure and processes and selected KHFs such as, attitude and morale, quality policy and innovation are presented in Table 5.21.

TABLE 5.21: Relationship between Organisational Structure and Processes and Selected KHFs

Sl. No.	Statistical Property	Attitude and morale	Quality Policy
1.	PCC	.583**	.304*
2.	Significance Level (2-tailed)	.000	.016

As the Table indicates organisational structure and processes exert a highly significant (P<0.01) and strong (.583) positive influence on the attitude and morale of people. The significance and strength of the relationship suggests that an organisation must be structured well so as to enable the people to develop right attitude towards TQM.

There is a significant (P<0.05) and moderate (.304) relationship between organisational structure and processes and quality policy and guidance. Thus, the hypothesis that there will be a positive relationship between these two variables is acceptable.

XIX. Total Quality Ecological Sustainability

Table 5.22 exposits the interrelationship between total quality ecological sustainability and people's delight with their job.

TABLE 5.22: Relationship between Total Quality Ecological Sustainability with Delight

Sl. No.	Statistical Property	Delight
1.	PCC	.275*
2.	Significance Level (2-tailed)	.031

Total quality ecological sustainability and people's delight are found to be well related. The PCC measure of .275 indicates that there is a moderate relationship between these two factors. The relationship is also significant ($P<0.05$). Thus, the hypothesis that good environmental conditions make the people delighted in tenable.

XX. Peer Team Support

Table 5.23 shows the interrelationships between peer team support and selected KHFs such as, empowerment and innovation.

TABLE 5.23: Relationship between Peer Team Support and Selected KHFs

Sl. No.	Statistical Property	Empowerment	Innovation
1.	PCC	.515**	-.013
2.	Significance Level (2-tailed)	.000	.919

The influence of peer team support on employees' empowerment is highly significant ($P<0.01$) and strong (.515). It indicates that the more the people are encouraged to work in team, the more they feel empowered.

However, the relationship between peer team support and innovation are found to be not well related. The PCC measure (-.013) shows that there is a negative relationship between these two variables. The relationship is also not strong as the significance level is .919. Thus, the hypothesis that peer team support encourages people to innovate is not tenable.

The Model in Figure 5.1 depicts the causal connection among the relevant KHFs.

IDENTIFICATION OF THE MOST CRUCIAL HUMAN FACTORS FOR SUCCESSFUL TQM IMPLEMENTATION

Another survey was made to find out the most important human factor responsible for the successful implementation of TQM in the company. For this purpose, a list of KHFs was prepared and the sample respondents (both executives and non-executives) were requested to rank them from 1 to 17 in

TABLE 5.24 (Contd.)

Sl. No.	KHFs	Executive (E)		Non-executive (NE)		Mean difference between E & NE	t-statistics		Significance level (two-tailed)	
		Mean	Standard deviation	Mean	Standard deviation		Equal variance assumed (a)	Equal variance not assumed (b)	(a)	(b)
13.	Empowerment	11.31	4.13	11.07	3.88	.24	.292	.286	.771	.776
14.	Teamwork	9.75	4.10	9.47	4.19	.28	.327	.329	.744	.743
15.	Customer relations	8.67	4.77	9.14	4.75	-.47	-.486	-.485	.628	.629
16.	Employee relations	12.31	3.85	11.89	4.20	.42	.499	.514	.619	.609
17.	Commitment & involvement	8.47	5.32	8.22	5.06	.25	.238	.234	.812	.816

Source: Compiled and collated from data collected during the opinion survey.

TABLE 5.25: Comparative Status of Various Motivating Factors

Sl. No.	KHFs	Executive (E)		Non-executive (NE)		Mean difference between E & NE	t-statistics		Significance level (two-tailed)	
		Mean	Standard deviation	Mean	Standard deviation		Equal variance assumed (a)	Equal variance not assumed (b)	(a)	(b)
1.	Improvement in work area	.247	1.58	2.64	1.37	-.17	-.567	-.541	.572	.591
2.	Identification and solution of work related problems	3.22	1.55	3.32	1.69	-.10	-.289	-.298	.773	.767
3.	Customer satisfaction	3.67	2.14	3.38	1.9	.29	.721	.693	.473	.491
4.	Need for achievement and recognition	7.0	1.37	6.99	1.36	.01	.050	.050	.960	.960
5.	Management instructions	5.81	1.64	5.99	1.62	.18	-.544	-.542	.588	.589
6.	Peer pressure	6.54	1.2	6.59	1.17	-.04	-.175	-.174	.861	.862
7.	Desire for involvement in decision-making	3.97	1.73	3.89	1.65	.08	.243	.239	.808	.811
8.	Enhance company image	3.33	1.85	3.43	1.96	-.10	-.248	-.252	.805	.801

Source: Compiled from data collected during the opinion survey.

Thus we fail to establish our hypothesis that the *more is the intensity of the desire for achievement and recognition, the greater would be the involvement of an employee in the TQM implementation in the organisation.*

SUMMARY

From the above discussion and analysis of survey findings it can be inferred that at present the organisation is at the '**Healing**" stage, therefore it requires regular check-up for further improvement. The process climate of the organisation is '**Supportive**' in nature. Except a few cases, the interrelationships among the KHFs have been positive and direct. But interestingly a negative relationship is found between leadership and resource allocation as well as between delight and reward and recognition.

Awareness, quality vision, and strategic leadership have been found to be the most crucial KHFs for successful TQM implementation. Similarly, it is also found that people get more involved in TQM programmes so as to bring improvement in their respective work areas. The other motivating factors are found to be identification and solution of work related problems, desire to enhance the company image, and desire for involvement in the decision-making.

REFERENCE

- Petrik, J.A. and Quinn, J.F. (1996). *Management Ethics and Organisation Integrity,* Sage Publications, Newbury Park, CA, pp. 56-60.

6

SUMMARY OF FINDINGS AND IMPLICATIONS FOR PRACTICE

The present chapter summarises the major findings of the study on human dimension of TQM conducted in RINL/VSP. Furthermore, attempt has been made to analyze the findings to uncover the implications of the study for practice. Accordingly a few recommendations has been offered, which may be helpful for a company to evolve operational strategies to strengthen the bondage between TQM and human resources. At the end, an effort has been made to indicate some pointers for further research in this field.

SUMMARY OF FINDINGS AND ANALYSIS

TQM is a holistic organisational approach to bring continuous improvements in organisational activities, processes and products to satisfy the customers. Quality experts have propounded different TQM models describing various components, core methods and principles of TQM. A review of all these models reveal that 'customer' is at the heart of TQM and the interplay of customer and supplier determines an organisation's strategy to achieve total quality. TQM encompasses certain basic principles such as, focus on customer, employee involvement, continuous improvement, defect prevention, performance measurement, continuous learning etc. which can be put into practice by using suitable methods.

TQM is a people-driven management approach that embodies the value of autonomy, real participation, humanisation of the work process, higher productivity, and quality in each and every aspect of work life. It realises the vigour of human potential and taps it in a scientific manner for the benefit of both the people as well as organisations.

TQM PRACTICES IN RINL/VSP

The journey of TQM in RINL/VSP was started on 15 September, 1995 with the establishment of TQM Cell, which was under the control of Works Department. The objective of the Cell was to propagate TQM movement in Works Division so as to continuously improve the quality of its work processes. A full-fledged TQM department in the company was born on January, 1997 under the nomenclature of TQM-ISO Cell.

TQM programme was implemented in the company in a phased manner. At the outset, quality awareness was created among executives (Phase-I), which was followed by the formation of a number of cross-functional Quality Action Teams (Phase–II). A survey was conducted to find out employees' attitude towards TQM (Phase-III) and subsequently a number of TQM related training programmes were organised by the company to expose the workmen and to create a positive attitude towards this novel practice (Phase–IV).

In order to coordinate the overall TQM efforts within the organisation and review its progress, one Core Group, Steering Committees, and Quality Council were constituted on 24 August, 1995, 28 January, 1997 and 28 January, 1997 respectively. Successful TQM implementation has enabled the company to get ISO-9001:2000 certifications from 4 January, 2001 onwards. In order to comply with the provision of ISO-9001:2002, the company has established, documented, implemented, and maintained a Quality Management System (QMS). The QMS operates through QMS Manual, Work Procedures, and Work Instructions. The Chief Executive, Management Representatives, and Heads of various departments are entrusted with the responsibility to implement QMS effectively. Internal quality audits and management reviews are carried out regularly to evaluate its efficacy.

At present, the TQM-ISO Cell comprises five members, who are responsible for identification and coordination of QIPs in different departments as well as monitoring and coordinating the functions of MOUs. The company has a well-defined and documented quality policy, which envisages upon **'commitment to meeting the requirements of customer as well as continuous improvement'**. The corporate quality policy and objectives provide the broad framework within which departmental quality the HODs determine objectives annually. These departmental quality objectives are subject to the approval of the Chief Executive.

With a view to bring continuous improvement in the quality of work process and product, the company has implemented a number of TQM tools such as, formation of QIPs, signing of MOUs, ISO certification, benchmarking, employee involvement schemes, and housekeeping. So far, different departments have taken up 292 QIPs, which have resulted in net financial saving of Rs. 156 crores of the company. During the year 2001-02, 11 MOUs were signed among the production departments with their customers/suppliers and for the year 2002-03, 22 MOUs have already been signed. The company embarks upon both external and internal benchmarking for improving its production, commercial, and financial performance. It benchmarks with British Steel Co., South Korea Steel Plant (POSCO), SAIL, and Tata Steel for reduction in the rejection rate, afforestation, and improving manpower productivity respectively. Internal benchmarking is done mostly in production units. Senior Officers of the respective departments prepare the list of benchmarking projects and submit the same to the ED (Works) for approval. For the year 2002-03, different departments for approval of the ED have already submitted 25 benchmarking projects. The Bureau Veritus Quality International, U.K has issued ISO-9001:2000, ISO-14001:1996, and ISO-18001:1999 certificates for manufacturing products in conformity with the international standard, environmental protection as well as for occupational health and safety respectively.

RINL/VSP has adopted a formal procedure in form of quality circles and suggestion schemes to encourage employees' involvement in the quality improvement process. During the year 2001-02, 3,450 Quality Circle Projects were formed, which resulted in Rs. 900 lakhs financial savings of the company. The management every year awards the best quality circle.

Similarly, in order to increase efficiency, productivity and bring about all-round progress in the company, a suggestion scheme named 'Suggestion Reward Scheme—*Srujan Vikas, 1996*' has been introduced with effect from 1 February, 1996. Employees have very well responded to the scheme, which is evident from the increasing number of suggestions received, implemented, and estimated savings over the years. Rs. 67.83 crores due to the implementation of employees' suggestions has benefited the company.

The company also lays emphasis upon good housekeeping. It has prepared a check sheet and distributed it among all employees for making orderly management of operations, tools, equipments, storage facilities, supplies, and maintaining cleanliness.

THE HUMAN DIMENSION OF TQM

TQM is a people-driven management strategy. It would never be successful in any organisation, unless people are seriously involved in its implementation process and show their passion about it. Realising this, RINL/VSP has envisaged an action plan to develop the wholehearted commitment, competence, and initiative of the personnel for better implementation of TQM in the organisation.

The Human Resource Professionals of the company have played a pivotal role at different stages of TQM implementation. They assisted the top management in creating and communicating the TQM vision, preparing the organisation as well as employees to implement TQM, creating quality awareness among the employees across the levels, functions, and departments, developing management support to quality action plans, organising quality workshops, formulating quality friendly policies, systems and procedures, changing the conventional mindset of employees, organising TQM training programmes (on teamwork, total quality advantage, FADE cycle, ISO procedures, instructions and documentation etc.), devising different communication exercises, encouraging team building activities, promoting employees involvement through suggestion scheme, quality circle and other participative forum etc.

In order to facilitate the TQM progress in the company, the HRD department has made on alignment with other departments. A number of Quality Action/Advantage Teams have been constituted in the company with managerial personnel from different departments including the HRD department. Quality policy of the company was also formulated in consultation with the HR Professionals. The HR Professionals in the company also act as internal consultants to other departments for better implementation of TQM. They act as facilitators and trainers in various quality workshops and advisors to other departments at the time of entering into MOUs with their customer/supplier departments. Implementation of TQM in the company has posed several unique human resource challenges to HR Professionals such as motivating employees who are mostly knowledge workers, mobilising managers who are hardly prepared to share with their power and delegate it, plethora of rules, regulations and directives by the Government, too much emphasis on formal communication system, and above all, the vastness of the organisation.

EVALUATION OF TQM PERFORMANCE

Efficacy can be gauged only when contribution of TQM to the organisation in terms of both tangible and intangible benefits are evaluated. TQM was implemented in the company to achieve twin objectives of enhancing quality, productivity, and total performance of the organisation, as well as enriching the quality of work life of the employees.

In terms of tangible monetary returns, the organisation has saved approximately Rs. 156 crores and Rs. 58.68 crores due to implementation of QIPs and QC projects respectively. Similarly, Rs. 67.83 crores has been saved due to the implementation of suggestions received from the employees under the *Srujan Vikas Suggestion Schemes*. Thus, the organisation has cumulatively saved approximately Rs. 282.51 crores due to the implementation of the QIPs, QCPs, and suggestions schemes. Implementation of TQM tools have not only resulted in financial savings of the company, but also on an average, it has increased the sales per year from Rs. 3263.66 crores to Rs. 7867.6 crores, reduced the manufacturing expenses from Rs. 394706.6 crores to Rs. 346158.86 crores, reduced the net loss incurred by the company from Rs. 697525.90 crores to Rs. 40094.58 crores, reduced the percentage of the defective blooms from 5.76 to 1.2, reduced the accident rates (both fatal and non-fatal) from 113 to 107, and increased the productivity rate (tonnes per man year) from 1.76 to 204 during the Pre-TQM period (1994-95 to 1996-97) to Post-TQM period (1997-98 to 2001-02). It has also declined the customer complaint rates from 0.27 to 0.13.

In terms of intangible returns, implementation of TQM has increased the employees' satisfaction with the quality of work life. At present, the overall employee satisfaction index is 75.26, which indicates the pronounced satisfaction of employees (both executives and non-executives). A number of QCs which are functioning in the organisation as a TQM strategy cover many areas such as, productivity maintenance, work methods, working conditions, energy-resource conservation, reduction in cycle time, housekeeping etc. They also deal with problems like habitual late coming, health and hygiene, plantation and environmental protection, inter-personal communication, maintenance of ethical standards at workplace etc.

TQM also has accrued benefits to the individual employees in terms of providing recognition, attitudinal changes, improved personality, better communication skills, and enhanced leadership qualities.

Thus, dividing the TQM benefits broadly into two categories, namely those which benefit the organisation and those which benefit the employees, it is found that around 90 per cent of the TQM initiatives directly benefit to the organisation and the rest to employees. The opinion survey results confirm to this findings. Yet, employees could foresee a bright future of TQM in the company.

RESULTS OF THE OPINION SURVEY

Analysis of Surveyed Data Relating to Different Dimensions of TQM

An opinion survey was conducted among 372 sample respondents relating to various dimensions of TQM implementation in the company. Inferences derived from analysis and interpretation of the survey data are summarised in Table 6.1.

TABLE 6.1: Summary of Findings on Different Dimensions of TQM

TQM Dimensions	Major Findings
Quality profile of the organisation	Healing stage
Organisational process climate	Supportive
Crucial KHFs for the success of TQM	Awareness, vision, and leadership
Crucial Motivating Factors for employee involvement in TQM	Desire to bring improvement in the work areas, identify work related problems, and involve in the decision-making process.

Note: The table is self-explanatory.

ANALYSIS OF SURVEYED DATA RELATING TO INTERRELATIONSHIP AMONG KHFs

Findings of the opinion survey relating to interrelationships among relevant KHFs are summarized in Table 6.2. The Table indicates that there exists highly significant relationship between awareness and training, awareness and innovation, vision and innovation, leadership and ethics, attitude and morale and system feedback coordination, attitude and morale and organisational structure and processes, customer satisfaction and system feedback coordination, empowerment, system feedback coordination and organisational structure and processes, empowerment and attitude and morale, empowerment and organisational structure and processes, training and organisational structure and processes, quality policy and guidance and system feedback coordination, quality policy and empowerment, organisational structure and processes and attitude and morale, and peer team support and empowerment.

Similarly, negative relationship has been found in between vision and delight, leadership and quality task resources, people's perception to quality culture and personal performance perception, as well as peer performance perception, stress and reward and recognition, delight and peer team support,

TABLE 6.2: Interrelationships among Key Human Factors: A Sum up

KHFs	i	ii	iii	iv	v	vi	vii	viii	ix	x	xi	xii	xiii	xiv	xv	xvi	xvii	xviii	xix	xx	xxi	xxii	xxiii
xxiii.				-														**					
xxii.											*												
xxi.				+										**						*			
xx.														**	*		**	**	*				
xix.									-	-							**						*
xviii.				+										**							**		
xvii.							+											**			**		
xvi.							+												*				
xv.																	**				*		
xiv.																	**		+		**		**
xiii.				-	+			+						-									
xii.				+							**												
xi.			+																				-
x.												-						+					
ix.					+													*		*	*		
viii.							+																
vii.							-	+															
vi.								-															
v.												+						+					
iv.			+			+				*											+		
iii.					**											-							+
ii.				**							-												+
i.				**						*									**				

Note:

(i) Awareness
(ii) Vision
(iii) Leadership
(iv) Innovation
(v) Ethics
(vi) Peoples' perception to quality culture
(vii) Personal performance perception
(viii) Peer performance perception
(ix) Communication
(x) Stress
(xi) Delight
(xii) Reward & recognition
(xiii) Maturity & breadth
(xiv) Attitude and morale
(xv) Customer satisfaction sensitivity
(xvi) Quality task resource
(xvii) System feedback coordination
(xviii) Empowerment
(xix) Training
(xx) Quality policy and guidance
(xxi) Organizational structure & processes
(xxii) Total quality ecological sustainability
(xxiii) Peer Team support

+ Positive relationship; - Negative relationship; * Significant (at 0.05 level); ** Highly significant (at 0.01 level)

maturity and breadth and innovation, maturity and communication, training and stress, and peer team support and innovation of employees.

This is worth-while mentioning here that the relationships derived from the surveyed data are in the context of TQM and purely tentative, hence cannot be generalised to all situations.

IMPLICATIONS FOR PRACTICE

The results of this study suggest important implications for better TQM implementation. Although some of the findings are tentative, they provide useful insight on how to make TQM more successful in the company.

Quality Profile of the Organisation—An Action Plan for Its Improvement

The following HRD actions are proposed to transmit the company into a 'whole' organisation:

- Generate more commitment among people towards TQM by providing TQM training, and organising more TQM workshops.
- Find out the reasons for deviations in the desired behaviours.
- Create a climate where everyone is prepared to accept his/her assigned responsibilities.
- Help people to perceive quality as a super-ordinate goal.
- Communicate the voice of customers to all employees through interaction.
- Reinforce the system for information sharing, suggestion scheme, monitoring results, accountability as well as the feedback coordination.

Transition from Supportive to Total Quality Organisation

At present RINL/VSP has a 'supportive' organisational process climate, which can be transformed into 'total quality' climate by adopting the following measures:

- Provide high degree of autonomy to employees to initiate, coordinate, and implement plans to accomplish TQM goals.

- Higher degree of sharing of power.
- More open and honest communication between employees and top management.
- Treatment of employees with trusts and respect rather than suspicion.
- Provide employees a sense of process ownership and pride in continually improving and learning.
- Redesign the present hierarchical structure of the organisation.

Adherence to these recommendations would create the 'total quality' process climate in the company that may result in the highest work productivity for the organisation and the highest quality of work life for responsible employees.

TQM-HRM Bond

The TQM-HRM bondage in the company can be further nurtured by adopting the following measures:

- HR managers should be trained as TQM trainers/ facilitators.
- Implementation of TQM should become a part of the assessment/appraisal of the performance of employees.
- TQM incentives should be introduced to trigger employees more in this direction.
- Trade unions should be involved in the TQM movement.
- Distribution of more literature to support TQM movement.
- Changing the conventional mindset of employees to focus on survival linkage to TQM.

Role of Key Human Factors (KHFs) and their Interrelationships

(i) *Awareness*

All the employees in RINL/VSP have been made well aware of TQM. For this purpose, the management has provided TQM awareness training, organised a number of quality workshops, and carried out different communication exercises such as, briefing groups, shop floor communication etc. The awareness programme helped to reduce the stress level of employees as well as in getting recommendations from them relating to effective TQM implementation.

It is recommended that more number of such awareness training programmes and quality workshops should be organised in the company at regular intervals.

(ii) *Vision*

It is important that TQM should be viewed as a new paradigm—a departure from the past, not an extension of the existing quality system of the organisation. Although the company has created a well-articulated vision, which has been communicated to all the employees, it is found that the vision has failed to delight the people and make them excited about their work.

Therefore, it is recommended that:

- The present vision of the organisation might be originated with the top management, but in future employees should be involved in the process of shaping the organisation's vision to build their commitment and create enthusiasm.
- The managers should not only talk about the vision, but also they must enact it. They must 'walk the talk' because employees are the watchers who look for managers' behaviours to symbolise values and expectations. The more consistent these behaviours are with statements, the more employees will believe and follow these statements. Moreover, walking the talk builds trust, thereby making people delighted towards their works. This might in turn encourage them to innovate.
- Teamwork should be made a part of TQM vision.

(iii) *Leadership*

Solid leadership and management are key to the success of TQM. Though in RINL/VSP, managers appear to be good leaders, they need to enhance and fine-tune their leadership qualities for more effective implementation of TQM. During the opinion survey, some leadership attributes essential for effective TQM implementation were identified and these are enlisted in Table 6.3.

TABLE 6.3: Essential Leadership Attributes for Effective TQM Implementation

Leadership Attributes	Narrative
• **Leadership vision**	
o Creating TQM vision	o Shape a strategic TQM with employees, customers, vision in consultation with suppliers and other constituents.
o Communicating the vision	o Communicate the meaning and elevate the importance of the visionary goals to the employees.
o Modeling the vision	o Legitimize the vision by enacting on it.
o Building commitment	o Build a communicable enthusiasm to energise people. Involve people in the process of shaping the vision.
• **Leadership motivation**	
o Power	o Share power through participative management.
o Accountability	o Delegation and joint decision-making.
o Resource allocation	o Allocation of sufficient resources—human, material and finance.
• **Leadership drive**	
o Achievement motivation	o Sky is the limit.
o Aspiration	o Being the best.
o Ingenuity	o Surmount the eventualities, be determined and dedicated.
o Vigour	o Hunting opportunities
• **Candor and veracity**	
o Ethical standards	o Credence, intelligibility, accessibility.
o Propensity	o Learning to achieve the TQM outcome straight.
• **Self-assurance**	o From glumness to over promising.

Source: The idea is fairly based upon the discussion made by Puffer, S.M. (1994), "Understanding the Bear: A Portrait of Russian Business Leaders", *Academy of Management Executive*, February, p. 42.

(iv) *Innovation*

Innovation is *sine qua non* for the long-term survival and success of an organisation. In RINL/VSP, people are definitely encouraged to innovate constructive ideas about TQM progress, which is evident from the increasing number of suggestions received by the organisation every year under the suggestion scheme. However, during the opinion survey some barriers to innovation have been identified by the sample respondents, which can be overcome by adhering to the guidelines provided in Table 6.4.

TABLE 6.4: Recommended Strategies to Overcome Barriers to Innovation

Barriers	Strategies to Overcome
Controlled environment	Create supportive and open environment. Allow mistakes (up to a permissible limits), experimentation and pro-typing as people always learn through mistakes.
Rigidity in organizational structure and processes	Provide autonomy, freedom, and flexibility to employees. Avoid excessive discipline.
Ideation is optional, not compulsory	Compel each employee to suggest ideas. Do not criticize the erroneous ideas, rather treat them as opportunities for learning.
Emphasis upon extrinsic, not intrinsic rewards	Though the present reward and recognition system of the organization is quite lucrative, but not sufficient in the sense that it does not provide sufficient intrinsic motivation to employees. Intrinsic motivation can be provided by making the work of people more interesting, challenging, enjoyable and showing appreciation and satisfaction over their work.
Insufficient opportunity for continuous learning	Provide people sufficient opportunity for continuous learning. Cultivate creativity through education and training.

Moreover, the top management must take the ultimate responsibility for stimulating and nourishing employees' creativity. Achieving total quality through innovation requires them to move away from unidimensional thinking to paradoxical thinking and learning to balance three kinds of roles: as a **conspirator, creator and conjurer**. As a **conspirator,** they must delve into the inherent abilities and capabilities of each employee and develop within them an innate belief in his/her own value. Only then, they will deliver unimagined products/services, thereby delighting their customers. The manager as a creator has to foster a congenial atmosphere in the organisation, and put together groups and coalitions in service of innovation and creativity. And finally, the manager as a **conjurer** has to build, integrate and settle the tensions and incongruity inherent to every organisation.

(v) *Ethics*

Ethics involves the study of morale issues and choices. It is concerned with right versus wrong, good versus bad, and the many shades of grey in supposedly black-and-white issues. Since, effective TQM implementation largely depends upon maintenance of ethical standards in the organisation, managers are challenged to make right decisions and to do the right thing that involves morale implications. Therefore, the managers are advised to make ethical decisions by adhering to the seven general moral principles popularly known as 'The Magnificent Seven' promulgated by Hodgson (1992) (Table 6.5).

TABLE 6.5: The Magnificent Seven: General Moral Principles for Managers

1. Dignity of human life	:	The lives of people are to be respected.
2. Autonomy	:	All persons are intrinsically valuable and have the right to self-determination.
3. Honesty	:	The truth should be told to those who have a right to know. Honesty is also known as integrity, truth, and honour.
4. Loyalty	:	Promises, contracts and commitments should be honoured.
5. Fairness	:	People should be treated justly, fairly, impartially, and equitably.
6. Humaneness	:	There are two parts: (i) our actions ought to accomplish good; and (ii) we should avoid doing evil. We should do good to others and to ourselves. We should show the concern in form of compassion, giving kindness, serving and caring.
7. The common good	:	Actions should accomplish the 'greatest good for the greatest number of people'.

Besides, an ethical organisational climate has to be created by managers by developing a meaningful code of ethics for employees, providing training to them to identify and deal with ethical issues, and reinforcing their ethical behaviour. However, it must be remembered by everyone that ethics is an everyday affair, not a one-time announcement of a new ethical code that gets filed away and forgotten.

(vi) *Perception*

Involvement of people in the TQM process depends upon their perception to the efficacy of the programme. By using one or more of the following recommendations can develop people's perception to TQM can be further developed by:

- Formal statements of TQM philosophy, mission, vision, values, and tools to be used. The statements must be clearly communicated and widely reinforced throughout the organisation. The organisational values should give priority to the interest of customers (both internal and external) and suppliers, continuously strive for quality in every activity, treating people with respect and dignity, promoting teamwork, adopting code of conduct that reflects the highest standards of integrity, and be good citizen.
- Create good work environment.
- Use slogans, language, acronyms and sayings that develop desire among employees to provide excellent customer service. The slogans may be like 'achieve customer satisfaction', or 'whatever it takes', which means employees are encouraged to do whatever it takes to exceed customer expectations.
- Different stories and myths that imbibe the value of doing whatever it takes to satisfy a customer may be narrated to employees to create enthusiasm.
- Deliberate role modelling, teaching, and coaching by managers and supervisors.
- Leaders reactions to critical incidents and organisational crises have a significant bearing on employees' perception. Therefore, they should think twice before they act and react.

(vii) *Communication*

It is said that management is communication. Every managerial function and activity involves some form of direct or indirect communication. Any managerial decision including the decision for improving quality through TQM would be ineffective, unless it is well understood by those responsible for enacting them. Therefore, in order to make TQM more effective, the communication system in the organisation must be strengthened. It is suggested that:

- The organisation should design a more effective communication system. Although it is not possible to demolish the existing one completely, along with that the revised communication system should be more open, honest, and reciprocal.
- Media selection is a key component of effective communication. Therefore, for obtaining and disseminating information about TQM, managers must determine which media is to be used. If an appropriate medium is not used, managerial decisions relating to TQM implementation may be based on inaccurate information and/or important messages may not reach the people who are regarded as the cornerstone of TQM progress.
- In order to encourage people to be more involved in the TQM process, managers should improve their communication competence by trying to be more assertive. An assertive communication style is more expressive and self-enhancing, but does not take advantage of others.
- The top management must communicate with employees at the grass-root level and convince them to enforce ethical standards within the organisation.

(viii) *Rewards and Recognition*

Rewards are the centerpiece of organisational life. Both extrinsic (financial, material and social) and intrinsic (self-granted and psychic, such as deriving pleasure from the work itself, experiencing a sense of competence, or self-determination) rewards motivate people to join and contribute to the quality efforts of an organisation. However, the relative importance of extrinsic and intrinsic rewards is a matter of personal values and tasks.

Although the present reward and recognition system in the company is quite lucrative, during the opinion survey, it was found that many employees are not highly satisfied with the present system. Therefore, the organisation must administer a better and well-structured reward system in order to motivate and guide them in the right direction to achieve total quality. The top management may keep the following tips in their mind while administering a good reward system in the organisation:

- Rewards should be tied to contributions/performance of both individual and team.
- Reward system should be based on clear and consensual exchange norms.
- Reward teamwork whenever possible.
- Reward teamwork behaviour (such as mutual support, cooperation, and group problem solving). Introduce team based pay incentives to avoid overload and frustration.
- Create a pay plan that blends individual achievement and team incentives.
- Provide reward having a long-term motivational impact on people.
- Every reward must have a 'deferential effect'.

(ix) *Mental State (Stress and Delight)*

It is believed that a relaxed frame of body and mind is the *sine qua non* for better quality of work. Stress acts as a major barrier to achieve total quality. It may arise from several sources such as, heavy workload, poor job and working conditions, role conflict and role ambiguity, lack of opportunity for career development, poor interpersonal relationship, aggressive behaviour of management, and conflict between work and other roles etc.

Every manager in the company must understand the causes and consequences of stress mainly because of two reasons.

First, from a quality of work life perspective, workers are more satisfied when they are not under a lot of occupational stress. Second, the morale imperative suggests that managers should attempt to reduce stress as it leads to several negative outcomes such as: physiological (increased blood pressure, high cholesterol, heart disease etc.), cognitive (poor decision-making, lack of concentration, forgetfulness etc.), and behavioural (job dissatisfaction, poor performance, higher rate of absenteeism, turnover, accident etc.).

In order to reduce the occupational stress, the company may adopt the following strategies:

- Identify the stressors that cause unnecessary tension and job burnout and remove them. Prepare a well-structured questionnaire and administer the same to all employees to identify the common stressors and receive suggestions for removing them may do this.
- Participative management can reduce occupational stress. Therefore, empower employees so that they will have more control over their work and work environment.
- Administer a well-structured reward and recognition system.
- Managers may also help to reduce the stress level of their employees by: (i) exhibiting supportive behaviour, (ii) showing concern for them, (iii) providing adequate guidance and direction, (iv) focusing on good performance, and (v) providing instrumental support such as, financial, material, and other required resources.
- Social support is one of the most effective stress management practices. It refers to a person's inter-personal transactions with others such as, co-workers, supervisors, family, friends, and others, who provide emotional or informational support to buffer the stress experience. This calls the need of the company to provide more opportunities to its employees to work through teams, so that they can establish good inter-personal relationship and, thereby obtaining necessary

social support. It will help them to reduce their stress level in at least four ways:

(i) *Venerate support*: Employees will experience that they are valued and precious. This sequentially will increase their self-esteem and perceived capability to handle the stressor.

(ii) *Informational support*: The peers will provide information to interpret, figure out, and possibly to confiscate the stressors.

(iii) *Poignant support*: People always look for the emotional support of others, when they face intimidating situations.

(iv) *Social comradeship*: It will provide opportunity to people to fulfil their social need that is need for endorsement and belongingness.

Besides, the predominant stress buster techniques such as, muscle relaxation, biofeedback, meditation and cognitive restructuring may be adopted at the work place.[1]

(x) *Maturity and Breadth*

The maturity level of people is exhibited in how they treat others, whether do they really demonstrate cooperative behaviour at the workplace, and the interest they show in different activities.

In this context, it is recommended that people must be trained and motivated in order to develop cooperative spirit, to treat others fairly and respectively, and to live up to high ethical standard in the organisation.

(xi) *Attitude and Morale*

Attitude of a person always affects his work performance. Work attitudes of people are reflected in their job satisfaction and morale as well as commitment to organisation. Satisfaction

1. Muscle relaxation technique refers to a conscious effort to relief muscle tension through slow and deep breathing. Biofeedback relies on a machine to train people to detect bodily signs of stress. Meditation activates the relaxation response by redirecting one's thoughts away from oneself. Cognitive restructuring entails identifying irrational or maladaptive thoughts and replacing them with rational or logical thoughts.

of employees and their morale are always associated with customer satisfaction which is the ultimate goal of TQM. During the opinion survey, it was gathered that satisfied employees provided better customer satisfaction for two reasons. First, job satisfaction affects the general mood of people. People who are in good mood are likely to communicate friendliness and positive feelings which customers appreciate. Second, satisfied employees are less likely to derelict their jobs. This allows the company to have employees with more experience and better skills to serve the customers. Therefore, in order to provide more job satisfaction to employees and uplift their morale level the company must ensure for:

- Providing equity and fairness in treatment.
- Building organisational comprehension. Affective commitment is likely to be strengthened when employees have a solid comprehension of the activities of their company. Employees should be regularly informed about various organisational activities and allowed personally experience the organisational crisis. People often develop apathetic attitude and feel themselves disconnected, when they do not know what is going on in the organisation.
- Providing more opportunities for employee involvement. People develop positive attitude when they feel that they are part and parcel of the organisation, and their action and decision guide the future of their company.
- Trusting employees. Put faith upon your employees. However, it is a reciprocal activity. To receive trust, the leaders/managers must demonstrate trust. Employees identify with and feel obliged to render quality work for their organisation, only when they trust their leaders/managers.
- Administering a good quality of work/life programme.

(xii) *Customer Satisfaction Sensitivity*

The ultimate goal of TQM is to delight the customers. Therefore, at the outset, the company must enhance the quality of customer services. Two important issues need to be addressed by the company while setting goals for obtaining customer satisfaction. First, it must bear in mind that customers are the sole judge of the quality of its products/services, which they assess by comparing the product/service they receive with the product/services they truly desire. Second, organisations tend to ignore product/service quality, when competitors start vying for their business. Therefore, every organisation must clearly state its customer service goal in terms of the following five criteria:

- *Fidelity*: improving the ability to perform the assured service accurately.
- *Corporeal*: Providing better physical facilities, tools, equipments, personnel, and communication materials.
- *Approachability*: Providing better and more opportunities to the customers to directly approach you, and develop more enthusiasm to help customers and provide them quick services.
- *Pledge*: Improving the knowledge and civility of employees and their ability to carry confidence.
- *Compassion*: Making the provision of caring and individualised attention to customers. Develop the abilities of employees through proper training to understand customer's feeling and desires.

(xiii) *Resources*

The old saying that 'he who has the gold makes the rules' sums up the idea that resources are power. There must be proper allocation and utilisation of resources such as, man, money, equipments, materials etc. in order to ensure effective implementation of TQM in the organisation.

Therefore, it is suggested that:

- The company should allocate more resources to the TQM-ISO Cell.
- Resources are central to the effectiveness of training programmes that prepare and motivate employees to achieve total quality. Therefore, the company must ensure that adequate resources are available to the HRD as well as Training and Development department to regularly organise TQM training programmes.

(xiv) *System Feedback Coordination*

Feedback improves role perceptions, ability, and motivation of people. Therefore, the company must carefully devise/ redesign the present feedback mechanism.

Managers should keep the following tips in mind while providing feedback to employees:

- Devise a value-based (value in terms of achieving excellence and competence) and objective feedback system for the company.
- Break away from the strict superior—to subordinate feedback.
- Provide feedback to employees from multiple sources.
- Relate feedback to existing performance goals and clear expectations.
- Provide feedback in explicit terms.
- Channel feedback to key result areas.
- Give feedback as soon as possible.
- Focus feedback on quality of performance, not personalities.
- Give both positive and negative feedback: positive feedback for encouragement, not just final results; and negative feedback for improvement, not criticism.
- Base feedback on accurate and credible information.

(xv) *Empowerment*

Empowerment leads to improved decision-making, commitment, development, and job satisfaction of employees as it creates the feeling of control and self-efficacy among them. During the opinion survey, it was revealed that the management does not value high to the concept of employee empowerment, which is absolutely essential for the successful implementation of TQM in the organisation.

The company should formulate a better empowerment plan and implement it. The proposed empowerment plan for the company has been given in Figure 6.1.

Information Sharing

- Share company performance information even with lower-level employees.
- Help people understand the business process.
- Build trust through information sharing.

Rearranging Organizational Processes

- Create a clear TQM vision in consultation with employees.
- Create new decision-making rules that support performance management processes.
- Clear communication.
- Job rotation.
- Job enrichment.

Re-engineering HRM Practices

- Provide direction and training for new skills.
- Provide encouragement and support for change associated with TQM implementation.
- Acknowledge the fear factor.
- Have managers, who do not hesitate to share power with their subordinates

Figure 6.1. The Proposed Empowerment Plan for RINL/VSP

(xvi) ***Training***

TQM is a company-wide activity. Adoption of TQM needs to focus on the concepts such as, concurrent engineering, benchmarking, quality function deployment, use of statistical tools etc. which must be disseminated among employees through proper training and education. As training is an effective medium of measuring communication competence, developing managerial and technical competence, and generating enthusiasm for implementing TQM effectively, the company must devise a better, well thought-out and properly organised training programme with a thrust on the aspects:

- Making effective use of various TQM tools.
- Multiple-skill development.

- Team building and group centred activities.
- Providing and receiving constructive feedback relating to the quality of performance.
- Stress management.
- *Managing communication competence*: improving the ability to use all the modes of transmitting, understanding, and receiving ideas, thoughts, and feelings (verbal, listening, non-verbal, written, electronic and the like) for accurate transmission and exchange of information and emotions.

(xvii) *Quality Policy and Guidance*

There are seven Key Business Drivers (KBDs) that form the nucleus of a company's quality policy and its strategic quality planning process. These seven KBDs are: customer satisfaction, employee satisfaction, process optimisation, fair profit, growth and survival, environmental consciousness, and external relations (quality and effectiveness of interactions with suppliers, community and other external agencies). The present quality policy of RINL/VSP is comprehensive enough to integrate all the KBDs except external relations.

Therefore, it is recommended to focus on external relations in the quality policy and objectives of the company.

(xviii) *Total Quality Ecological Sustainability*

At present, the company shows a lot of concern for environmental protection, promotion and ecological sustainability. In addition to that it should show more concern to raise the living standards of people by finding better ways to reduce and eliminate pollution that create ecological hazards.

(xix) *Organisational Structure and Processes*

At present, the organisation is structured according to the traditional chain-of-command principle. However, this traditional pyramid shaped structure tends to be too slow and inflexible and moreover, it does not suit to an organisation that embraces TQM principles. A TQM organisation needs a leaner and more organic structure that can accommodate strategic balancing act between cost, quality, and speed. Therefore, the company has to restructure itself so as to become more customer-focused, dedicated to continuous improvement and learning, which hopefully would enable it to mimic the speed and flexibility of a total quality organisation.

In this context, some strategies are recommended by the researcher which are enlisted in Table 6.6.

TABLE 6.6: The Desired Shape of RINL/VSP to Achieve Total Quality

Sl. No.	Characteristics	Present	Desired
1.	Design of the organisation	To meet customers' requirements	To satisfy and delight the customer
2.	Task definition and knowledge required	Narrow, technical	Broad, general
3.	Task flexibility	Relatively rigid and routine	Flexible and varied
4.	Degree of hierarchical control	High	Low (more emphasis on self-control)
5.	Specifications of techniques, obligations, and rights	Specific	General
6.	Primary communication pattern	Hierarchical and vertical	Lateral and multi-directional
7.	Primary decision-making style	High authoritarian and less participative	Less authoritarian and more participative
8.	Emphasis on obedience and loyalty	High	Low
9.	Nature of work	More individual-oriented	More team-oriented and less individual centred
10.	Information hoarding	Less Sharing	Information rich and more sharing
11.	Reward & recognition	Time, effort and rank	Skill, contribution and result
12.	Feedback system	Single source—from top to bottom, and rarely from peers and subordinates	Multiple sources

(xx) *Peer Team Support*

TQM is based upon the core principle of teamwork, trust and mutual respect. A TQM organisation uses some methods and tools, which require the players from different departments to get together and plan, develop, and regulate the organisational activities. It means people need to learn how to work together in a team and accordingly they should be trained to polish their team skills. In RINL/VSP, there are two major team formats operating in the workplace, Quality Circles and Self-managed Cross-functional teams/Quality Improvement Projects (QIPs). While Quality Circles involve limited empowerment in form of consultation, in contrast QIPs enjoy a high degree of empowerment through delegation. Regarding membership, quality circles rely on volunteers, while employees are assigned to QIPs. Both quality circles and QIPs are regarded as the key to higher productivity, lower cost, increased savings, employee development, and improved job attitude. However, they have a much greater chance of being more effective, if they are properly nurtured and facilitated well by the organisation. Table 6.7 contains few recommendations that may be useful for the company to make teamwork more effective.

POINTERS FOR FUTURE RESEARCH

As a sequel to the present work, further work could be carried out in the following directions:

- In the present study, negative relationship has been found between leadership and resource allocation, which contradicts the expectation of the researcher based on the earlier research findings. Hereafter investigation could be made to verify this finding.
- Training does not seem to effect reduction in stress level of people as expected. Nevertheless, earlier literature and interaction with people implementing TQM suggest that there is some problem with this finding. This is perhaps because this study could not separate effects of TQM training from the influence of the technical training, thus confounding the relationship. Further investigation is required to resolve the contradiction.
- TQM arena is also extended beyond the boundaries of an organisation, i.e. to the families and the society. A further empirical study could be made to find out the relationship between quality of life and TQM.

- Further work on TQM-HR interface could be done in some service industries where operations are managed though logistics like defence, health, hotels, transport, as well as educational institutions.

TABLE 6.7: Recommendations to Facilitate Teamwork in the Context of TQM in RINL/VSP

• Mission and Vision	The mission, vision, objectives or task of the team must be clearly defined and accepted by everyone. However it should be compatible with the organisation's overall purpose and strategy.
• Ambience	An open, transparent, informal, flexible, and trusting environment.
• Involvement	Each team member should be encouraged to involve in the functioning of the team.
• Listening	The members should be good listeners*.
• Decision-making	As much as possible, decision should be made through open discussion of every one's ideas. Hold off rating or simple compromises. Use brainstorming and synectics method.
• Communication	Team members should feel free to express their views on matters concerned. Develop good inter-personal skills (assertive rather than aggressive communication).
• Translucent roles	Fairly distribute work among team members. Clearly explain the role expectations. Avoid role ambiguity.
• Leadership	The team may have a formal leader, but the leadership functions should shift from time to time depending on the circumstances, the needs of the team, and the skills of the members.
• Exterior liaison	The teams should spend more time in developing outside relationships, mobilising resources, and building credibility with important players in other parts of the organisation or other teams.
• Self-appraisal	From time to time the team should make a self-appraisal of how well it is carrying out, and what are the impediments to their effectiveness.

Note: *Indicates every member must be trained in making effective use of listening techniques such as, avoiding interruptions, maintaining interest, postponing evaluation, organising information, showing interest, and providing feedback.

Source: Adapted in part from Parker, G.M. (1990), *Team Players and Team Work: The New Competitive Business Strategy*, Jossey-Bass, San Francisco.

Annexures

ANNEXURE I

The Human Dimension of Total Quality Management: A Study

SCHEDULE TO THE MANAGEMENT

A. I. Organisational Profile

1. Geographical Location
2. Date of Establishment
3. Various Units in the Plant
4. Raw Material Linkages
5. Manufacturing Products
6. Area Covered
7. Historical Growth and Development of the Organisation
8. Technology Used
9. Market Policy
10. Locational Advantages
11. Mission of the Organisation
12. Vision of the Organisation

II. Workforce

1. Total Workforce
2. Employees
   (a) Managerial
   (b) Supervisory
   (c) Clerical
   (d) Others
3. Workers
   (a) Skilled
   (b) Semi-skilled
   (c) Unskilled
4. Contractual relationship
   (a) Permanent
   (b) Temporary
   (c) Contract
   (d) Casual

III. Organisation Structure

1. Kindly provide the details of your organisation structure
2. Line and Staff Functions
3. No. of Functional Departments
4. Communication System
5. Nature of Delegation of Authority

B. TQM Department: Structure & Functions

Do you have (Q1-9)	Yes	No
1. Corporate level quality plans with goals and objectives.	☐	☐
2. A written quality policy embodying vision, mission, values and guiding principles of organisation regarding quality.	☐	☐
3. Proper communication of quality policy to all employees, vendors and customers.	☐	☐
4. A full-fledged TQM department headed by a		
(a) Top management representative/ task force/Steering committee.	☐	☐
(b) Any staff authorities/consultant for TQM.	☐	☐
5. Well-defined roles, responsibilities and objectives for those responsible for quality.	☐	☐
6. Free and frequent flow of two-way communication between TQM staff & top management.	☐	☐
7. Adequate verification of resources and competent and trained person are provided for quality related activities.	☐	☐
8. A system for management review for quality systems organisation-wide.	☐	☐
9. Committed leadership from top for TQM.	☐	☐

C. TQM Practices in Different Departments

I. Materials

1. What is the present procurement policy of your company?

Do you (Q2-6)

	Yes	No
2. select suppliers on the basis of quality of materials to be supplied?	☐	☐
3. inspect the materials supplied and accept?	☐	☐
4. properly identify materials and do the documentation at all stages of work order, supply and arrival time?	☐	☐
5. treat supplier as a business partner promoting quality image?	☐	☐
6. maintain cordial relationship with the suppliers?	☐	☐

II. Manufacturing

1. Whether emphasis is given on quantity and cost of production?	☐	☐
2. Whether emphasis is given on quality of the product?	☐	☐
3. Do you identify the processes, conditions and variables that affect manufacturing of quality product directly? If yes, how do you?	☐	☐
4. What are the regular process analysis for continuous process improvement?	☐	☐
5. Do you regularly verify methods, equipment and quality Of work of operators for special processes? If yes, how do you?	☐	☐
6. How do you do the documentation of work instructions?	☐	☐
7. Is your company concerned for meeting the target given?	☐	☐

III. Marketing

Do you ensure (Q1-3)

1. mass marketing? ☐ ☐
2. niche focus? ☐ ☐
3. mass advertisement? ☐ ☐

Are you concerned (Q4-8)

4. on market share? ☐ ☐
5. for being closer to customers? ☐ ☐
6. for increased market share? ☐ ☐
7. for competitive market creation ☐ ☐
8. for thriving in the market? ☐ ☐

IV. Finance

Do you carry out (Q1-3) Yes No

1. centralised/decentralised management of financial matters? ☐ ☐
2. function of financial staff as policeman? ☐ ☐
3. approval and control at multiple level/only of high spreading authority? ☐ ☐

V. *A. Customer Feedback, Servicing and Satisfaction*

1. Have you established some determinants for customer satisfaction. ☐ ☐
   If yes, specify.

Do you carry out (Q2-6)

2. recording of customer returns and complaints within and outside warranty? ☐ ☐
3. systematic compilation of feedback from post installation servicing to customer? ☐ ☐
4. analysis and referral of feedback to concerned functional group in plant by proper identification. ☐ ☐

5. training and awareness programmes for customers regarding use and maintenance of product.
6. delivery, analysis and review of instruction manual for handling with packaging itself to prevent unintended misuse, mishandling and misinterpretation by customer.
7. Do you have a formal mechanism to settle disputes with/claims from customers? If yes, specify details.

B. Internal Customer Satisfaction (ICS)

Do the (Q1-3) — Yes / No

1. organisation operate any ICS model? If yes, specify details of its functioning.
2. various departments/employees render their sister departments/employees effective quality service in order to ensure successful operation of the ICS? If yes, specify details.
3. departments have signed MOU(s) in this regard?
4. What is the role of ICS model in delivering quality products/services to the external customers?
5. Please provide statistical inormation with regard to qualitative and quantitative benefit that accrued from the model.

D. TQM Srategies in the Organisation

I. Bench Marking — Yes / No

1. Has the management adopted any technique of Benchmarking?
2. What benefits did the company gain through benchmarking so far?

3. What are the different areas that are benchmarked?
4. Please provide cases with regard to benchmarking.
5. How it enables organisations to learn from others?
6. Before opting for benchmarking have you considered the socio-cultural environment?

II. Business Process Reengineering

	Yes	No
7. Has the organisation gone for any fundamental rethinking and radical redesigning of business processes to achieve dramatic improvements in critical contemporary measures or performance such as, cost, quality, service and speed?	☐	☐
8. Specify different steps that are adopted by the company in the reengineering processes.		
9. Do the operations of reengineering match the customer wants?	☐	☐
10. Have you created any structure or team work for BPR? If yes, specify.	☐	☐
11. Does this process require top-down and bottom-up initiatives?	☐	☐

III. Kaizen

12. Is Kaizen practised in the organisation? If yes, specify how is it done?		
13. What are the areas in which Kaizen is done?		
14. Who are the people working for Kaizen?		
15. Does Kaizen yield good results for the organisation? If yes, give details.	☐	☐

IV. ISO Series

	Yes	No
16. Has the organisation certified with ISO series?	☐	☐

If yes, what are they?

17. When it got certified?
18. What were the steps taken by the company to obtain the certificates?

19. Whether any training is given for awareness of ISO standards? If yes, please specify details.	☐	☐
20. Does the company has any qualified and experienced internal auditors?	☐	☐

21. Has the company realised any benefits after certification of ISO standards? If yes, specify details.

E. The Human Side of TQM

I. Role of HR Department

1. How do you define your role in successful implementation of TQM practice?
2. Do you feel that the employees play a key role in TQM?
3. Sight some cases where the other departments sought your help for successful implementation of any TQM strategy.
4. What are the factors that act as barriers for successful implementation of TQM?

II. Training

Does your organisation have a system for (Q1-3)—

	Yes	No
1. Identification/assessment of training needs of all personnel performing activities directly affecting quality.	☐	☐

2. Giving training to personnel not primarily concerned for manufacturing quality e.g. marketing / finance / personnel. ☐ ☐

One level All level

3. Periodic training programmers in quality awareness and ☐ ☐

appreciation at all levels. One area All area ☐ ☐

III. Employee Empowerment

4. Do you have a policy of employees empowerment to get the best from employees regarding quality?

Yes No

5. Kindly provide the details of employee involvement programme launched in your organisation. ☐ ☐

6. How do the programmes ensure employees Involvement?

IV. Motivation

Is there a (Q7-9):

Yes No

7. sense of pride/quality consciousness in workers as regards workmanship by delegation of quality responsibility. ☐ ☐

8. satisfactorily high level of morale/ motivation in workers in your opinion. ☐ ☐

9. (a) job rotation scheme to facilitate mobility of workers to work with more than one machine.

Both Fin. Non-fin. Nil

(b) scheme of financial/non-financial incentives for suggestion in quality improvement. ☐ ☐ ☐ ☐

10. If any other job enrichment Scheme followed, specify...

V. Leadership

11. In your opinion does leadership play a crucial role in the successful implementation of TQM?
12. If yes, who should play the role of a leader:
    Top management/
    Middle management/
    Lower level managers
13. What is the role of a leader in the following process:
    (a) developing organisational vision
    (b) resource allocation
    (c) motivating employees for close involvement in implementation of TQM process
    (d) team building
    (e) employees empowerment
    (f) education and training of employees
    (g) creativity and innovation
    (h) managing change
14. Which leadership style do you mostly adopt:
    Democratic/Autocratic/Partcipative/Free rein

VI. Team Approach

	QCs	CFTs	SGAs	Nil
15. As an initiative to partcipation in group activities for quality improvement, do you have QCs/CFTs/SGAs.	☐	☐	☐	☐

16. Any other, specify.

VII. Change Management for TQM

17. Salient problems regarding quality are traceable to

	Always	Generally	Sometime	Rarely	Never
(a) knowledge and skills of employees	☐	☐	☐	☐	☐
(b) attitude/ work culture of employees					

18. Are you in the process of implementing TQM?

	Yes	No
If yes, did you:	☐	☐
(a) face resistance to change during implementation of TQM from workers?		
(b) use any O.D. intervention strategy for managing this change?	☐	☐

If any other, specify.

VIII. Role of Creativity and Innovation in TQM

	Yes	No
19. Do you encourage employees to innovate ideas for better implementation of TQM?	☐	☐

If yes, what strategies do you adopt for this purpose?

20. So far how many new ideas you have received from employees?
21. How many innovative ideas you have so far been implemented?
22. If any other, specify.

Thanking you.

ANNEXURE II

The Human Dimension of Total Quality Management: A Study

QUESTIONNAIRE

We are conducting a study on 'The Human Dimension of Total Quality Management'. Hence, we need your kind co-operation. Please feel free to give frank opinion on the following statements. If you feel so, you may not reveal your identity. The findings of the study shall be used purely for academic purpose.

PART-A

Profile of the Sample Respondent

1. Name
2. Age
3. Sex: Male/Female
4. Designation
5. Total work experience
6. The present organisational tenure.

PART-B

Employee's Attitude towards the Status of the Organisation (In terms of quality)

Directions: Given below a list of 5 characteristics. Please put a "✓" mark on your choice of alternative in order to indicate your opinion.

Characteristics	That's us all the way	Some is true	We're not like that
1. Our services and/or products normally contain waivers, deviations and other indications of their not conforming to requirements.	☐	☐	☐

2. We have a "fix it" oriented field service and/or dealer organisation.	☐	☐	☐
3. Our employees do not know what management wants from the concerning quality.	☐	☐	☐
4. Management does not know what the price of non-conformance really is.	☐	☐	☐
5. Management believes that quality is a problem caused by something other than management action.	☐	☐	☐

PART-C

Organisational Process Climate

Directions

Read each dimension of organization process climate and consider the descriptions at both ends of the scale. Circle the number on the scale that reflects your evaluation of conditions in your organisation at this time (1 is the lowest evaluation possible and 20 is the highest evaluation possible).

1. Reward System: The degree to which employees, as individuals and as teams, feel they are being recognized and rewarded for good work rather than being ignored, criticised, or punished when something goes wrong.

Rewards are not in line with effort and performance	1	2	3	4	5	6	7	8	9	10	11	12	13	14	15	16	17	18	19	20	Employees are recognized and rewarded positively.

2. Standards of Performance: The emphasis placed upon quality performance and achieving results, including the degree to which employees feel meaningful and challenging goals are being set at every level of the organisation.

Performance standards are low	1	2	3	4	5	6	7	8	9	10	11	12	13	14	15	16	17	18	19	20	Performance standards are High

3. Warmth and Support: The feeling that friendliness is a valued norm and that employees trust, respect and offer support to one another. The feeling that good human relationships prevail in the day-to-day work of the organisation.

There is little warmth and support in the organisation	1	2	3	4	5	6	7	8	9	10	11	12	13	14	15	16	17	18	19	20	Warmth and support are characteristic of the organisation

4. Leadership: As needs for leadership arise, people feel free to take leadership roles and are rewarded for shared successful leadership. The organization is not dominated by or dependent upon just one or two individuals.

Leadership not respected or rewarded; organisation dominated by or dependent upon just 1 or 2 individuals	1	2	3	4	5	6	7	8	9	10	11	12	13	14	15	16	17	18	19	20	Leadership is accepted and rewarded based on expertise of individuals and teams

5. **Organisational Clarity:** The feeling among employees that things are well organised and goals and responsibilities are clearly defined rather than being disorderly, confused, or chaotic.

The organisation is disorderly, confused, and chaotic	1	2	3	4	5	6	7	8	9	10	11	12	13	14	15	16	17	18	19	20	Organisation is well organised, with clearly defined goals and responsibilities

6. **Communications:** Important information is shared quickly and accurately—up, down, and sideways—in the organisation.

Information is wrong, censored, or unavailable	1	2	3	4	5	6	7	8	9	10	11	12	13	14	15	16	17	18	19	20	Information is accurate, open and available

7. **Creativity**: New ideas are sought and used in all areas of the organisation. Employees creativity is encouraged at every level of responsibility.

The organisation is closed and unresponsive to change	1	2	3	4	5	6	7	8	9	10	11	12	13	14	15	16	17	18	19	20	The organisation is innovative and open to new ideas

8. Job Stress: Employees are neither overworked nor underworked. Stress levels are appropriate for the job.

Stress levels are harmful	1	2	3	4	5	6	7	8	9	10	11	12	13	14	15	16	17	18	19	20	Stress levels are optimum

9. Ethics: The emphasis the organisation places upon high standards of moral behaviour at all levels of responsibility.

Double standards exist; ethics are low	1	2	3	4	5	6	7	8	9	10	11	12	13	14	15	16	17	18	19	20	High standards of conduct are expected at all levels.

10. Tolerance: The degree of open-mindedness that exists towards different people, ideas and customs in the organisation.

Prejudice and discrimination are the norm	1	2	3	4	5	6	7	8	9	10	11	12	13	14	15	16	17	18	19	20	Nonprejudice and non-discrimination are the norm

11. Feedback and Controls: The use of reporting, comparing and correcting procedures, such as employee evaluations and financial audits.

Controls are used for policing and punishment	1	2	3	4	5	6	7	8	9	10	11	12	13	14	15	16	17	18	19	20	Controls are used to provide guidance and solve problems

12. Resources: Sufficient financial and physical resources are available to accomplish the job.

Insufficient funds, equipment and supplies	1	2	3	4	5	6	7	8	9	10	11	12	13	14	15	16	17	18	19	20	Supplies, equipment, and funds are sufficient

13. Employee Growth: Personal and professional development is emphasized at all levels and in all classifications in the organisation.

Employee growth is a low priority in the organisation	1	2	3	4	5	6	7	8	9	10	11	12	13	14	15	16	17	18	19	20	Employee growth is a high priority in the organisation

14. **Physical Working**: Conditions (lighting, space, heat, washroom facilities, etc.): Safe and comfortable working conditions exist throughout the organisation.

Working conditions are poor	1	2	3	4	5	6	7	8	9	10	11	12	13	14	15	16	17	18	19	20	Working conditions are good

15. **Teamwork**: The amount of understanding and co-operation between different levels and work groups in the organisation.

Teamwork is poor	1	2	3	4	5	6	7	8	9	10	11	12	13	14	15	16	17	18	19	20	Teamwork is high

16. **Employee Pride**: The degree of pride that exists—pride of individual workmanship and pride of organisation goals and accomplishments.

Pride is low	1	2	3	4	5	6	7	8	9	10	11	12	13	14	15	16	17	18	19	20	Pride is high

17. **Employee Involvement**: Responsibility for decision-making is broadly shared in the organisation. Employees are involved in decision that affect them.

Low employee participation in decision-making	1	2	3	4	5	6	7	8	9	10	11	12	13	14	15	16	17	18	19	20	High employee participation in decision-making

PART-D
The Human Dimension of Total Quality Management

Directions: Use the following scale to indicate your answers to the statements below:

1.	2.	3.	4.	5.	6.
Strongly disagree	Disagree	Somewhat disagree	Somewhat agree	Agree	Strongly agree

There are no right or wrong answers. Write the number (1, 2, 3, 4, 5 or 6) that best indicates the extent of your agreement with the statement.

I. Awareness

1. People are aware of the top priority accorded quality strategy. ________
2. People in the organisation are aware of how their jobs contribute to the organisation's quality mission. ________
3. Meeting and exceeding customer expectations is accorded a higher strategic priority than short-term financial gain. ________
4. People in the work unit can describe the organisation's quality and sustainable productivity policies. ________
5. People in the work unit know how to define the quality of work they produce. ________

II. Vision

6. People in the organisation try to plan ahead for changes (such as customer expectations) that might impact the organisation's future performance. ________
7. People in the organisation try to plan ahead for technological changes (such as new developments in computer software) that might impact the organisation's future performance. ________

8. People in the organisation regularly work together to plan for the future. ________

III. Leadership

9. Leader(s) in the organisation ask people about ways to improve the work produced. ________
10. Leader(s) in the organisation encourage people to voice their concerns. ________
11. Leader(s) in the organisation follow up on suggestions for improvement. ________
12. Leader(s) in the organisation set examples of quality performance in their day-to-day activities. ________
13. Leader(s) in the organisation regularly review the organisations progress toward meeting its goals and objectives ________
14. Leader(s) in the organisation attempt to find out why the organisation may not be meeting a particular goal or objective. ________
15. People in the work unit turn to their supervisors for advice about how to improve their work. ________
16. People in the work unit know that their supervisors will help them find answers to problems they may be having. ________
17. People in the work unit are challenged by their supervisors to find the ways to improve the system. ________
18. Supervisors in the work unit provide guidance to make the continuous improvement of the work produced top priority. ________
19. Supervisors in the work unit regularly ask the customers about the quality of work they receive. ________
20. Supervisors encourage people in the work unit to share their opinions and ideas about work improvement. ________

IV. Innovation

21. Creativity is actively encouraged in the organisation. ________
22. Innovators are the people who get ahead in the organisation. ________

V. Ethics

23. People in the organisation live up to high ethical standards. ________
24. The organisation has an ethics development system in place. ________
25. People in the organisation are used to fair treatment at work. ________

VI. People's perception of quality culture

26. The work unit has few bureaucratic barriers to getting the job done properly. ________
27. Work expectations for the work unit are fair. ________
28. People in the work unit are committed to producing high quality work. ________

VII. Personal performance perception/system stability results

29. I know the amount of work I produce is within the approved/expected range of variation for anyone in my position. ________
30. I know the quality of work I produce is within the approved/expected range of variation for anyone in my position. ________
31. I know the efficiency of my work habits is within the approved/expected range of variation for anyone in my position. ________

VIII. Peer performance perception/system stability results

32. My work unit peers know the amount of work out unit produces is within the approved/ expected range of variation for any comparable work unit. ________
33. My work unit peers know the quality of work our unit produces is within the approved/ ________

expected range of variation for any comparable work unit.

34. My work unit peers know the efficiency of their work habits is within the approved/expected range of variation for any comparable work unit. ________

IX. Communication

35. People in the work unit are involved in decision-making and listen to what others have to say. ________
36. The facts and information needed to do a good job are available to the people in the work unit. ________

X. Stress

37. People in the organisation experience moderate stress (rather than feeling overstressed or understressed) in meeting workload responsibilities. ________
38. People in the organisation are encouraged to experience a healthy balance between work and life obligations. ________

XI. People's Delight

39. People in the work unit are delighted with their supervisors. ________
40. People in the work unit are delighted with other persons in their work group. ________
41. People in the work unit are delighted with their jobs. ________

XII. Rewards and Recognition

42. The pay scale is fair for people in the work unit. ________
43. The reward/recognition policies contribute to a stable quality system with widespread satisfaction. ________

44. People in the work unit receive promotions because they earn them. ______
45. There is quick recognition of people in the work unit for outstanding performance. ______
46. The organisation rewards the people in the work unit for working together. ______

XIII. Maturity & Breadth

47. People in the work unit demonstrate cooperative behaviour. ______
48. People in the work unit treat each other fairly and respectfully. ______

XIV. Attitude and Morale

49. People in the work unit take pride in their work and rarely demonstrate cynical attitudes. ______
50. People in the work unit share responsibility for the success or failure of the work produced. ______
51. People in the work unit believe that their work is important to the success of the organisation. ______

XV. Customer Satisfaction Sensitivity

52. People in the organisation know who their internal and external customers are. ______
53. People in the organisation care about meeting or exceeding their customers expectations. ______
54. In general, all customers know that the organisation cares about what they think. ______
55. The organisation's customers are asked for their opinions about the work (services, products) they receive from the organisation. ______

XVI. Quality Task Resources

56. The right tools, equipment and material are available in the work unit to get the job done. ______

57. The distribution of work among the people in the work unit is well balanced. ________
58. There is ample time for people in the work unit to perform jobs in a professional manner. ________

XVII. System Feedback Co-ordination

59. There are good working relationships between work units in the organisation. ________
60. Rapid feedback reduces the cycle time for improvement in all parts of the system. ________
61. The organisation has good working relationships with other organisation. ________

XVIII. Empowerment

62. People in the organisation make decision with sufficient information. ________
63. The information they get is rarely ambiguous in nature. ________
64. The organisation encourages them for free and frank exchange of information. ________
65. The management values the concept of employee empowerment. ________

XIX. Training

66. My work unit periodically conducts surveys to assess training needs of employers relating to quality problems. ________
67. Training helps me to work as a team member using various tools with different quality processes and follow ups with specific use on the job. ________
68. There is no emphasis on quality in training sessions. ________

XX. Quality Policy/Guidance

69. The quality of work produced is the primary focus of the organisation. ________
70. People in the organisation see the continuing improvement of work produced as essential to the success of the organisation. ________

71. The organisation emphasises doing things right the first time. ________

XXI. Organisation Structure and Processes

72. The structure of the organisation makes it easy to focus on improving processes. ________
73. People know how the processes in their work unit fit in with the processes of other work units. ________
74. Key processes in the organisation are regularly measured and qualified. ________
75. Key processes in the work unit are regularly measured and qualified. ________
76. Key processes in the organisation are regulary benchmarked and undergo quality auditing. ________

XXII. Total Quality Ecological Sustainability

77. In this organisation, the natural environment impact of strategic decisions is regarded as important. ________
78. Sustainable development rather than unmanaged growth or stagnation is typical of this organisation's approach to nature. ________
79. There are numerous "greening" (i.e., recycling) policies and practices in this organisation to promote ecological sustainability. ________

XXIII. Peer Team Support

80. People in the work unit encourage each other to work as a team. ________
81. People in the work unit hold each other accountable for work produced. ________

PART–E

Assessment of the Leadership Style

Directions: Read each of the statements below and tick ☑ the response that you believe best describe your answers.

My QIP/QC leader:	Strongly agree	Agree	Neutral	Dis-agree	Strongly disagree
• Focuses attention on irregularities, mistakes, exceptions and deviations from what is expected of me.	☐	☐	☐	☐	☐
• Engages in words and deeds that enhances his/her image of competencies.	☐	☐	☐	☐	☐
• Monitors performance for errors needing correction.	☐	☐	☐	☐	☐
• Serves as a role model for me.	☐	☐	☐	☐	☐
• Points out what I will receive if I do what is required.	☐	☐	☐	☐	☐
• Instills pride in being associated with him/her.	☐	☐	☐	☐	☐
• Keeps careful track of mistakes.	☐	☐	☐	☐	☐
• Can be trusted to help me overcome any obstacles.	☐	☐	☐	☐	☐
• Tells me what to do to be rewarded for my efforts.	☐	☐	☐	☐	☐

• Makes me aware of strongly held values, ideals, and aspirations which are shared in common.	☐	☐	☐	☐	☐
• Is alert for failure to meet standards?	☐	☐	☐	☐	☐
• Mobilises a collective sense of mission.	☐	☐	☐	☐	☐
• Works out agreement with me on what I will receive if I do what needs to be done.	☐	☐	☐	☐	☐
• Articulates a vision of future opportunities.	☐	☐	☐	☐	☐
• Talks about special rewards and good work.	☐	☐	☐	☐	☐
• Talks optimistically about the future.	☐	☐	☐	☐	☐

PART-F

Identification of the most Crucial Human Factor

Directions: Given below a list of human variables essential for successful TQM implementation. Kindly rank them in accordance of your preference (for instance, the variable which you think is of utmost importance rank it '1', the next important human factor as '2' and so on).

Human Variables	**Rank**
• Quality Awareness	______
• Vision	______
• Leadership	______
• Innovation and creativity	______
• Ethics	______

- Communication ________
- Perception of quality culture/performance/ peer support. ________
- Mental condition (such as delight, stress etc.) ________
- Reward and recognition ________
- Attitude and morale ________
- Maturity & breadth ________
- Training ________
- Empowerment ________
- Team work ________
- Customer satisfaction sensitivity ________
- Employee relations ________
- Commitment and involvement ________

PART–G

Identification of the Motivating Factors for TQM Implementation

Why I am totally involved in implementation of TQM in the organisation? Rank the following reasons in order of their priority from 1 to 8:

1. It helps to bring improvement in my work area ________
2. It helps to identify and solve work related problems ________
3. To enhance customer satisfaction ________
4. Desire for achievement and recognition ________
5. The management instruts me to be involved in ________
6. Peer pressure and pressure of the team leader ________
7. Desire for more involvement in decision-making ________
8. To enhance company image ________

Thanking you.

ANNEXURE III

Role of HR Professionals in TQM Implementation

INTERVIEW GUIDE

1. Please specify the role of HR professionals in successful TQM implementation.
2. Please specify the unique human resource challenges associated with TQM implementation.
3. In your organisation, is there any specific connection between HR policy and TQM policy?
4. Do you think that HR department should partner with other departments to support TQM? Please justify your stand.
5. Do you act as an internal consultant to other departments including TQM? Please substantiate your statement.
6. What role do you play in the following matters:
    - Systematic identification and assessment of training needs
    - Employees' education
    - Team building
    - Employees' empowerment
    - Communication?
7. In your opinion, how can the human resources play a better role in effective TQM implementation?

Thanking you.